THE NORDIC CONSTITUTIONS

This book analyses the Nordic constitutional systems of Denmark, Finland, Iceland, Norway and Sweden in a comparative context. It has two main aims: first to fill a gap in the literature by providing an accessible English language account of the Nordic constitutions, and second to provide a comparative analysis of them, revealing their similarities and differences within their political, historical and cultural contexts. In this respect, the book challenges the assumption that the Nordic countries form a homogeneous constitutional system due to their cultural and historical affinities, a view not necessarily supported by a close comparative examination. A key issue is EU membership—where the Nordic countries have made different choices at different times—and the book will show how this has affected the individual countries and whether a divide between EU member states (Denmark, Finland and Sweden) and non-members (Iceland and Norway) has appeared. Another key issue is how the ECHR has impacted the Nordic constitutional systems and whether the convention draws the Nordic systems closer to each other. The book represents a first of its kind in the English language, and will provide constitutional scholars with a valuable comparative resource on the Nordic region.

Volume 23 in the series Hart Studies in Comparative Public Law

Hart Studies in Comparative Public Law

Recent titles in this series:

Human Rights in the UK and the Influence of Foreign Jurisprudence
Hélène Tyrrell

Australian Constitutional Values
Edited by Rosalind Dixon

The Scope and Intensity of Substantive Review
Traversing Taggart's Rainbow
Edited by Hanna Wilberg and Mark Elliott

Entick v Carrington
250 Years of the Rule of Law
Edited by Adam Tomkins and Paul Scott

Administrative Law and Judicial Deference
Matthew Lewans

Soft Law and Public Authorities
Remedies and Reform
Greg Weeks

Legitimate Expectations in the Common Law World
Edited by Matthew Groves and Greg Weeks

The Dynamics of Exclusionary Constitutionalism
Mazen Masri

Constitutional Courts, Gay Rights and Sexual Orientation Equality
Angioletta Sperti

Principled Reasoning in Human Rights Adjudication
Se-Shauna Wheatle

Human Rights and Judicial Review in Australia and Canada
Janina Boughey

The Foundations and Traditions of Constitutional Amendment
Edited by Richard Albert, Xenophon Contiades and Alkmene Fotiadou

The Federal Idea
Public Law Between Governance and Political Life
Edited by Amnon Lev

The Nordic Constitutions

A Comparative and Contextual Study

Edited by
Helle Krunke and Björg Thorarensen

•HART•
OXFORD • LONDON • NEW YORK • NEW DELHI • SYDNEY

HART PUBLISHING

Bloomsbury Publishing Plc

Kemp House, Chawley Park, Cumnor Hill, Oxford, OX2 9PH, UK

HART PUBLISHING, the Hart/Stag logo, BLOOMSBURY and the Diana logo are trademarks of Bloomsbury Publishing Plc

First published in Great Britain 2018

A catalogue record for this book is available from the British Library.

A catalogue record for this book is available from the Library of Congress

ISBN: HB: 978-1-50991-093-9
ePDF: 978-1-50991-095-3
ePub: 978-1-50991-094-6

Typeset by Compuscript Ltd, Shannon
Printed and bound in Great Britain by TJ International Ltd, Padstow, Cornwall

MIX
Paper from responsible sources
FSC www.fsc.org FSC® C013056

To find out more about our authors and books visit www.hartpublishing.co.uk. Here you will find extracts, author information, details of forthcoming events and the option to sign up for our newsletters.

PREFACE

The idea for this book appeared four years ago. It was initiated by a strong wish to conduct a comparison between the Nordic constitutional systems—a missing link in legal literature—and to provide English-speaking readers with an insight into this field—another missing link in legal literature. We had both experienced much interest in the Nordic constitutional systems from colleagues abroad and very little literature to which we could refer them. One of the perspectives, which we wanted to explore, was how the European Union and the EEA Agreement as well as human rights conventions have had impact on the Nordic constitutional systems and whether they are drawn closer to each other or further apart. Coming from Iceland (Björg) and Denmark (Helle), we contacted our colleagues and researchers in constitutional law from the other Nordic countries Eivind Smith (Norway), Tuomas Ojanen and Marku Suksi (Finland) and Thomas Bull (Sweden) and this led to a long, fruitful and pleasant process of writing this book together. We owe them our greatest thanks for the engagement and commitment they showed throughout the four years. Like any other book project which runs over four years and requires on-going cooperation among the authors there have been 'ups and downs' in the process. However, our common interest in Constitutional Law and our friendship always carried us forward.

We would like to thank the Centre for European and Comparative Legal Studies (CECS), Faculty of Law, University of Copenhagen, which funded two Nordic seminars in Copenhagen with the purpose of discussing and coordinating the project. We would also like to thank project student Stine Hellqvist Frey (CECS) for handling the manuscript in the last phase. Finally, we owe thanks to Hart Publishing for their good, professional and patient support.

With this book, we hope to put the Nordic constitutional systems on the global map and to deepen the Nordic understanding of our constitutional systems. The cover of the book has a wonderful resemblance with the Northern Lights, which many of the Nordic countries share.

Björg Thorarensen and Helle Krunke
Reykjavik and Copenhagen, April 2018

CONTENTS

LIST OF CONTRIBUTORS

Thomas Bull is Justice of the Supreme Administrative Court of Sweden.

Helle Krunke is Professor of Constitutional Law, Centre for European and Comparative Legal Studies (CECS), Faculty of Law, University of Copenhagen.

Tuomas Ojanen is Professor of Constitutional Law, University of Helsinki.

Eivind Smith is Professor of Public Law, University of Oslo.

Markku Suksi is Professor of Public Law, Åbo Akademi University.

Björg Thorarensen is Professor of Constitutional Law, University of Iceland.

1

Introduction

HELLE KRUNKE AND BJÖRG THORARENSEN

I. The Purpose of this Book

The aim of this book is to present the Nordic constitutional systems in a comparative context, which reveals similarities and differences. The Nordic countries include Denmark, Finland, Iceland, Norway and Sweden. Despite the seemingly widespread interest in the Nordic constitutional systems from the outside world, little literature on the constitutional systems of these states exists in English. At the same time, the Nordic constitutional systems are often viewed as similar from the outside because of the closeness of their culture and languages, and their interwoven history to an extent not necessarily supported by a closer look.

The purpose of the book is twofold: first, it aims at making each of the Nordic constitutional legal systems accessible to the rest of the world in English; second, it aims to show which features are similar in all or some of the Nordic constitutional systems and in which areas limited or no coherence exists. The analyses will be embedded in their political, historical and cultural context.

The book focuses on selected aspects, particularly on how European and international cooperation through the European Union (EU), the European Economic Area (EEA) and international human rights conventions (mainly the European Convention on Human Rights (ECHR)) has impacted the Nordic constitutional systems. On an important issue such as EU membership, the Nordic countries have made different choices and at different times. Among other things, we will discuss how this has affected the individual country and whether a divide between EU Member States (Denmark, Finland and Sweden) and non-members (the EEA states—Iceland and Norway) has appeared in relation to the development of the respective constitutional systems. All the Nordic countries have incorporated the ECHR, whereas only some Nordic countries have incorporated other international human rights conventions. The impact of this development on the individual constitutional systems and on the unity of the Nordic constitutional systems will be examined.

The Nordic national parliaments, the key actors in the constitutional systems, have increasingly been challenged by the internationalisation of politics and in particular the ongoing process of European integration. Closely related to this are the increased powers of the judicial branch in the exercise of judicial review, involving obligations deriving from European treaties which are placing greater restraints on the legislator. The growing Europeanisation of politics will be discussed and compared, particularly how Nordic parliaments have sought to compensate for their alleged decline in legislative activity by developing their oversight and control mechanisms with respect to EU affairs. Meanwhile, the EEA states are in a weaker position in terms of strengthening their parliamentary oversight in EU/EEA affairs, due to many factors.

Together, these analyses will contribute to an overview of the complex contemporary constitutional setting in the Nordic countries based on national constitutions, EU/EEA law, international human rights conventions and a special Nordic constitutional identity, which is, among other things, reflected in a Nordic free movement zone.

This brings us to the main thesis of the book and the methodology chosen to test this thesis and achieve the book's purpose.

II. The Main thesis and Methodology of this Book

This book compares the constitutional systems of the Nordic countries. The main thesis of the book is that viewed from the outside—a European or global perspective—the Nordic constitutional systems share some common features both at a more functional level and at a deeper level of values. However, viewed from a closer Nordic perspective, differences appear in the aforementioned general pattern. This volume aims at identifying both the broader common features and the more detailed differences, in this way presenting a rich analysis of the Nordic constitutional systems seen both from a macro- and a micro-perspective.

Methodologically, a contextualised functionalism approach[1] is chosen. We have identified some key features of constitutional systems. Within each of these fields, we will conduct a comparative study. The chosen key features are the following:

- Institutional structure and division of powers.
- Mechanisms for parliamentary control of the executive.
- Judicial review of legislation.
- Human rights in Nordic constitutions and the impact of international obligations.
- The impact of the EU/EEA on the Nordic countries.

[1] VC Jackson, 'Comparative Constitutional Law: Methodologies' in M Rosenfeld and A Sajo (eds), *The Oxford Handbook of Comparative Constitutional Law* (Oxford, Oxford University Press, 2012) 72.

Although each field has a main author, all the authors—who together represent all the Nordic countries—have cooperated on each chapter.[2] This cooperation ensures the quality of the comparison, including our emphasis on performing a contextualised functionalism comparison. This approach will require a deep understanding of each constitutional system and the values and identity it builds on. The chosen main author is an expert in his or her specific field. Furthermore, we support our analysis in a chapter on the common roots and foundations of the Nordic constitutional systems. Each chapter explains the structure of the analysis carried out, possible delimitations and other analytical choices the author has had to make.

All the comparative studies of specific constitutional features are in the end included in a general comparative study of the Nordic constitutional systems. Here we will also be able to show the interaction between the sub-studies. The overview given in the last concluding chapter will allow us to make some more general observations on whether the similarities are strong enough to form a 'Nordic constitutional model' which at least, seen from a European or global perspective, has some distinct features.

In this way, our comparative analysis process will be somewhat similar to peeling an onion. We will work our way through the different layers of history, culture, values, constitutions and practices, which are closely interwoven and together form the Nordic constitutional systems.

Throughout the book, a number of important distinctions will play a special role in our comparative analysis. These distinctions are inherent components in our comparative study and therefore deserve a few words. First, as mentioned above, we make a distinction between the macro-level and the micro-level. The idea is to distinguish between an outside perspective and an inside perspective.[3] Viewed from the outside—a European or global perspective—the Nordic constitutional systems might appear very similar. However, following a closer look, it becomes clear that these similarities are not all based on similar constitutional provisions, but just as much on shared culture, values and policy outcomes, which are expressed in European and international fora. Furthermore, a closer look also shows that though some general constitutional features can be identified, a further comparative study uncovers many nuances and differences in the Nordic constitutional systems. The macro-/micro-perspective forms part of the main thesis of this book. Second, an East/West distinction serves as a helpful tool in our analysis throughout the book. Traditionally, the Nordic constitutional systems have been grouped into a Western (Denmark, Norway and Iceland) and an Eastern (Sweden and Finland) constitutional tradition. We still find some distinct constitutional

[2] The responsibility of each chapter remains solely with the chapter author.
[3] M Suksi, 'Markers of Nordic Constitutional Identity' (2014) 37(4) *Retfaerd* 66, 67.

features in the East and in the West, especially as regards institutional structure. However, as our analyses will show, similarities and differences also appear across this East/West structure and new distinctions are formed, among others, based on the EU/EEA cooperation and international human rights conventions. Third, our comparative analysis pays special attention to the distinction between EU Member States and EEA Member States among the Nordic countries. This distinction serves as an analytical instrument throughout our analyses. As the chapters will show, the EU/EEA distinction is perhaps not as dominant as one might expect, and another important distinction between formality and reality seems to form part of the picture. Even though the aforementioned distinctions do not find a clear and consistent expression—or maybe precisely for that reason—they serve as fruitful instruments in terms of structuring and carrying out our comparative analysis, revealing new insights in the complex processes that the Nordic constitutional systems are undergoing in the context of history, contemporary constitutional thought and impacts caused by outside forces in the form of EU/EEA and international human rights conventions. By combining the functional analysis of a number of carefully chosen constitutional features with the aforementioned main distinctions, we are able to focus our comparative study even further and draw attention to new relevant layers of comparison.

As mentioned above, an important feature of this volume is the focus on whether and how the EU/EEA and international human rights conventions impact the Nordic constitutional systems, and whether this leads to new distinctions or more unity in the Nordic constitutional order. In this way, our constitutional analysis has several layers and the time perspective plays an important role. In order to identify the impact of the EU/EEA and international human rights on the Nordic constitutional systems, both individually and seen together, we need to carry out a comparative analysis of the constitutional systems before and after the emergence of this outside influence. As a result, our comparative analyses will reflect different stages in the development of the Nordic constitutional systems in light of Europeanisation and internationalisation. In the conclusion, we will add a further dimension by attempting to look into the future in terms of further unity or diversity in the Nordic constitutional systems.

Finally, some remarks on the final comparative analysis in the concluding chapter. As mentioned above, all the comparative studies of specific constitutional features are in the end included in a general comparative study of the Nordic constitutional systems. The purpose of this chapter is to combine the sub-studies into a broad overview of some more general observations on whether the similarities are strong enough to form a 'Nordic constitutional model' which at least from a European or global perspective has some distinct features. Furthermore, we focus especially on how the EU/EEA and international human rights (in particular the ECHR) impact the Nordic constitutional systems, and whether this impact creates new differences and similarities in the Nordic context. The analysis will be structured and carried out in the following way. First, we draw upon historical analysis and extract the main common features. Second, we compare the findings in the functional analysis across all the chapters, mapping:

— first, some main features, which we find or do not find in all the Nordic constitutional systems;
— second, areas where the East/West divide still exists;
— third, areas in which we find differences across the Nordic countries and the East/West divide.

We use diagrams to provide overviews of the results of this mapping of similarities and differences of constitutional features. The concluding chapter provides a general overview and the reader will need to consult the topic-based chapters for more detailed information on the similarities and differences between the individual Nordic systems. Following the comparative mapping, we turn to the question of whether the EU/EEA and international human rights conventions are creating new divides or more unity in the Nordic constitutional systems. Here we draw not only on the specific chapters (Chapters 6 and 7) in relation to these questions, but also on the other chapters, which have all approached the impact of such European and international cooperation. We conduct this analysis through the following steps:

— First, we map areas in which an East/West division seems to exist across the EU/EEA division and attempt to explain this.
— Second, we map ways in which a strengthened unity appears as a result of the EU/EEA.
— Third, we map areas in which international human rights conventions seem to create new divides.
— Fourth, we map ways in which international human rights conventions create unity in the Nordic human rights protection.
— Fifth, we combine our observations in order to provide an overall complex picture of the processes in the Nordic constitutional systems when influenced by the EU/EEA and international human rights conventions.

In the final conclusion, we revisit the historical context and briefly reflect on it in relation to the Nordic approach to EU/EEA cooperation and international human rights conventions, and then turn to reflections on future Nordic movement towards new constitutional divisions, differences or further unity.

When summarising our methodological approach, it should be noted that by choosing to organise and structure our constitutional study of the Nordic constitutional systems as a functional *topical-based* analysis, we deviated from the common *country-based* comparative approach. In the country-based comparative approach, the comparative study is normally structured with chapters on each of the countries compared, ending with a general chapter in which a general comparative analysis is carried out. Each country-specific chapter will normally discuss the same functional elements, making the comparison in the last chapter easier to carry out. In the topical-based approach, the functional analysis is carried out across all the compared legal systems in each chapter.

The concluding chapter in this volume will then be based on the comparative analyses already carried out throughout the book and will contain some general comparative analyses on the entire legal systems across countries. Both approaches have their strengths and weaknesses. The strength of the country-based approach is that it provides a good and easy-to-access overview of many specific features of each legal system. The strength of the topical-based approach is that it provides a possibility to reach a deep level of comparison in specific areas since the comparison is carried out at two levels—throughout the book and in the final comparative analysis. One might say that the topical-based approach demands a little more from the reader as well as the authors. At the same time, the aforementioned strengths indicate the weaknesses of the two approaches. Our choice to apply a topical-based approach in our comparative analysis of the Nordic constitutional systems was based on several factors: the wish to create a dynamic, innovative and interesting book, which already from its very outset combines the Nordic constitutional systems in its narrative, thereby choosing a methodology which reflects the presumption that the Nordic countries share a certain common constitutional tradition (even if it does not apply to all fields).

By starting the comparison already in the functional analyses, we hope to reach a deeper level of comparison. We attempt to counter the possible weaknesses of the applied methodology through the close cooperation between experts from all the Nordic countries in reading and commenting on the chapters written by each other and by choosing an expert on each chosen topic (who already has knowledge of the Nordic countries in that particular field) to write that particular chapter. During the writing process, the group of authors met twice in Copenhagen at seminars on the book project—at the start of the project and towards the end—to discuss the overall design of the book, methodology, individual chapters and how to coordinate the project. No matter how much effort we have put into designing the methodology and the process in the best possible way in order to facilitate the comparative study, we have no desire to try to disguise that we have set out on an ambitious task and our work should be seen in that light.

III. Structure of the Book

The structure of the book has already indirectly appeared through the previous sections. After this introductory chapter (Krunke and Thorarensen), in which we have described the purpose, main thesis, methodology and structure of the book, is Chapter 2 on the common roots of Nordic constitutional law (Suksi). This chapter analyses legal-historical developments and relations between the constitutional systems of the five Nordic countries. Chapter 3 (Bull) provides the reader with a comparative overview of political institutions and division of powers. Chapter 4

(Thorarensen) compares parliamentary control mechanisms of the executive. Following this, a comparative analysis is carried out in Chapter 5 in relation to judicial review of legislation (Smith). The book then moves from the primarily institutional focus to the area of human rights. Chapter 6 (Ojanen) compares human rights in the Nordic constitutions and the impact of international human rights obligations. After having addressed human rights, Chapter 7 (Krunke) focuses on the impact the EU/EEA have had on the Nordic countries. Drawing on the earlier chapters, the concluding chapter (Krunke and Thorarensen) combines the historical analysis and the functional analysis to provide a general comparative overview of the common features, differences and impact of EU/EEA cooperation and international human rights conventions on the Nordic constitutional systems.

IV. Before We Start: The Nordic Legal Systems as a Legal Family?

The Nordic legal systems are sometimes characterised as a separate legal family.[4] Other authors define the Nordic legal systems as primarily belonging to the legal systems in continental Europe, having more in common with the civil law tradition than the common law tradition.[5] The following characteristics of the Nordic legal systems have been emphasised:

— the limited importance of legal formalities;[6]
— Scandinavian realism;[7]
— a 'specific legal method, its mixture of statutory and case law and its, in relation to most continental EU countries, less theoretical and conceptualised approach to legal problems';[8]
— the absence of an actual reception of Roman law;[9]
— no civil codes;[10]
— the fact that 'all-embracing legal principles play a more limited role in Nordic law than in, for example, French or German law';[11]

[4] See, eg, K Zweigert and H Kötz (eds), *Introduction to Comparative Law*, 3rd revised edn (Oxford, Oxford University Press, 1998); D Tamm, 'The Nordic Legal Tradition in European Context' in P Letto-Vanamo (ed), *Nordisk identitet—Nordisk rätt i europeisk gemenskap* (Helsinki, KATTI, Institute for International Economic Law at Helsinki University, 1998) 15 ff; Å Malmström, 'The System of Legal Systems: Notes on a Problem of Classification in Comparative Law' (1969) 13 *Scandinavian Studies in Law* 127.

[5] See, eg, M Bogdan, *Komparativ rättskunskap*, 2nd edn (Lund, Norstedts Juridik, 2003) 82 f.

[6] See D Tamm, 'The Nordic Legal Tradition in European Context' in Letto-Vanamo (n 4) 15 ff.

[7] See Zweigert and Kötz (n 4).

[8] U Bernitz, 'What is Scandinavian Law? Concept, Characteristics, Future' (2007) 50 *Scandinavian Studies in Law* 14, 28.

[9] See D Tamm, 'The Nordic Legal Tradition in European Context' in Letto-Vanamo (n 4) 15 ff.

[10] See Bernitz (n 8) 20; and see also Zweigert and Kötz (n 4).

[11] Bernitz (n 8) 20.

- frequent use of analogies taken from available legislation, particularly within the law of obligations;[12]
- the importance attached to preparatory legislative material (*travaux préparatoires*) when interpreting legislation.[13]

Most similarities between the Nordic legal systems are found within the field of private law and Nordic cooperation on legislation has traditionally taken place within this field.[14] Therefore, it is normally private law that is presented as an argument for the existence of a special Nordic legal family. The field of constitutional law is normally not used as an argument in this regard. When it comes to understanding and comparing constitutional law in the Nordic countries, Kaarlo Tuori's theory on 'the three levels of law' is sometimes applied.[15] The idea is that three levels of law exist: surface law (legal norms), the middle layer (legal culture) and the deep structure (general principles and values). It has been stated that if the Nordic constitutional systems are compared, the likeness grows the further one moves down into these three levels, meaning that the differences are most significant at the legal norm level expressed through the constitutional text, that we find more similarities at the level of legal culture and the most similarities at the level of general principles and values.[16] Seen in this light, the reason why the Nordic constitutional systems might appear alike to the foreign observer is because the Nordic countries share general principles and values at a deeper level. One might also add that the Nordic constitutional systems share certain features which clearly make them stand out from other constitutional systems—for instance, in the field of judicial review of constitutionality—and this attracts attention from the outside.[17] However, the Nordic constitutional systems as such have not been the subject of extensive comparative studies so far,[18] and our task in this book is precisely to carry out such a comparison. Hopefully, this will lead us closer to an understanding of how close to each other the Nordic constitutional systems actually are—historically, traditionally, contemporarily and in light of EU/EEA integration and international human rights conventions—and how similarities, differences and developments might be explained. In the following chapters, this is precisely what we set out to do and we invite the reader to follow us on this comparative journey into the Nordic constitutional systems.

[12] ibid.

[13] See ibid 8.

[14] See the overview in Bernitz (n 10) 16.

[15] See K Tuori, 'Introduction to the Theme: Constitutional identity' (2014) 37(4) *Retfærd* 3; and F Sejersted, 'Grunnlovens funktion i de nordiske land' (2014) 127(5) *Tidsskrift for Rettsvitenskap* 535, 559.

[16] Sejersted (n 15).

[17] See, eg, R Hirschl, 'The Nordic Counternarrative: Democracy, Human Development and Judicial Review' (2011) 9(2) *International Journal of Constitutional Law* 449.

[18] An interesting recent comparison of the Nordic constitutional systems can be found in Sejersted (n 15) and in a special issue of *Retfaerd* on constitutional identity in the Nordic countries: (2014) 37(4) *Retfærd*.

2

Common Roots of Nordic Constitutional Law? Some Observations on Legal-Historical Development and Relations between the Constitutional Systems of Five Nordic Countries

MARKKU SUKSI

I. Introduction

Looking at the Nordic countries from the outside, the viewer would easily arrive at the conclusion that the five states are very similar to each other. Yet from the inside, the picture is more varied: although commonalities exist, features distinguishing the five states also exist. In spite of the differences, the operation of the various constitutions produces results that are very similar, such as a welfare state that tries to look after every member of society.[1] Similarities exist to the extent that the Nordic states have been willing to open up even their citizenship law for some exceptions in terms of residence requirements for granting citizenship in some respects: the requirement of four or five years of residence in the state in which citizenship is being applied for may be waived if the applicant can show residence in one of the other current Nordic countries. The core of what constitutes a state—the right to define the conditions of citizenship—is thus opened up so as to recognise the similarity of the other Nordic countries for the purpose of fulfilling the residence requirement. Hence, it is not only from the outside that the five countries look alike; internally, there is an understanding that the five countries

[1] Internal analysis also proceeds from this assumption. See, eg, U Bernitz, 'What is Scandinavian Law?—Concepts, Characteristics, Future' (2007) 50 *Scandinavian Studies in Law* 13, 16, available at www.scandinavianlaw.se/pdf/50-1.pdf: 'The Nordic countries share a common culture and heritage, based on common democratic and social values, nowadays also the welfare state.'

and the way of life in these countries are so similar that in some situations involving becoming a citizen of another Nordic country, the residence requirement can be completely or partially waived. But is that a result of commonalities in constitutional history?

Although early on, the so-called Kalmar Union united the areas that now comprise the five states, the Nordic space has been militarily characterised by strife between the two old or original states in the region, Denmark and Sweden. However, the last Nordic war was fought in 1814 between Sweden and what had become Norway after separation from Denmark in the Napoleonic Wars in relation to an attempt at Norwegian secession from Sweden. From the middle of the nineteenth century, the ideology of Scandinavism grew stronger and resulted in thoughts of joint law-drafting projects that emphasised cooperation rather than dispute.[2] In spite of a military build-up on both sides of the border, the separation of Norway from the union with Sweden in 1905 was finally regulated in a peaceful manner by means of a treaty concluded at Karlstad between the two parts of the realm.[3] The dispute between Finland and Sweden over the national affiliation of the Åland Islands did not escalate into an armed conflict because both states agreed to submit to dispute resolution by the League of Nations that resulted in the so-called Åland Islands Settlement in 1921.[4] Taken together, the Nordic countries have not wasted their national wealth on wars between themselves during the past 200 years.[5] After the Second World War, the idea of a union between the Nordic countries was realised at the international level in the Nordic Council and the Nordic Council of Ministers, two formally different organisations. This cooperation resulted, inter alia, in a passport-free zone of free movement, including the free movement of labour.

[2] For an analysis of the development of periodic Nordic lawyers' meetings from 1872 onwards, as well as mentions of Nordic legislative cooperation and the Nordic monetary union, see L Björne, *Den konstruktiva riktningen. Den nordiska rättsvetenskapens historia, del III: 1871–1910* (Lund, Institutet för rättshistorisk forskning, 2002) 22–24. I wish to thank Dr Björne, Professor Emeritus of Legal History, University of Turku, Finland, for his insightful comments on a draft version of this chapter. All remaining errors are, of course, my own responsibility.

[3] For the relevant documents related to the Karlstad Convention, including the abdication of the Swedish king and subsequent amendments to 112 § of the Norwegian Constitution, see www.nb.no/baser/1905/dokumenter/uoinnh.htm.

[4] The Åland Islands Agreement before the Council of the League of Nations. V. Minutes of the Seventeenth Meeting of the Council, 27 June 1921. League of Nations Official Journal, September 1921, 701.

[5] When Finland was attacked by the Soviet Union in 1939 in what became the Winter War of 1939–40, there was a significant show of solidarity from the other Nordic countries. Support from Sweden to Finland, totalling 1,970 million marks (some of which may formally have been purchase of materials), amounted to around 57 per cent of the ordinary expenses budgeted in peacetime in 1938 for the 1939 state budget of Finland. The combined support from all Nordic countries was 2,120 million marks, which was more than 61 per cent of the ordinary expenses estimated for the budget for 1939. In addition, volunteers arrived from Denmark, Iceland, Norway and Sweden.

From the point of view of comparative constitutional history until approximately the Second World War, the following research questions are of interest (with specifications to follow further below):

1. What is the historical relationship between the constitutional systems in the Nordic countries? Is this relationship reflected legally in the constitutions? What role has cross-fertilisation from other legal systems outside the Nordic countries historically played?
2. Is there a cultural relationship between the constitutional systems in the Nordic countries? If so, how is this cultural relationship reflected legally in the constitutions, in particular the constitutions in force today?
3. How can we explain similarities and differences between the Nordic countries?

These research questions should enable us to uncover common roots of Nordic constitutional law, if they exist, in order to establish features that might unite the constitutional orders of the Nordic countries for the purposes of creating a sense of Nordicness and a Nordic constitutional identity at the level of constitutional law. Common roots are here understood as constitutional features that the Nordic countries would have shared in their constitutional history and that are today reflected in the constitutions that are in effect, as outlined in the other chapters in this volume.

Methodologically, this chapter reviews the five Nordic countries by using the comparative method of an ordinary kind,[6] namely that of horizontal comparison, but in a longitudinal setting in which the legal-historical component is strong. In this respect, the Peace of Westphalia is used as a first 'tipping point' between the 'old' and the 'new', the proposition being that the state in the modern meaning of the term as a subject of international law and as a constitutional entity started to develop (before and) around the year 1648. However, the idea is not to suggest that the Nordic countries were, during the seventeenth century, in any way aware of the significance that later times have attached to the Westphalian system. A second 'tipping point' is less a particular year or even era, but rather a series of instances in the constitutional evolution of the five countries during which core features of a modern constitution were introduced, often as a reaction to autocratic rule or external dominance.

From the point of view of materials, constitutional documents mentioned in the text constitute primary sources, complemented by literature mentioned in the footnotes from the fields of legal history, history and law. Scholarly work from Professor Nils Herlitz focusing, inter alia, on the constitutional features of the Nordic countries deserves a separate mention as an important source of information for this chapter. His *Elements of Nordic Public Law* is intended for an

[6] Because of the inter-governmental link of the Nordic Council that unites the five states, some measure of vertical comparison will be present in the inquiry.

international audience,[7] but is largely based on his thorough analysis in several volumes of *Nordisk offentlig rätt*,[8] that is, Nordic public law. It is hardly possible to do justice in a limited piece like the current one to the constitutional history of the various Nordic countries, and therefore this current piece is a collated view of one author, while the background can be accessed in greater detail through the work of Herlitz and through research and documentation referenced in the footnotes.

II. The Time before Westphalia

From the Middle Ages, three crowns, the precursors to those of Denmark, Norway and Sweden today, were in control over the Nordic space, albeit not necessarily within those geographical borders that demarcate the Nordic states today. In the aftermath of the dispersed organisation of the Viking era, population groups started to gather in units with somewhat larger territorial scope where chiefs and warlords wielded local power and formed alliances that eventually led to formations that could be called kingdoms. In these kingdoms, a king exercised the highest power. This is at least the ordinary explanation, although the focus on the one king prevents us from detecting other ways to govern the relatively scarce population of those times, even if these other ways are likely to have existed. The earlier nationalistic construction of history also tried to push back the creation of the kingdoms and states as far back in history as possible in order to establish a clear lineage of kings, the one more heroic than the other, even when such lineage did not always exist, a feature which at least in Sweden led to fantastic tales about the origins of the kingdom.[9] However, the 'state' and thus also the 'constitution' in the general and modern meaning of the term is probably a somewhat later phenomenon than is commonly thought, at the same time as the 'starting point' of the state may be different in the Nordic countries.

Although in Norway, the office of king may have conformed to the expectation of a hereditary kingdom from as early as 1163, the opposite was true in Denmark

[7] N Herlitz, *Elements of Nordic Public Law* (Stockholm, PA Norstedt & Söners förlag, 1969).

[8] N Herlitz, *Nordisk offentlig rätt. I. Historisk inledning* (Stockholm, PA Norstedt & Söners förlag, 1958); N Herlitz, *Nordisk offentlig rätt. II. Riksdagarna och tingen* (Stockholm, PA Norstedt & Söners förlag, 1958); N Herlitz, *Nordisk offentlig rätt. III:1. Regeringsmakt och förvaltningsorganisation* (Stockholm, PA Norstedt & Söners förlag, 1963); N Herlitz, *Nordisk offentlig rätt. III:2. Regeringsmakt och förvaltningsorganisation* (Stockholm, PA Norstedt & Söners förlag, 1963).

[9] See, eg, D Juslenius, 'Aboa vetus et nova', dissertation, Kungliga Akademin i Åbo, 1700 (reissue, Helsinki, Åbo Akademi & Suomalaisen kirjallisuuden seura, 2005) 47, where reference is made to times after the flood, when the population increased (Genesis 9:1 and 7) and 'descendants of Japheth, who received Europe for themselves, migrated to the north under the leadership of Magog and occupied Finland', after which they began to build towns. Reference is also made to the rule of King Siggo III of Sweden at the beginning of the fourth century after the flood, but there is no evidence of such a king ever having existed, nor for that matter that Sweden would have existed at that time.

and Sweden, where the office of king was at least in principle elective. This feature may signal an earlier evolution of Norway towards a more unified state structure than in the other two countries, where the king remained dependent on integral parts of the territory until a later time. In Sweden, the hereditary kingdom was instituted in 1544 and in Denmark as late as in 1660. Until then, the various parts and segments of the state had at least some say in electing the main king, who often came from among lesser chiefs and warlords who were in control of particular parts of the country. For instance, although an election of a king of Sweden was practised during the twelfth and the thirteenth centuries, only in the mid-fourteenth century was this person identified as a king of Sweden, and in 1362, the representatives of what is now Finland were invited to participate in the election of the king, which means that the process of integrating the traditional parts of Sweden was well under way at that point in time (although it was by no means complete at that point in time). In the Codes of the 1350s and 1442, there were provisions concerning the king, his election and various governmental matters, preceded by similar provisions in some older regional codes.

The king, in particular the elected king, remained dependent of his support groups, the most important of whom developed into nobility. At this point in time, the Catholic Church was a central power factor in society, which resulted in the clergy forming into another privileged group. With the importance of trade increasing, the burghers also became a group to reckon with, at least in the towns where the trade was concentrated, while in the countryside, landed peasants were traditionally involved in at least some measure of self-administration in respect of their common matters. These forms of organisation of the peasantry were later on incorporated into the structures of the state, except in Denmark, where the regular peasantry was drawn into a system of servitude of the kind practised elsewhere in Europe and which was only abolished in 1788. Servitude did, however, not develop into anything significant elsewhere in the Nordic space, leaving a good portion of the population in the countryside in formal possession of their lands. This is a feature that is sometimes offered as an explanation of the relatively egalitarian nature of the Nordic states.

There were some alliances between Sweden and Norway as well as Denmark and Norway earlier in the fourteenth century, but in 1397, the Nordic space formed itself into the so-called Kalmar Union, created with the purpose of stemming the increasing German influence in the Baltic Sea area. The three crowns were loosely united, with the council of each country as the power-wielding body, but early on in the Union, it started to be dominated by the Danish crown. This created frictions in particular in relation to the Swedish nobility and, as a consequence, the Kalmar Union broke up in 1523 into two states, Denmark and Sweden. The current territories of Norway and Iceland (which had been joined with Norway in 1262) remained part of Denmark through a personal union, while what was then Sweden also contained parts of current Finland. Therefore, it is possible to say that the independence of Sweden actually began in 1523, when it left the Kalmar Union. The relationship between the king and 'the people' was constitutionalised in the pledges of the king when he ascended to the throne, which was from this point onwards hereditary.[10] The heritage of the three crowns from medieval times is, however, still today reflected in the monarchical constitutions of Denmark, Norway and Sweden with figurehead royalties, while the independence of Finland and Iceland in the form of republics was a more natural choice during the twentieth century than monarchy. Although the Finnish president wielded considerable powers until the 1990s, it seems that the two Nordic presidents are situated in a more all-European tradition with relatively limited powers, almost figurehead-like positions.

The geopolitical situation that resulted from the break-up of the Kalmar Union determined for centuries the aggressive tone between Denmark and Sweden: the southern and south-western parts of what today is Sweden, including the island of Gotland in the Baltic, continued to remain part of Denmark, and with the Danish possessions in Norway close by, Sweden had only a tiny outlet to the North Sea, approximately where the city of Gothenburg is situated today. Because Denmark stretched its sovereignty along the Norwegian coast to the northernmost part of Scandinavia and from there eastwards towards Russia, and because Denmark controlled the Danish straits, Sweden felt itself in many ways encircled by Denmark, without proper customs-free access to other countries and ports than those on the Baltic Sea. War was a constant feature of the relationship between Denmark and Sweden, and also during formal peace, diplomatic efforts were undertaken in relation to other countries in order to forge alliances that would block the moves of the other neighbour. Sweden often found itself outflanked by Denmark.

The Reformation altered the traditional relationship between the Church and state. Originally, the Catholic Church had wielded a fair amount of power in society and saw itself as standing above the king. Religion enhanced the legitimacy of the king, who in turn was in charge of ruling the subjects according to the faith. With the Evangelic-Lutheran Reformation, this was turned upside down, placing the king clearly at the helm of the affairs of the state and also of the Church. The king was still constitutionally supposed to rule according to the faith, but there was no pope or other religious authority that would stand above the king. In Denmark, the Reformation took place in 1536, and in Sweden, coupled with the confiscation of the properties and valuables of the Church to the crown, from 1527 onwards. The Lutheran variant of the Christian faith is still entrenched in the Constitutions of Denmark[11] and Iceland,[12] while section 2 of the Constitution of Norway makes reference to the value base found in the Christian and humanistic heritage.

[10] See, eg, RE Henry and KE Miller, 'Denmark, Including Greenland and Faroe Islands' in AP Blaustein and GH Flanz (eds), *Constitutions of the Countries of the World* (Dobbs Ferry, NY, Oceana Publications, 1985) 1 f.

[11] Section 4: 'The Evangelical Lutheran Church shall be the Established Church of Denmark, and, as such, it shall be supported by the State.'

[12] Section 62: 'The Evangelical Lutheran Church shall be the State Church in Iceland and, as such, it shall be supported and protected by the State.'

In Finland, section 76 of the Constitution of Finland concludes that provisions about the organisation and administration of the Evangelic-Lutheran Church are given in a separate Church Act. In addition, the section places the determination of the legislative process concerning the Church Act in this Act, thereby to some extent sidelining the matters of the Church from the regular scope of the Constitution. Amendments of the 1974 Instrument of Government (Constitution) Act of Sweden have separated the state and the Church entirely and have brought about a situation where the church, until 2000 formally a state church, now approximates the status of any other religious community, albeit on the basis of a separate statute, the general operations of which are, according to Chapter 8(2), subject to provisions in law. However, the king (or queen, as the case may be) is required, under the Succession (Constitution) Act of 1810, as amended, to profess the pure evangelical faith.[13] Hence, although religion today plays an insignificant role in the constitutional life of the Nordic states, there are still today clear traces in the Nordic constitutions of the former supreme significance of religion, in particular the Evangelic-Lutheran religion.

III. The Sovereign State Taking Shape

The medieval state structures started to evolve towards more formal procedures of governance during the seventeenth century. The Thirty Years' War, which in principle and on the surface was a struggle between Protestants and Catholics (but in reality was probably an ordinary power struggle between kingdoms), suddenly established Sweden as a major military and political power in Europe. Sweden was a warring party and thus a party to the Treaty of Westphalia, while Denmark was not (although it entertained diplomatic designs against Sweden throughout). As a consequence, Sweden was a signatory to the Treaty, which is, in a more recent construction, thought to have defined the state in the modern meaning of the word. The Westphalian state is an entity which is sovereign in relation to other states and a subject of public international law, a quality that would obviously also apply to Denmark, although it was not a party to this great treaty.

In the internal 'constitutional' sense, the Westphalian idea of the state became, in part, visible in a more stringent organisation of the state, a quality that evolved during the Thirty Years' War, which forced both Denmark and Sweden to develop their armies and also the collection of taxes to support armed action over time.

[13] Section 4: 'In accordance with the express provision of Article 2 of the Instrument of Government of 1809 that the King shall always profess the pure evangelical faith, as adopted and explained in the unaltered Confession of Augsburg and in the Resolution of the Uppsala Meeting of the year 1593, princes and princesses of the Royal House shall be brought up in that same faith and within the Realm. Any member of the Royal Family not professing this faith shall be excluded from all rights of succession.'

The definition of the privileges granted to different groups of persons that were formed into estates grew in importance and were understood as constitutional pledges or constitutional conventions amendable only with the consent of the estate concerned. In Denmark, the estates consisted of the nobility, the clergy and the burghers, while in Sweden, due to the absence of serfdom, there was an additional fourth group of persons, the land-owning peasants. The actual government was in both countries in the hands of the nobility—more specifically, of the high nobility, which was constituted in the Council. The Council was a body of advisors to the king and gained this position originally through military services made to the king. To a great extent, the Council became the administrative nexus of the state in both kingdoms.

A certain regularisation and constitutionalisation of the state and the affairs of state took place in Sweden with the adoption of the 1634 Instrument of Government Act, which contained organisational provisions about the construction of the state. While the functioning of the Diet of Sweden was first regulated in the Rules of Procedure of 1617, the Instrument of Government, created during the exigencies of the war when the king was away from Stockholm, was a document that became more necessary during the minority of the subsequent ruler, Queen Christina. Drafted largely by Chancellor Axel Oxenstierna, the Instrument of Government of 1634 represented a model of rational and efficient organisation of the state that many other European powers, including Denmark, wanted to imitate, although in modified forms. The variant and unstable administrative arrangements inherited from medieval times were becoming more solidly organised.

Several of the institutional arrangements recorded in the first Instrument of Government are still today present in the Swedish Constitution and to some limited extent also in the Finnish Constitution. However, at that juncture, the idea of a separation between normative enactments of a constitutional and an ordinary kind had not yet developed. Therefore, several modifications and exceptions to the Instrument of Government emerged some years after the document was adopted.

An important and general exception (albeit temporary) to the previous models of rule was the era of autocracy or absolutism, which commenced in Denmark in 1661 and in Sweden in 1680. While it ended in Sweden in 1718, the era of absolutism prevailed in Denmark until as late as 1848. One characteristic feature of autocracy of this time was the centralisation of the state and the very detailed and direct rule by the king in a manner which left little space, for instance, for the Diets in the two countries: in practice, the operation of the Diets ended during the time of absolutism (in reality, however, absolutism seems to have facilitated the strengthening of the position of civil servants). This direct rule with attention to detail was not only a feature of the Danish and Swedish monarchs towards the end of the seventeenth century, but was a feature also known in France (under Louis XIV) and Prussia. At least in Denmark, absolutism was philosophically motivated by reference to the writings of Jean Bodin and some other authors who justified government by reference to a contract of government between the king and the population,[14] while in Sweden, the position of the king was still given a religious justification.

Internally, the 'Westphalian' focus on the state in combination with autocratic rule may also have meant that the existence of sub-national parts or sub-countries within a state with their own legal orders or variants to the legal order of the state became more difficult to entertain. As a consequence, the state may have become more unified, unitary and monolithic, which would have affected at least Norway and Iceland, which early on in their position as part of the Danish crown could maintain separate or at least traditional jurisdictions. However, the real reason for a more unified state was probably the absolutism of the king in Denmark, which made it abundantly clear that normative enactments stemmed from the Danish crown, not from any of the sub-parts. For Norway and Iceland, this had already actually been the case since the mid-sixteenth century, although both sub-parts of Denmark were allowed to keep some public servants and public bodies under their local names and probably also under some local laws, at least in Iceland: after all, the absolute monarch lacked the capacity to streamline all legislation and institutions across the vast kingdom. Norway was actually explicitly made a regular province of Denmark in the same way as the provinces of Denmark proper. For the eastern part of Sweden, which is today known as Finland, this was never any issue, because Finland was clearly an integral part of Sweden without any partial legislative jurisdiction of its own. At any rate, the two states, Denmark and Sweden, were subjects of contemporary international law.

IV. Constitutionalisation of the Life of the State

A. Background

An important step in the constitutionalisation processes of the Nordic countries is the point when a distinction between ordinary law and constitutional law emerges. No doubt, earlier provisions about codes containing mentions of the king and his administration can be understood as being of constitutional nature, along with the pledges between the king and the estates and the privileges guaranteed for different segments of the populations, such as the nobility, the clergy, the burghers and, in Sweden, the land-owning peasants. However, as evidenced during the period of so-called autocratic rule in both Denmark and Sweden, such provisions in ordinary law were easily broken by the king, a feature which perhaps contributed to the need to establish legislation of a higher order, amendable only by special procedures.

[14] D Tamm, *Retshistorie: Danmark—Europa—globale perspektiver* (Copenhagen, DJØF, 2005) 200–05.

The distinction between ordinary law and fundamental law was at least partly based on the notion of privileges of the estates, the amendment of which required, on the basis of section XIX of the 1723 Rules of Procedure Act, the unanimous decision of the four estates in Sweden, while other legislation was decided by a majority of three out of four estates. In Denmark, the Royal Act of 1665 is often referred to as the unique case of a constitutional act for an absolute king on the basis of which other legislation was adopted.

Until the beginning of the nineteenth century, Nordic constitutional history is the history of Denmark and Sweden, two states that do not have too much in common in terms of constitutional history. However, from 1808 onwards, things start to change. The Napoleonic Wars resulted in two territorial adjustments in the Nordic space that were of great constitutional relevance. In the Finnish War of 1808–09 between Sweden and Russia, fought on the basis of the Treaty of Tilsit concluded between Russia and France in order to force Sweden to join the continental system against Great Britain, Sweden lost its eastern part, Finland, to Russia. In 1814, the Treaty of Kiel transferred Norway from Denmark to Sweden in a measure that can at least in part be regarded as compensation to Sweden for the loss of Finland, at the same time as it was a measure to reward Sweden for participation in the alliance against Napoleon.[15] Denmark was at that point in time an ally of France, so the measure also had the character of a punishment for Denmark. As a consequence, two sub-state jurisdictions emerged—one with a legal order of Swedish provenance as an autonomous part of the Russian Empire and another with a new legal order as a part of Sweden, but both displaying an evolution towards independence at the beginning of the twentieth century.

It has been noted that through the break-ups of the two realms in 1809 and 1814, two new 'states' emerged—the Grand Duchy of Finland and the Kingdom of Norway—and that the emergence of new states was commonplace during the Napoleonic Wars. What appears unusual in comparison with state formations of the Napoleonic era is that these embryonic states have lasted until the present day.[16] It was also unusual that the two sub-state entities emerged as independent states around the same point in time, 1917 and 1905, respectively. The position of Iceland in relation to Denmark started to develop after the period of absolutism and resulted in sub-state status for Iceland. However, the independence of Iceland in 1944 was a consequence of the Second World War under the 1918 Self-Government Act, which in practice made Iceland an independent entity: from the occupation of Denmark in 1940 by the Third Reich, the ties between Denmark and Iceland were effectively severed, paving the way from a move towards personal union to complete independence. From that vantage point, the Icelandic evolution

[15] In fact, the deal concerninh Norway was finalised and confirmed between the Russian Tsar and the Swedish crown prince at a meeting held in Turku/Åbo in August 1812. See NE Villstrand, *Furstar och folk i Åbo 1812* (Stockholm, Atlantis, 2012).

[16] L Björne, *Hotet från öster. Drag i finsk och även norsk konstitutionell historia fram till 1809/1814* (Oslo, Akademisk publisering, 2014) 145.

resulted in a break-up of a similar nature to that of Finland's independence in 1917. In all three cases, the severing of ties from the old country by means of independence paved the way for the evolution of modern constitutions. Against this background, it would also be possible to expect that the Nordic space, in terms of constitutional tradition, consists of two parts: an eastern constitutional tradition (Sweden and Finland) and a western constitutional tradition (Denmark, Norway and Iceland). The presentation of the five Nordic countries below follows the chronological order of emergence of the five countries, supplemented by a consideration of self-government for sub-state entities and municipalities.

B. Denmark: From Eternal Absolutism to Rigid Constitutions

The 1665 Danish Royal Act was preceded by the 1661 Act of Succession of Absolutism, which already at that stage referred to itself as a fundamental law, while at the same time identifying the jurisdiction so as to cover Denmark and Norway (with Norway including the Faroe Islands, Iceland and Greenland). It is, however, not clear from this Act that a distinction between this constitutional act and ordinary acts was foreseen, although that certainly would seem to have been the consequence. At the same time, the Act extinguished the ancient tradition of the elective king and made prescriptions about the order of succession. The 1665 Royal Act identifies itself as an instrument of government and already makes reference to itself as a fundamental law in the Preamble. Section II of the Royal Act establishes the sovereignty of the absolute power of the king of Denmark and Norway, based on hereditary succession, over all law.[17] This is further specified in section III, which goes on to say that the king alone shall have the highest power and authority to make laws and ordinances according to his own will and wish, and to explain, amend, expand, circumscribe and even revoke previous legislation granted by him or his predecessors. The king could also exempt what and whom he liked from the general prescriptions of the law.

However, according to section III, the Royal Act itself was to be exempted from the absolute powers of the king, because the Royal Act should remain as the true Constitution and Constitutional Act of the kingdom and therefore would be unamendable and unaltered. Section III was thus framed to function as an eternity clause of some sort: although the king in principle had unlimited legislative powers, these powers were not effective in relation to the very basis of his absolute authority, the Royal Act, which could not be amended by anyone. It is therefore possible to reach the tenuous conclusion that in Denmark since the 1660s, there existed an understanding that the Constitution and the ordinary enactments were at different normative levels. This understanding did not, however, play out in the way that ordinary constitutional law would expect. When the era of absolutism came

[17] See also Henry and Miller (n 10) 3.

to an end in 1848 (notwithstanding the eternity clause in section III of the Royal Act), the then-prevailing understandings in Europe of the meaning of a constitution became visible in the Danish context in the text of the 1849 Constitution,[18] which introduced constitutional monarchy with legislative powers vested in a two-chamber parliament and the king. Some foreign models considered in this context were the Norwegian Constitution of 1814 (see below) and the 1831 Belgian Constitution. It might be possible to identify 1849 as the most recent point of *pouvoir constituant* in Denmark, that is, as a point from which the current constitutional order derives its continuity.

The 1849 Constitution established in section 100 a complicated procedure of amendment in three phases by the bicameral legislature: after the adoption of an amendment proposal in both chambers of one legislature, the measure is submitted to the next parliament and if adopted and agreed to by the king, the parliament shall be dissolved and the amendment proposal submitted to the third parliament for final adoption. This method of amendment certainly signals a wish to create a very clear difference between constitutional enactments and ordinary law. The introduction in the amendment clause of the new 1915 Constitution of a compulsory constitutional referendum was perhaps at the time perceived as a simplification of the earlier amendment procedure, because the referendum replaced the third decision-making procedure in the parliament:[19] the dissolution of the entire parliament was no longer needed in order for the third stage of constitutional amendment procedure to be completed. However, the decision-making rule of this mandatory constitutional referendum is not a simple majority of those voting, but instead a quorum requirement and an approval threshold are established that require a high level of popular involvement: if a majority of persons taking part in the voting and at least 40 per cent of the electorate has voted in favour of the amendment as passed by the parliament, and if the amendment receives the royal assent, it shall form an integral part of the Constitution.

Therefore, it seems that this method of amendment (1/2 + elections + 1/2 + referendum with qualified approval rules) has not alleviated the rigidity of the Danish Constitution because no amendments have been made to the Constitution after 1953, when the current Constitution of Denmark was enacted. There is a considerable risk of failure of an amendment in a referendum. This probably means that the Danish Constitution is mainly evolving through organic development within the existing provisions. With the introduction of the Constitution of 1953,[20] the Danish Parliament was made unicameral, based on proportional election combining the seat allocation methods of d'Hondt and Sainte-Laguë into a very complicated system for the distribution of mandates. The Danish Constitution is the only one amongst the Nordic constitutions to require a referendum for

[18] See also ibid 4 f.
[19] See also ibid 7 f.
[20] See also ibid 10–14.

an amendment of every aspect of the Constitution and is also otherwise formally speaking a very referendum-friendly system, although the legislative referendum has not been used since 1963. However, it has been noted that while the constitutional possibility of holding a legislative referendum has only been used once, the provision enabling a parliamentary minority to request such a referendum may press the government to seek broad majority support in Parliament in order to eliminate the 'threat' of a legislative referendum. In this way, the provision on the legislative referendum in the Danish Constitution may be understood as significant, although it is rarely activated.[21] Because the actual use of the referendum in Denmark has mainly been in the area of international treaties, in particular membership of the EU, the constitutional system of Denmark stands out as one which is as representative in nature as those in the other Nordic countries, where consultative referendums are sometimes held on important issues, such as EU membership.

C. Sweden: From Vague Principles to Firm Application

In Sweden, the understanding that there is a normative difference between ordinary legislation and constitutional legislation started to develop during the eighteenth century, in particular during the so-called Age of Liberty, inaugurated in 1718 as a reaction to the autocratic rule of the king. Unlike other documents, the 1719 and the 1720 Instruments of Government identified themselves in the Preambles and in the confirmations undersigned after a unanimous vote by the estates and the king as a general fundamental law that the king would observe. Section 13 of the 1719 Instrument of Government established this idea in particular for the relationship between the king and the Council when it maintained that the king should act with the advice of the Council, never outside of such advice or against the advice, notwithstanding rules and practices that had existed in the past. In addition to the same provision in section 13 of the 1720 Instrument of Government, there were also references to fundamental law in sections 14 and 37, but the context indicates some degree of confusion about the concept of the fundamental law, because the Instrument of Government and a number of other legislative enactments and privileges are mentioned in the same provision. At this juncture, the 1723 Rules of Procedure of the Diet were also regarded as fundamental law.[22]

However, the first time that this understanding manifested itself more clearly was the adoption of the 1766 Freedom of the Press Ordinance. As such, the term

[21] JP Christensen, JA Jensen and MH Jensen, *Grundloven med kommentarer* (Copenhagen, Jurist- og Økonomforbundets Forlag, 2015) 290. See also M Suksi, *Bringing in the People: A Comparison of Constitutional Forms and Practices of the Referendum* (Dordrecht, Martinus Nijhoff Publishers, 1993) 200–01.

[22] See also F Sterzel, *Författning i utveckling—Tjugo studier kring Sveriges författning* (Uppsala, Iustus förlag, 2009) 94.

'Ordinance' indicates that rules exist at the level of a decree, that is, below the level of an act. However, the Ordinance was enacted under the sovereignty of the Diet, which at that point in time was undisputable, and therefore the Ordinance is, in fact, an act of the Diet. In addition, section 14 of the Ordinance defines itself as an irrevocable fundamental law.

In order to understand the meaning of 'irrevocable fundamental law', it is necessary to know that Acts passed by the Diet required the majority of three of the four estates in the Diet (the nobility, clergy, burghers and land-owning peasants). This principle was established on the basis of the 1720 Instrument of Government Act and the 1723 Rules of Procedure of the Diet Act. Both of these Acts were considered fundamental laws, and the 1766 Ordinance can be understood as a complementary fundamental law in relation to them.[23] By the time of the adoption of the Ordinance, the concept of fundamental law was still developing concerning the enactment procedure, and it seems reasonable to think that the Ordinance already became a fundamental law according to the 'traditional' idea of fundamental law that originated at the beginning of the Age of Liberty. In addition, a principle for the enactment of fundamental law was established by the Diet in the Resolution of 15 October 1766, according to which a constitutional act enacted at a Diet required, during the following Diet, a super-majority of four estates, that is, unanimity of the four estates for confirmation as a constitutional act.[24]

This process for 'explaining, adding to or improving' constitutional acts was adopted by the Diet only a month before the Freedom of the Press Ordinance was enacted. Because neither freedom of the press nor access to public documents was part of the two constitutional acts and because no absolutely clear distinction between a formal constitutional act and an ordinary act existed concerning the procedure of adopting constitutional acts, the 1766 Ordinance was not antithetical to the material constitution (in particular, the privileges of any of the estates) and could therefore be adopted by three estates as a fundamental law in spite of the fact that the nobility was opposed to some parts of it.[25] Nevertheless, the Ordinance could be understood as a fundamental law of the same order as the Constitutional Acts of 1720 and 1723. In fact, the nobility had also supported freedom of the press and the Ordinance, although it preferred a slightly altered version of it, so at the end of the day, it was possible for the king to promulgate the Ordinance as

[23] See A Brusewitz, *Frihetstidens grundlagar och konstitutionella stadgar* (Stockholm, PA Norstedt & Söner, 1916) iii; and Sterzel (n 22) 95. The preamble to the 1720 Instrument of Government Act identifies the Act as a fundamental law enacted by the unanimous decision of the four Estates. The 1723 Rules of Procedure Act was also considered to be a constitutional act. On the clear understanding of the fundamental laws of 1720 and 1723 as constitutional documents of a superior nature in relation to previous documents, see M Roberts, *The Age of Liberty: Sweden 1719–1772* (Cambridge, Cambridge University Press, 1986) 61 f.

[24] See the decision of the Diet of 15 October 1766, para 6, in which the process of enacting constitutional acts is outlined. See Roberts (n 23) 68, 168–70.

[25] P Virrankoski, *Anders Chydenius—Demokratisk politiker i upplysningens tid* (Stockholm, Timbro, 1995) 193.

a fundamental law. The irrevocable nature of the fundamental laws indicated the existence of an eternity principle of some sort, but at that juncture, it was commonplace to think that such an enactment by the sovereign Diet was permanent.[26]

Formally, during the Age of Liberty, the decisions of the Swedish Diet were made by means of the four collective votes, one from each of the estates. So when the (conservative) political party of the Hats dominated the Diet, they did so by dominating at least three of the estates, and when the (liberal) party of the Caps finally gained an overall majority, they had to dominate at least three of the estates.[27]

However, the nature of the 1720 Instrument of Government, the 1723 Rules of Procedure of the Diet and the 1766 Ordinance as fundamental laws could not withstand the coup d'etat performed by the king, together with the military, in 1772. At that point, the young king Gustav III had grown weary of his role as a figurehead and longed for the restoration of royal powers, staging a swift campaign that ended in the wholesale revocation of all those fundamental laws that had been enacted after 1680, including the Ordinance of 1766. The 1772 Instrument of Government, adopted by the Diet at gunpoint, referred to itself as a constitution and a fundamental law, and the 1789 Guaranty and Security Act made reference to itself as an unamendable constitutional act by which the 1772 Instrument of Government was partly amended and, in addition, confirmed. In reality, however, these two Gustavian constitutional acts were the products of a king who was becoming increasingly autocratic: the proto-democratic Age of Liberty turned into a period of absolutism that lasted until 1809.

The constitutional breakdown of the Gustavian order in 1809 was of a revolutionary nature and resulted in the re-introduction and confirmation of the idea of the constitution. The 1809 Instrument of Government Act of Sweden defined itself as a constitutional act and also did so in section 85 for the Freedom of the Press Ordinance, the Rules of Procedure of the Diet/Parliament and the Succession Act, thus making the Swedish Constitution multi-documentary. The 1809 Instrument of Government identified itself in the Preamble as the constitution, and this was also established in the confirmation of the regent. At the same time, the Constitutional Acts of 1772 and 1789 as well as the 1617 Rules of Procedure of the Diet were revoked (it can be said that from this point onwards, the idea of fundamental law started to matter in practice). A new Rules of Procedure of the Diet was enacted in 1810, being replaced in 1866 by a new set of rules introducing the reform of the representation in the second chamber based on single-member constituencies, which was changed in 1909 into proportional representation using the d'Hondt method for the allocation of seats (the members of the first chamber

[26] Sterzel (n 22) 95.

[27] Therefore, control by one political party of all four estates would have guaranteed the possibility of passing more progressive legislation at the level of formal constitutional law. In such a situation, the enactment of rules in the new constitutional order according to the formula 3/4 + 4/4 would in any future party constellation of the different estates have made it virtually impossible to secure unanimity for the revocation of a fundamental law.

were appointed by electoral colleges). Thus, it is possible to conclude that 1809 seems to be the point of *pouvoir constituant* in Sweden from which the current constitutional order derives its continuity. The amendment formula of section 81 with the temporal partition in two decisions concerning the contents of the constitutional amendment by two consecutive parliaments, in the last instance by the unanimity of all four estates, followed the principle established in the resolution of 1766. At the same time, the idea of the irrevocability of fundamental law was dropped, resulting in many amendments to the Constitution between 1809 and 1974, when a new Instrument of Government (Constitution) Act was enacted.[28]

The Swedish Parliament turned from a bicameral into a unicameral one from 1971. The variant of the early principle of constitutional enactment now recorded in section 8:14 of the 1974 Instrument of Government Act is that the amendment proposal be adopted by a simple majority by two consecutive parliaments, leading to the formula of '1/2 + elections + 1/2', with at least nine months elapsing between the first parliamentary introduction of the amendment proposal and the elections. However, under section 8:16, a minority of MPs may request a referendum on a pending constitutional amendment, a decisive vote designed as a popular veto which leads to a defeat of the amendment proposal if an absolute majority of voters vote against the proposed amendment. If a referendum is organised, the next parliament will not decide on the matter. In comparison with the rigidity of the Danish Constitution, the Swedish Constitution is definitely more flexible—in fact, it is the most flexible in the Nordic space, leaving the Finnish, Icelandic and Norwegian Constitutions to lie between the two extremes. Although a reform of representation in national decision-making was effected in 1866, at which point the Diet based on estates was replaced by a two-chamber parliament with a directly elected lower chamber, a modern unicameral parliament emerged only by means of the Instrument of Government (Constitution) Act of 1974, when the upper chamber with regional and municipal representation was abolished. Since then, the method of proportional election has been based on party lists with adjustment seats to ensure correct proportionality over the country that can be described as a modified Sainte-Laguë (adjusted odd-number) method of distribution of mandates with a support threshold of four per cent.

D. Finland: From Sub-state Existence to Emphasis of Continuity

In fact, the separation from Sweden of what in 1808–09 emerged as Finland threatened to place this part of the Nordic countries outside of the Nordic space. In the Russo-Swedish war of 1808–09, Sweden ceded its eastern part to Russia, and under ordinary circumstances, the autocratic emperor of Russia would have incorporated this territory into the Russian Empire as a regular province.

[28] See Sterzel (n 22) 97–100.

This, however, did not happen, because the Tsar willed something else, namely to rule over Finland under the provisions of the Swedish law that had been in force in Finland until 1809. In March 1809, exactly at the same time as the Swedish King Gustavus IV Adolf was deposed and the old constitutional order was coming to an end in Sweden, the Tsar pledged to uphold the Christian faith, the Constitutional Acts and the privileges of each of the estates, and referred explicitly to the term 'Constitution'.[29] He also expressed the opinion that this moment was the beginning of the existence of Finland as a state. He pledged to govern Finland according to the laws of Finland, which meant, for instance, that the Swedish General Code of Laws of 1734 remained in force with its chapters on various areas of law, such as criminal law, contracts, family law, etc.[30] The estates of Finland, while recognising the Emperor and the Grand Duke of Finland as the only real authority, pledged in return not to destabilise the constitution or the form of government.

The various interpretations of all these pledges converge on the understanding that the 1772 Instrument of Government and the 1789 Act of Union and Security as well as the 1617 Rules of Procedure of the Diet were maintained as the fundamental laws of Finland. When the Diet was concluded in August 1809, the Tsar and Grand Duke explained that Finland was henceforth to be placed in the category of nations. Thus, a curious situation emerged: despite being an autocratic ruler in the rest of Russia, the Tsar and Grand Duke was at least in principle a constitutional monarch within the particular jurisdiction of Finland under those Swedish Constitutional Acts which had been revoked in Sweden.[31] The Gustavian constitutional legislation lived on in Finland, and because it did not necessarily limit the actions of the ruler too much, the arrangement was no serious impediment for the Tsar and Grand Duke. In this respect, a comparison could be made with the period of autocratic rule in Denmark between 1661 and 1848,[32] but it seems that the legal position of the autonomous Finland was unclear and, in particular from a Russian point of view, it might have been an absurd idea that Finland could be a particular state in a union of some sort with Russia.[33] At the same time, the population

[29] For the text, see Björne (n 16) 78. According to Björne, the Swedish usage of fundamental law (Swe: *grundlag*) was established, while the term 'constitution' was not entrenched in legislation, but was only a part of literature in the area of constitutional law (see Björne (n 16) 79).

[30] See ibid 82 f concerning the broad scope of Swedish norms re-instituted in the particular jurisdiction of Finland. A prelude to this pledge was published in a manifesto to the inhabitants of Finland from the Russian Tsar in June 1808, in which the Tsar on the one hand said that these inhabitants have now taken a place amongst those different peoples that exist under the Russian crown and that together constitute an empire, but on the other hand promised to uphold the laws and privileges of their old country. See ibid 71.

[31] An even stranger situation would have emerged if what remained of Sweden would have kept the Gustavian constitutional legislation in force. In terms of timing, this was a very likely outcome, because the Swedish king was deposed around the same time as the Tsar made his pledges, and the new Instrument of Government for Sweden was only decided on 6 June 1809.

[32] See Björne (n 16) 83; for the discussion about whether Finland emerged, in 1809, as a state or a province, see Björne (n 16) 91–102.

[33] ibid 88, 90.

of Finland, especially the political and administrative segments, countered the potential threat and, towards the end of the era of autonomy, the real threat of Russification posed by autocratic rule by developing a legalistic approach on the basis of Swedish law to the troubles that emerged at the end of the nineteenth century. A recognition and a codification of the particular constitutional position of Finland as an autonomous jurisdiction within the Russian Empire came with the 1906 Constitution of Russia, the first written one, which in section 2 stated that the 'Grand Duchy of Finland, while it constitutes an indivisible part of the Russian State, is governed in its domestic affairs by special institutions on the basis of special legislation'.[34]

The development of the constitution was halted after 1809 until the 1860s, when the Diet was summoned the first time after 1809, and in 1869, a new Rules of Procedure of the Diet was enacted. This act identified itself as a constitution and was in principle following the Swedish model from 1809 and the 1810 Rules of Procedure. When the great reform of representation took place by means of the enactment of the 1906 Parliament (Constitution) Act, establishing universal suffrage and proportional election for a unicameral parliament on the basis of the d'Hondt method of distribution of seats, and by means of the 1906 Act on Civil Liberties introducing the freedoms of assembly, association and the press, it seems that the models followed were the 1866 Rules of Procedure of Sweden as well as the 1814 Constitution of Norway (see below). The latter was visible in the attempts to build in a 'second chamber' of some sort in the unicameral parliament by means of a grand committee and potentially also in the amendment provisions, requiring in the ordinary procedure a qualified majority of two-thirds.[35] The amendment formula, however, was modelled against the background of the idea of the temporal division in decision-making and the requirement of a super-majority, here placed in conjunction with the final decision, made after the first decision has been left in abeyance over the next parliamentary elections. The formula was thus '1/2 + elections + 2/3', showing some affinity with the old Swedish amendment formula of 1766. At the same time, however, a fast-track procedure was designed that made it possible for one parliament to decide on the amendment without having to wait for the final decision concerning the next elections. This expedited amendment procedure was premised on a declaration of the matter as urgent with a super-majority of five-sixths, after which the amendment could be decided by a super-majority of two-thirds by the same parliament, that is, 5/6 + 2/3.

When, in the unclear situation caused by the Russian Revolution in the autumn of 1917, Finland declared independence, the general point of departure was that the 1772 Instrument of Government (Constitution) Act and the 1906 Parliament (Constitution) Act remained in force. In fact, the Parliament proceeded to elect a

[34] See M Szeftel, *The Russian Constitution of April 23, 1906: Political Institutions of the Duma Monarchy* (Brussels, Les éditions de la librairie encyclopédique, 1976), 84.

[35] A Jyränki, *Lakien laki* (Helsinki, Lakimiesliiton kustannus, 1989) 461. See also Herlitz (n 7) 30, 35.

king as required by the norms of 1772 and, in 1918, there was a serious discussion on whether to remain monarchical or become a republic. A new Instrument of Government (Constitution) Act was enacted in 1919 along republican lines, but in a manner that retained strong, almost royal powers for the president, making the constitution semi-presidential until the 1990s. It was apparently politically necessary to try to preserve strong executive powers in the presidency in order to secure the adoption of the new Instrument of Government (Constitution) Act in 1919. Although a case can be made for a breach of constitutional continuity at the moment of independence in 1917, the 1919 Instrument of Government (Constitution) Act was formally enacted with reference to the amendment formula in the 1906 Parliament (Constitution) Act, clinging to the idea of *pouvoir constitué*.[36] This Act repealed the constitutional acts of Swedish origin. Therefore, it is also possible to locate the moment of *pouvoir constituant*, at least in its internal sense, in the events of 1809 and, more particularly, in the act of will of the Tsar. Later on, the multi-documentary formal Constitution of Finland was broadened by the 1922 Ministerial Responsibility (Constitution) Act and the 1922 Court of the Realm (Constitution) Act. Finally, the 1906 Parliament (Constitution) Act was replaced by the 1928 Parliament (Constitution) Act.

The Finnish Constitution, laid down in the four above-mentioned constitutional Acts, remained largely unamended in a formal sense, but was affected by so-called Acts of Exception or exceptive acts, by which it was possible to introduce provisions into ordinary law that were contrary to the formal constitution. Only from the 1980s onwards can an increasing level of amendment activity be recorded, using the amendment formula in section 67 of the 1928 Parliament (Constitution) Act, requiring the '1/2 + elections + 2/3' model, which is again replicated as the main method of amendment in section 73 of the Constitution of Finland of 2000. This constitution, however, is now the only constitutional Act in Finland that identifies itself as one, which means that the constitutional order is no longer multi-documentary.

E. Norway: From Unwanted Personal Union to Established Constitutional Rule

When Norway was separated from Denmark and transferred to Sweden by means of the Treaty of Kiel in 1814, it was in no way unconventional that the construction of public authority in Norway would be premised on the existence of a constitution. The idea of fundamental law was clearly present in the Nordic context

36 During the Civil War of 1918, the Reds actually attempted to bring about a breach of constitutional continuity and create an instance of *pouvoir constituant* by means of their draft constitution. Thus, the conflict in the Civil War between the Reds and the Whites could be characterised, from a constitutional point of view, as a conflict between the *pouvoir constituant* of the Reds and the *pouvoir constitué* of the Whites.

through the evolution in Denmark and Sweden of the idea of fundamental law as separate from ordinary law. The understanding that constitutional laws could exist that set the rules for the enactment of ordinary laws and establish state institutions such as the king, the parliament and the courts was well known from the constitutions adopted in the aftermath of the 1789 French Revolution and also from the constitutions that emerged in the former British colonies in America after the 1776 Declaration of Independence and, in particular, with the 1789 US Constitution, including its 1791 Bill of Rights. Although existence as a sub-state within Sweden was not in line with the wishes of the Norwegians, the internal solution found in the form of a personal union where the king of Sweden was also the king of Norway ultimately became a relatively satisfactory solution, except at the very end of the era of the union. In addition, a sub-state existence on the basis of a constitution other than the constitution of the state was at that point in time evolving in Finland.

In 1814, the jurisdictional existence of Norway was by no means self-evident. The transfer from Denmark, which at that point in time was ruled following the principle of absolutism, implied the incorporation of Norway into the state of Sweden without any particular status. Yet at the same time, Norway had some constitutional traditions to fall back on and, in some respects, local traditions had been maintained that differed from those in Denmark.[37] However, the Danish Constitution at that time was hardly a model for Norway, except concerning the organisation of courts. Supported by the Danish crown prince of the time, who had his own ambitions and interests in the matter, it was not difficult to persuade Norwegians to call together a constituent assembly with the aim of creating a constitution for Norway.[38] The constituent assembly met at Eidsvoll during the winter and spring of 1814 and in May 1814, the Constitution of Norway was approved by the assembly and signed by the crown prince, who at the same time accepted to become king of Norway. However, Sweden did not accept the loss of its treaty-based acquisition to independence, sending in troops that forced the Norwegian authorities to reach another solution in August 1814: the crown prince abdicated and moved to Denmark, the Constitution was slightly amended in November 1814 so as to allow for a loose personal union bordering to independence, and the Swedish king was appointed as king of Norway.

The details of the 'domestic' union between the jurisdictions of Norway and Sweden were outlined in the 1815 Act of the Realm.[39] In section 12 of the Act, it is

[37] See Björne (n 16) 108.

[38] See also ibid 137–45 for a discussion of the deconstruction of the 'secession-nationalism' in Norway that would already have been built up during the eighteenth century. At the same time, nationalism was also present in Sweden and fomented sentiments against Norway by the time of the break-up of the union in 1905.

[39] Some commentators have been of the opinion that the Act of the Realm was a treaty under public international law and that Norway after 1814 fulfilled the requirements of a subject of international law, presumably of that period of time. See Björne (n 16) 146.

concluded that the provisions of the Act are, in part, exceptions and in part additions to the Constitution of Norway. Therefore, the Act of the Realm was identified as an Act that would have the same status and force as the Constitution and it could be amended only in the order determined in section 112 of the Constitution.[40] In addition, in 1814, the Swedish Succession Act was adopted as a constitutional act in Norway. Hence, the Norwegian Constitution was also multi-documentary until independence in 1905. In principle, section 1 of the Act of the Realm defined the Kingdom of Norway as a free, independent, indivisible and inalienable realm which is joined with Sweden under one king. However, section 4 of the Act placed foreign affairs and military affairs in the hands of the king, which in effect meant that relations with third states were the responsibility of state of Sweden (however, both parts had their own military forces).[41] In addition, under section 5, the prime minister of Norway and two other Norwegian ministers attached to the king had seats and consultative votes in the Swedish government when such matters were dealt with that concerned both realms, while three members of the Swedish government would have seats and votes in the government of Norway when joint matters were dealt with. These forms of cooperation between the two governments under the same king, as well as some other consultation arrangements, tried to bring some measure of coordination into what was otherwise two separate jurisdictions with their own law-making powers, public administration and court systems.

This relatively equal internal or domestic existence of Norway in relation to Sweden passed, with some disturbances in the beginning, with a generally positive spirit until the 1860s, when the sub-state status of Norway in relation to the foreign affairs of Sweden that also affected Norway started to cause problems. More specifically, the issue was whether or not Norway could have its own consulates in third states.[42] Although there was no outright repression of Norwegians by Sweden and although Norway was ensured some measure of participation in the exercise of foreign powers, the conviction nonetheless grew in Norway that independence was the only possible solution to the problem, and was effectuated in 1905 by means of a parliamentary situation that supposedly left Norway without a government. After approval in a referendum in Norway, the personal union was dismantled in a manner that could be characterised as unilateral secession, which resulted in full subjectivity under international law. Constitutionally this meant that the 1814 Constitution continued in force as the constitution of the independent Norway. Therefore, for Norwegians, the original point of the exercise of the *pouvoir constituant* is May 1814. It appears, however, that those immediate

[40] According to Björne (ibid 146), the Act of the Realm was not a constitutional act in Sweden.

[41] However, Norway had a limited international capacity to conclude agreements. For practical examples, see *Sveriges och Norges traktater med främmande makter jämte andra dit hörande handlingar* (Stockholm, Kungl. Boktryckeriet, PA Norstedt & söner, 1934).

[42] See E Vedung, *Unionsdebatten 1905—En argumentationsanalys* (Uppsala, Uppsala universitet, 1994), available at www.diva-portal.org/smash/get/diva2:173415/FULLTEXT01.pdf.

constitutional modifications necessitated by the separation from Sweden were not made in complete harmony with the requirements of the Constitution. This could have made the Norwegian Parliament of 1905 a constituent assembly also exercising the *pouvoir constituant* of Norway at this point in time.[43] Therefore, although constitutional continuity seems to have existed during the past two centuries, there might even be some element of discontinuity.

Originally, the Parliament of Norway was divided into two sections (of which the smaller one was involved in the reading of draft laws and in criminal cases against ministers of the government), but without becoming a bicameral legislature. In 2009, this internal division within the two parts was abolished. The Norwegian Parliament is a unicameral parliament elected in proportional elections following the modified Sainte-Laguë method for the distribution of mandates, with a support threshold of four per cent. The original formulation of the amendment formula for the Constitution of Norway was established in section 110 and started by stating that when the assembly has approved this Constitution, it will become the fundamental law of the realm. Concerning amendments, the section stated that the proposal to that effect shall be presented at one session period and then published, while the final approval during the next session period was by a super-majority of two-thirds. Hence, the amendment formula was 'tabling + elections + 2/3'. This same amendment formula is now found in section 121 of the Constitution of Norway.

F. Iceland: From a Territory via Enhanced Self-Government to Independence

Although Iceland can be proud of its parliamentary tradition of more than 1,000 years since the year 930, provided that a decision-making body with both norm-making and judicial powers counts as a parliament, the period of absolutism in Denmark also affected Iceland, at least formally, by trying to press Iceland into the same mould of legal order as other parts of Denmark. Therefore, an evolution of the position of Iceland became possible only after 1848. In spite of Danish absolutism, it seems that Iceland could also keep some of its jurisdictional specialities during that time (1660–1848), although formally speaking it was a part of the unitary state of Denmark, ruled by the king under the Royal Act, which did not leave any space for constitutional particularities.

From the mid-1850s onwards, the constitutional status of Iceland as a part of Denmark started to develop relatively rapidly. Soon after the end of absolutism in Denmark in 1848, a dispute arose between Iceland and the Danish government regarding the definition of Iceland's position in relation to Denmark. Icelanders declined to acknowledge the Danish Constitution adopted in 1849 and demanded

[43] E Holmøyvik and D Michaelsen, *Lærebok i forfatningshistorie* (Oslo, Pax Forlag, 2015) 251 f.

their own constitutional assembly for the purpose of drawing up an Icelandic constitution, convened in 1851, where Icelanders demanded control of all matters that were decided by Parliament and the electorate. They refused to submit to the authority of the Danish electorate and Parliament, although they accepted what remained of royal authority. Denmark turned down all the demands of the Icelanders, thereby starting a long campaign for independence during the subsequent decades. In 1874, King Christian IX of Denmark presented Iceland with the 'Constitution concerning the special affairs of Iceland'. It was unilaterally granted by the monarch and its contents were not in line with the proposals adopted by the Alþingi for a new constitution. However, it was an important step as it restored the legislative power of the Alþingi in Icelandic affairs, although the highest executive and judicial powers remained with the Danish institutions.

In 1904, Iceland achieved home rule according to amendments to the Constitution of 1903. The highest executive power was transferred to Iceland, which acquired its own minister instead of being governed by the Danish government. The Ministry for Iceland, which had been located in Copenhagen, was transferred to Reykjavík as the new government ministry. Simultaneously, the principle of parliamentary government, which had already been recognised in Denmark, was established in the Icelandic constitutional system as an unwritten rule. The Minister of Iceland, who should be writing and speaking the Icelandic language, was appointed by the king and was answerable to Parliament, and not the monarch. However, Denmark retained control over various matters, such as foreign affairs and the highest judicial powers.

In 1918, Iceland was granted sovereignty and recognition of its equal status in a union with Denmark under a joint monarchy by means of a union treaty between Iceland and Denmark that implied a more personal union or a 'Realunion' with the rest of Denmark than had previously been the case. A new Constitution of the Kingdom of Iceland was adopted in 1920, following the 1918 Union Treaty. It is generally considered to be the most important step towards the full independence of Iceland. Section 76 of the Constitution of 1920 (and section 61 of the 1874 Act) included an amendment formula according to which the two parts of the Alþingi, the upper part and the lower part, had to separately support the amendment, after which elections were organised. After the elections, the new Alþingi was expected to confirm through its both parts the approval of the amendment initiated in the previous Alþingi. Hence, already from 1874, two orders of domestic norms existed in Iceland: a constitutional one and another one with ordinary legislation. A particular provision concerning the dismantling of the relationship between Iceland and Denmark was featured in sub-section 2 of section 76, according to which an approval by the Alþingi to separate from Denmark would be submitted to a referendum. The same procedure would apply to amendments to the status of the Evangelic-Lutheran Church.

The self-government acts of Iceland first established Iceland as a sub-state of Denmark, initially with a weaker status of the kind granted to the Faroe Islands and Greenland (see below), and later on with an increasingly stronger status in

1918/1920. In 1940, the German armed forces occupied the main parts of Denmark and, after that, Britain occupied Iceland (as well as the Faroe Islands). This meant that the ordinary link between Iceland (and also the Faroe Islands and Greenland), on the one hand, and the German-controlled government in Denmark proper, on the other, was cut off. In 1941, US forces replaced the British troops in Iceland. This de facto independence of Iceland from the Danish king eventually led to the dismantling of the personal union in 1944, when a referendum was held in Iceland about formal independence under forms foreseen in the Constitution Act of 1920. In fact, in addition to the referendum on dismantling the personal union, another referendum was held simultaneously on whether or not to approve the republican draft constitution. Both measures secured near-unanimous support.

The current Constitution of Iceland, the more exact translation of which is an instrument of government or form of government, was thus enacted in 1944 following a referendum, and it is possible to say that this was the point of the exercise of the *pouvoir constituant* in Iceland. Because of the special circumstances that prevailed at the height of the Second World War, only minimal amendments were made to the Constitution in 1944 compared with the Constitution of 1920, the purpose being to give effect to the transformation from a constitutional monarchy to a republican form of government with a directly elected president. The idea was to postpone any comprehensive revision to a more favourable point in time. As stated in section 79(1) of the Constitution of Iceland, a proposal to amend or supplement the Constitution shall first be adopted in one parliament, after which elections shall be called for a new parliament, which then has to adopt the same formulation in order for the amendment to take effect. The formula for constitutional amendment in Iceland is thus '1/2 + elections + 1/2'. The seats in the Parliament of Iceland, which has been unicameral since 1991, are distributed in proportional elections according to the d'Hondt method.

G. Evolution of the Various 'Country-Embryos'

The starting point after Westphalia was the two Nordic kingdoms, Denmark and Sweden, which established themselves as the generic and 'genetic' bases from which three other states, Finland, Norway and Iceland, have developed. In an attempt to venture into further layers of Nordic state organisation, Professor Kári á Rógvi from the Faroe Islands proposed a dynamic map of various 'countries' in the Nordic space that have been in the process of developing in various ways.[44] With the caveat that the mapping exercise proposed by á Rógvi seems to be premised on a teleological outcome of independence as a state in all these cases, the progression indicated in Table 2.1 is nonetheless interesting and at the same time provocative

[44] Kári á Rógvi, 'Revideringar av självstyrelselagstiftningen för Färöarna' in S Spiliopoulou-Åkermark and G Herolf (eds), *Självstyrelser i Norden i ett fredsperspektiv—Färöarna, Grönland och Åland* (Mariehamn, Nordiska rådet och Ålands fredsinstitut, 2015) 157–58.

in its attempt to use the terms 'land' (country) and 'biland' (co-country) to illustrate the position of what used to be different parts of Denmark and Sweden. The table below is modified and corrected with respect to a couple of years mentioned and does thus not reproduce his table in every aspect.

Table 2.1: The dynamics of constitutional evolution

Country	Co-country	Pressure	Self-government	Commonwealth	Independence
Norway	1380	1814		1814 (Nov.)	1905
Iceland	1262	1851	1874, 1903		1918
Faroe Isl.	1271	1851	1940, 1948	1994, 2005	–
Greenland	1200s, 1721	1952	1979	2009	–
Schleswig	1230	1852	1849	1855	[1864, 1920]
Finland	1362	1700s	1809, 1906	–	1917
Åland Islands	–	1809, 1856, 1919, 1995	1920–21	–	–
The Sami	1600s	1800s	1990s	–	–

This table points out some tendencies of 'fragmentation' in the Nordic countries which in the first instance result in self-government arrangements that can be termed 'autonomy' and in some cases in independence as the last instance. Three of the current Nordic countries have achieved a state of independence from a previously sub-state existence (Norway and Iceland from Denmark, and Finland from Russia) and at the beginning of the twenty-first century, several autonomy arrangements prevail in the Nordic countries, with territorial autonomy in Denmark and Finland, and non-territorial autonomy for the indigenous population of the Sami in Finland, Norway and Sweden.

This feature of self-government is supplemented and augmented by the relatively strong local self-government of municipalities. Municipalities are afforded explicit constitutional protection of a stronger or a weaker kind in Denmark, Finland, Iceland and Sweden, but they are not protected in the same way by the Constitution of Norway, although municipalities are an important feature of Norwegian public administration and are mentioned in the Constitution in conjunction with the organisation of elections and as public authorities with the duty to provide openness and transparency for everyone. Overall, when the constitutional position of municipalities is combined with the particular position of different territorial and non-territorial autonomy arrangements in the Nordic countries, a general picture emerges which indicates that in spite of its unitary nature, the Nordic state is generally not especially fearful of the 'particular' or the 'local'. Instead, self-government is an important constitutionally legitimate response to administrative needs at the local and regional levels.

Two Nordic states in particular are characterised by sub-state self-government solutions, namely Denmark and Finland, while Iceland, Norway and Sweden are more clearly in conformity with the regular unitary state. However, with Denmark and Sweden as the original states, the account of á Rógvi underlines the evolutionary tendencies of the three more recent states, Norway, Iceland and Finland, and of territorial and non-territorial autonomies.

For Norway, the account provided by á Rógvi indicates an evolution towards a subordinated area within Denmark up to the point when external forces in 1814 compelled Denmark to transfer Norway to Sweden, resulting in an uneasy relationship towards the end of the nineteenth century, a development that evolved ultimately with independence in 1914 as the end result. It is nonetheless possible to maintain that the separate existence of Norway in conjunction with Sweden displayed a commonwealth-like relationship between the two entities. Iceland was also chipped away from Denmark in an evolution that appears almost inevitable, albeit facilitated by the Second World War: the recognition of the position of Iceland as a commonwealth-like part of Denmark prepared the population for independence in 1918 in a manner similar to the autonomy of Finland between 1809 and 1917 and the position of Norway between 1814 and 1905. In the same account, Iceland is considered to have taken all the steps in the evolution of its status in a logical and methodical order over a period of some 60 years. This development is in part attributed to the fact that the local authorities of Iceland were staffed with individuals from Iceland, something that helped create pressure in the protests of 1851.

In the context of Denmark, it is also necessary to mention Schleswig, the Faroe Islands and Greenland. Schleswig was for a long time a possession of the king of Denmark and was to some extent outside the ordinary Danish jurisdiction.[45] However, as a consequence of Schleswig's geographical position on the border between Denmark and Germany (Prussia), the wars of 1848–50 and 1864, which actually sparked the idea of Scandinavism, and the First World War left the national affiliation of that particular territory to be determined by means of a series of referendums held in 1920 on the basis of the Treaty of Versailles, by means of which the present-day border between Denmark and Germany was drawn. After that territorial challenge, Denmark was forced to deal with yet another territorial consequence of wars when the Faroe Islands were held by the Allied forces during the Second World War (mainly Britain), because of a referendum organised there in 1946 which resulted in a slim majority for independence. Denmark managed to assert its sovereignty over the Faroe Islands, but passed legislation in 1948 that

[45] Between 1855 and 1863, a confederal 'comprehensive constitution' of some kind existed for four different parts of Denmark, namely Denmark proper, Schleswig, Holstein and Lauenborg, but the construction was unsustainable and was replaced by a joint government of some kind between Denmark proper and Schleswig, where the enumerated powers were held by the parts, while the joint government was in charge of the residual powers. This joint government lasted until 1864, when Schleswig was lost to Germany.

granted autonomy for the Faroe Islands. Since then, the self-government of the Faroe Islands has, according to á Rógvi, encountered many challenges, but has often been developing in a very real direction. A similar development can be noted for Greenland, which in the aftermath of the Second World War was first considered a colony and has, since 1979, been granted autonomy, which since 2009 has been recognised as a mechanism for the indigenous Inuit population because of their right to self-determination under public international law. According to á Rógvi, Greenland has experienced a remarkable formal change in its status, but is facing economic and structural challenges. From a constitutional point of view, however, the three parts of Denmark—namely Denmark proper, the Faroe Islands and Greenland—are considered a commonwealth (but without forming a federation).

For Finland, á Rógvi explained that the country managed to develop a relation with the extra-Nordic Russia, in principle by means of a dynamic and peaceful process. The pressures indicated in the eighteenth century probably is a reference to the several wars between Sweden and Russia during which it started to become clear to at least parts of the population that the central powers of Sweden could not be counted upon to provide protection against the threats from the east. Arguably, independence in 1917 was no great improvement in that respect, given the two wars, the Winter War of 1939–40 and the Continuation War of 1941–44, against the Soviet Union. The pressures noted for the Åland Islands starting in 1809 underline the particular position of the territory as a part of Finland, with EU membership in 1995 on the basis of some exceptions to the primary law of the EU. This self-governing jurisdiction has a constitutionally entrenched autonomous position, originally created in 1920, which may be strong from a formal point of view amongst the Nordic autonomies, but, according to á Rógvi, is perhaps weaker in reality than those of the Faroe Islands and Greenland, at least in terms of the material scope of the legislative powers that the Åland Islands possess.

The non-territorial autonomy of the Sami in each of the Nordic countries is a form of self-government that seemingly unites Finland, Norway and Sweden. However, while the Sami Assemblies, directly elected by the Sami in each country, are independent statutory bodies in Finland and Norway, in Sweden the Sami Assembly is a state agency. Moreover, these Sami Assemblies do not normally have any significant public powers and do not deliver any significant number of public services for the Sami populations in the three countries. These features leave the Sami Assemblies mainly in the position of consultative bodies in relation to governmental organs at the national, regional and local levels. However—and as was also suggested by á Rógvi—the Sami are facing a territorial challenge, although their cultural identity is growing stronger: most of the Sami in the three Nordic countries live outside of the traditional Sami areas and are perhaps not always within reach of their self-governing bodies.

As is clear from this account, the Nordic countries display complex institutional structures, both past and present, but all in very different ways. Municipal self-government—that is, local self-government—is a more or less joint constitutional feature, regulated in the Constitutions of Denmark, Finland, Iceland and Sweden, where rules regulating local government have to be passed by an act of parliament, but this is not quite so in Norway, where the Constitution presumes the existence of municipalities without protecting their self-government in any particular way.[46] The strong undercurrent of municipal self-government at the local government level is thus a feature that underlines the position of municipalities in the constitutional fabric of the Nordic countries and the relatively high degree of administrative decentralisation of the Nordic countries. The constitutional position of municipalities is particularly strong in Finland and Sweden, where the Constitutions contain, inter alia, the right to elected decision-making bodies and the right of taxation as material components of the constitutional protection of municipalities.

Against this background, and recognising that the strength of municipal self-government in the five countries may, for an outside observer, signal a relatively high degree of autonomy, it may perhaps be said that Iceland is clearly a unitary state, while Norway and Sweden only slightly deviate from that pattern because of the non-territorial autonomy of the Sami. In Finland and Denmark, the self-government arrangements of the Åland Islands and non-territorially for the Sami, on the one hand, and the Faroe Islands and Greenland, on the other, add constitutional layers to the governance of these countries that defy the straightforward logic of the unitary state, but that nonetheless allow these countries to operate in good order.

As one possible explanation for similarities amongst the Nordic countries, the importance of self-organisation may be offered. By the mid-nineteenth century, the Nordic countries were rural societies which the advent of industrialism left without significant capital, at least outside of larger cities. At the local level, associations of various kinds, such as cooperatives, were used to pool together the resources of agricultural society. As a consequence, banks, dairy plants, shops, insurance companies, social assistance institutions, water corporations, electricity corporations, entities for the maintenance of roads and other entities were created at the local level. They were often not organised as limited corporations, but as associations of some kind that facilitated the activities of modernity in the countryside.

This local self-management of various issues, carried out as a result of general legislation concerning associations or under particular legislation enacted or tailor-made for the function, created a feeling for the local collective that legitimised local self-government in the municipality and, ultimately, self-government in the form of the state. In Finland at least, the model effect of Sweden has been considerable in municipal matters, the legislation concerning municipalities from

[46] However, the Norwegian local government legislation of 1837 appears to have been considered when the Swedish local government legislation was enacted in 1843, which in its turn stood as a model for the Finnish local government legislation of 1865 and 1873.

1865 and 1873 being directly modelled on the basis of Swedish local government law. In addition, this self-management or self-organisation may have contributed towards making the Nordic countries sympathetic to such special forms of self-government that break up the unitary nature of the state, such as the self-governing territorial autonomies with law-making powers proper (the Faroe Islands and Greenland in Denmark, the Åland Islands in Finland, and historically Iceland between 1874 and 1944) and the non-territorial and cultural self-government accorded to the indigenous Sami population of Finland, Norway and Sweden.[47]

V. Concluding Remarks: Fewer Common Roots than Expected

The evolution of the states in the Nordic space from two to five, with decentralisation of powers and functions to the sub-state and local government levels, has, in each of the countries, passed through a constitutional moment of the *pouvoir constituant* of one kind or another at some point from which the constitutional continuity of the current constitutional set-up can proceed (Sweden 1809; Finland 1809/1917; Norway 1814/1905; Denmark 1849; Iceland 1918/1944). The rigidity of the five constitutional orders varies in relation to the formal mechanisms of constitutional amendment. Denmark and Sweden can be viewed as extremes on a scale of rigidity and flexibility, while Norway, Finland and Iceland may be viewed as occupying a middle ground between these two extremes, perhaps in this order (although Iceland is in practice as flexible as Sweden, subject to the confirmation of amendments by the president of the republic). The Danish Constitution is the only one that creates a (very demanding) mandatory referendum for amendment (and the Icelandic Constitution does so for the position of the Evangelic-Lutheran Church), while the other constitutions operate on the basis of amendments by parliament, requiring at least a temporal distance between two points of adoption, with intermittent elections.

The introduction of ordinary legitimacy-building representations of the people took place at different points of time (Norway 1814; Denmark 1849; Iceland 1874/1918; Sweden around the turn of the twentieth century; Finland 1906/1917). Today, the Nordic parliaments are all unicameral, after upper chambers (Denmark, Sweden and Iceland) or other sections (Norway) of parliaments had been abolished by means of subsequent constitutional amendments. The parliaments are elected by means of proportional elections using the d'Hondt or Sainte-Laguë

[47] Of course, Greenlandic autonomy should be grounded in the indigenous character of the population of Greenland.

methods (or a combination thereof) for distributing the mandates in the parliament. Under the principle of the legislative sovereignty of the elected parliament, three of the five countries are nominally monarchies, while two are republics with relatively weak presidencies (Finland and Iceland). All five countries follow the principle of parliamentary answerability, but the introduction of the mechanism that places the government under the requirement of the confidence of the parliament only took place sometime after the emergence of the representative parliaments. This took place in Norway in a gradual process since the beginning of the twentieth century: in Denmark in 1901 (at which point it started to form itself into a legally binding constitutional convention), in Iceland in 1904, in Sweden more definitively after 1918 and in Finland in 1917/1918.[48] The written Constitution of Finland already recorded this mechanism in 1919, but the other countries did so only much later (Denmark in 1953, Sweden in 1974 and Norway in 2007), while the mechanism is not recorded at all in the written Constitution of Iceland. Of these countries, only Finland practises positive parliamentarism (actually since 1991, but more clearly from 2000), requiring a vote for the government by the time of its formation. The other countries practise negative parliamentarism, normally allowing the party that wins the elections to govern with or without a coalition until a point in time when it becomes clear that there is no support for the government in the parliament. In part because of negative parliamentarism, minority governments have been relatively frequent in the Nordic countries.

None of this reveals any clear common roots for Nordic constitutional law, except that the creation of the law separates between constitutional law and ordinary law (which is also commonplace elsewhere in the world) and that the constitutional position of the Evangelic-Lutheran Church, or at least of the faith, has been (and to some extent still is) a common denominator between the countries.

Also, in spite of the fact that the original two states, Denmark and Sweden, have become five after Finland, Iceland and Norway became independent, it is difficult to see any clear consequence of a divide into a western and eastern constitutional tradition. The Danish and Swedish Constitutions have evolved separately from each other, as can be expected on the basis of the history of the two countries, and for that reason, there could be a divide into a western and an eastern tradition. However, the 1814 Constitution of Norway cannot generally be attributed to the Danish Constitution of absolutism, because the constitutional ideas came from elsewhere. The 1944 Icelandic Constitution seems, in terms of its contents, to have a clearer Danish provenance via the 1920 Constitution that created a personal union. The constitutional history of Finland has a Swedish provenance, but instead of the Swedish Constitution of 1809, its background lies in the Gustavian constitution of the late eighteenth century, a constitution overthrown in Sweden in 1809.

[48] Herlitz, *Nordisk offentlig rätt I* (n 8) 96.

None of this prevents the possibility of regarding the Nordic space as forming an eastern (Sweden and Finland) and a western (Denmark, Iceland and Norway) Nordic tradition, for instance, in terms of court organisation, the powers of the Ombudsman and some other features.[49] In fact, such an east-west constellation may, for its part, speak against the notion of common roots of constitutional law for the five Nordic countries. In that sense, our inquiry may have uncovered at least a dimension of legal culture that operates in the background of the constitutions of the east and of the west in the Nordic countries—potentially even a deep structure, in the words of Kaarlo Tuori.[50] Against that background, the current constitutional rules and practices at the surface of the law appear to be poised to bridge (for instance, by means of Nordic cooperation in the area of the law) the east-west divide and to develop common solutions. However, at the same time, reference to east and west in the Nordic context helps to explain differences and to understand possible similarities between the countries. Notably, one interesting difference is visible in the relationship of the five countries to NATO: the countries of the west are members of NATO, while those of the east are not. Perhaps the fact that the western countries were subject to occupying forces during the Second World War (while those of the east were not; Sweden has actually never been under foreign domination) may help explain their understanding of the importance of collective security guarantees from like-minded countries. However, the east-west divide does not appear to be relevant in terms of the EU issue, because Denmark, Finland and Sweden are Member States of the EU, while Iceland and Norway are not (although they are passive recipients of EU norms through their membership of the EEA).

It is quite surprising that the Nordic constitutions are so disparate in terms of their evolution throughout constitutional history. There are few common roots to refer to, although some cross-fertilisation has taken place. When Denmark created a new constitutional order after absolutism in 1849, the searchlight was, inter alia, on the 1814 Constitution of Norway, and when Finland's Parliament (Constitution) Act was drafted in 1906, the Norwegian Constitution and its separation between two sections of the Parliament seems to have been considered. Generally speaking, however, it is difficult to point at common constitutional roots. What is interesting is that at least a few mechanisms commonly found in other constitutional systems outside the Nordic countries are currently absent in the Nordic space, such as a separate constitutional court entitled to review the constitutionality of legislation and inter-institutional contacts and procedures, the right of

[49] See, eg, J Husa, *Nordic Reflections on Constitutional Law: A Comparative Nordic Perspective* (Frankfurt am Main, Peter Lang, 2002) 131, 179 f. See also Kári á Rógvi, *West-Nordic Constitutional Judicial Review* (Copenhagen, DJØF, 2013) 273; and Bernitz (n 1) 16.

[50] K Tuori, *Critical Legal Positivism* (Aldershot, Ashgate, 2002) 147, 150, 183 f, 192, 193, 194, 196. The two original states, Denmark and Sweden, and the 'turfs' they established before the nineteenth century have impacted legal culture, perhaps even deep structures of the law, in the other three countries and in country-embryos in a manner that shows itself in the surface layer of the law and becomes visible in the court organisation and in other legal institutions.

individuals to use an individual complaint of unconstitutionality before such a court, federalism, presidentialism (although the Finnish Constitution was semi-presidential until the 1990s), lofty aims of the constitution and the state recorded in preambles of the constitutions, and so forth. The Nordic countries have been cautious in formulating such new features to their constitutions the existence of which are not indicated by their own previous constitutional tradition.[51] The attitude to law seems pragmatic to the extent of creating the image that the five countries might be speaking with one voice. More importantly, because law exists in texts formulated in the language of a country, the Nordic languages (except Finnish, although Swedish is the other national language of Finland, including the language of law) can in practice be forged to a *lingua franca* that facilitates the existence of a Nordic legal community.

However, this picture may change when particular mechanisms and the material contents of constitutions are studied. Hence, at the same time as there might not be any greater commonalities in the constitutional history, different areas of constitutional law may display a greater degree of material or procedural proximity, as is reviewed in the other chapters of this volume. Such material areas would be, for instance, emphasis on parliamentary sovereignty, the manner in which parliamentary accountability influences the separation of powers by establishing a link between the legislative and executive power,[52] the judicial accountability of ministers of the government in special judicial proceedings, the independence of the judiciary and the restraint that the judiciary has shown towards reviewing the constitutionality of legislation passed by the sovereign parliament, the review performed by the Ombudsman in relation to the public administration and courts,[53] and the position of the constitutional rights in the legal orders of the five countries.[54] In areas of this kind, similarities (and certainly also differences) exist at the constitutional level, but they do not stand out as particularly significant from the perspective of common constitutional history.

The evolution of the Nordic constitutions during the past century has been based on an idea of continuity, and no dramatic breaches of that continuity or

[51] The conclusion here is similar to that concerning the characterisation of Nordic legal scholarship in L Björne, *Realism och skandinavisk realism. Den nordiska rättsvetenskapens historia, del IV: 1911–1950* (Stockholm, Institutet för rättshistorisk forskning, 2007) 568, where he follows B Hjejle, *Nordisk retsfællesskab* (Copenhagen, Norden, 1946) when writing that there are some commonalities in Nordic law. They consist, in part, of indicating distance from extreme solutions and from logical consequence at any cost as well as from rhetoric, but, in part, of a tendency towards everyday realism, towards dull 'business-as-usual' and towards protection of the individual against the public powers and of protection of the weaker against the stronger.

[52] The 1974 Instrument of Government Act of Sweden is, according to its travaux preparatoires, not based on the principle of the separation of powers, but on the principles of the sovereignty of the people and parliamentarism in its relation to the executive power.

[53] The institution of the Ombudsman was first introduced in the Swedish Instrument of Government of 1809 and was adopted in the Finnish Constitution in 1919 and thereafter in the other Nordic countries.

[54] Husa (n 49) 178 f.

collapses of constitutional orders have taken place in the Nordic space (save for the attempt in the Civil War of Finland in 1918 that ultimately did not manage to bring about a revolutionary collapse of the Constitution, which later on survived even the Second World War). Also, the Nordic constitutions do not seem to have any such particular aims, recorded in, for instance, preambular texts, which would try to determine the direction or general contents of national decision-making or to identify the constitutional subject in terms of a 'We the People' of some sort. Against this background, it would be daring to suggest that there is 'a Nordic Constitution'. They are all different, and so is their historical background, although they organise national decision-making in a similar manner. Therefore, it cannot be said that one constitution of a Nordic country would reflect a constitutional identity based on common constitutional roots that is recognised as Nordic in a way that is also relevant in all the other Nordic countries. In light of the fact that the outcomes of legislation and policy are similar, this indicates that the reasons for the current similarities between the Nordic countries, for instance, in the form of the welfare state that they all represent, should be sought elsewhere than in the historical commonalities of their constitutions. Perhaps similarities are instead due to more recent events and trends, such as the impact of a social-democratic political trend and the wish of the Nordic countries to work within the Nordic Council and the Nordic Council of Ministers, two inter-governmental organisations that provide an institutional umbrella for the Nordic countries.

The outside observer is therefore informed about the fact that the Nordic constitutions may be very different in terms of their rules concerning such core constitutional features as the electoral systems (which are proportional, but nonetheless different from each other), the position of the referendum in national decision-making (where the Constitution of Denmark in particular, but also the Swedish Constitution are more permitting of referendums), and the construction of the court system (which is unitary in Denmark, Iceland and Norway, but in Finland and Sweden is divided between civil and criminal courts, on the one hand, and administrative courts, on the other hand). Yet at the same time, significant similarities exist in terms of policy outcomes to the extent that an outside observer might justifiably think that the five countries are very similar. If the function of the constitution is to provide a legal framework for the operation of politics and if the constitutional history of the Nordic countries is relatively divergent, then the operation of politics in the five countries can perhaps be attributed with responsibility for producing largely similar results in the legislation of the Nordic countries.

However, in the current Nordic constitutions (understood in the material sense), there may exist a more current common root in the area of citizenship law, which is a core part of constitutional law. The Nordic constitutions create separate citizenships for the five states as established in ordinary legislation passed by the parliaments of the five Nordic countries. Although the citizenship acts of the Nordic countries are not completely identical and display a slight variance in their rules concerning the treatment of other Nordic nationals (albeit that the outcomes of application of the various rules may be close to identical), the pattern in Nordic citizenship legislation is clear. Each Nordic country has a string of provisions in its citizenship legislation that grants preferential treatment to citizens of the other Nordic countries in the acquisition of citizenship by waiving residence requirements to a great extent. The legal explanation for this is that there is a Nordic convention between Denmark, Finland, Iceland, Norway and Sweden concerning citizenship, the latest version of which was signed in Copenhagen on 13 September 2010.[55] The stated aim of the Convention according to Article 1 is to facilitate the possibilities of Nordic citizens to acquire or re-acquire citizenship in another Nordic country. In this respect, reference is explicitly made to the close cooperation between the Nordic countries. What the text of the Convention reflects is a common understanding between the Nordic countries concerning commonalities and an understanding that citizenship and residence in another Nordic country prepares the applicant for citizenship in the country of application, because the countries are so similar to each other.[56] As a practical matter, the five Nordic countries seem to think of themselves as sharing common roots, but the understanding of commonalities between the five countries is perhaps after all so recent that constitutional history cannot be of much assistance in uncovering many of these common roots of Nordic constitutional law.

[55] The Convention of 2010 replaced a similar Convention of 2002 and an original one concluded in 1950 between Denmark, Norway and Sweden, which Finland joined in 1969 and Iceland in 1998. Nordic cooperation in citizenship matters had already started in 1880. See sub-chapter 23.1 of the Bill of the Swedish Government for the enactment of a citizenship act, 1999/2000:147.

[56] M Suksi, 'Markers of Nordic Constitutional Identity' (2014) 37 *Retfærd* 66, 68–74.

3

Institutions and Division of Powers

THOMAS BULL

I. Introduction

This chapter will provide a brief overview of the basic constitutional institutions of the Nordic countries. By 'institutions' we mean nothing more complicated than the usual actors in a formal constitutional context: heads of state, parliaments, governments and courts.

As none of the Nordic countries is a federal state, the actors discussed here are all national institutions. This might seem a very formal way of delimiting the discussion on distribution of powers and institutions, but it is relatively clear-cut and avoids the danger of a text with a lot of details and exceptions that only cloud the view of what is characteristic of the constitutional systems in the north. Regional and local institutions are thus only mentioned when they are of particular interest from a constitutional point of view.

As a further caveat, it must be pointed out that many of the issues covered in this chapter are more complex and nuanced than it is possible to fully express within the limited space allowed. Therefore, it is a simplified and to some degree incomplete picture that will be painted here. However, the exceptions—and the exception to the exceptions—not mentioned here do not, in our opinion, change the ambition or ability to provide a factually correct description and draw substantiated conclusions from that.

II. Head of State

A. Background

Three of the Nordic states—Denmark, Norway and Sweden—are constitutional hereditary monarchies in which the king or queen is the head of state. Finland and Iceland are republics with elected presidents who function as heads of state. It is obvious that this division is not the common East/West split that we come across so frequently when dealing with the Nordic countries. Instead, the split is somewhat connected to history, as Denmark, Norway and Sweden are old states with long-standing royal houses, and to chance. Both Norway and Finland became fully independent states in the beginning of the twentieth century and both opted for a monarchy, choosing their royalty from Denmark and Germany. In Norway this was done by referenda in 1905 in which a clear majority voted for a monarchy. In Finland, the choice of a German prince as future king was stopped by the end of the First World War as the prince conveniently declined the throne and instead a republic was formed. Like Norway, Iceland was under Danish rule for several hundred years and became fully independent first in 1944. Following a referendum Iceland opted for a republican form of government.

B. Royal Inheritance and Presidential Election

A new king or queen will ascend the throne on the death of the previous holder or in the event that the previous holder is unable to fulfil his or her duties. In Norway and Denmark, the rules of succession are found in the country's constitution, while Sweden's Succession Act is a constitutional act in its entirety. Sweden was the first monarchy in Europe to establish an order of succession that was fully equal in 1980, meaning that the eldest child of the monarch, whether female or male, ascends to the throne (full cognatic primogeniture). Norway followed suit in 1990 and Denmark in 2009. The king or queen comes of age at 18 in all three countries.

The three monarchies also have in common a constitutional regulation of the monarch's religious affliction. In Norway and Denmark, this is achieved by a short stipulation on Evangelic-Lutheran affiliation in the constitutional text. In Sweden, a more detailed provision demands that the monarch has a 'pure' evangelistic faith based on the Augsburg Confession as received in Sweden in 1593. Thus, perhaps somewhat surprisingly, the monarchs of the Nordic countries are some of the very few people in Europe who do not enjoy full freedom of religion. Another common feature is that the royal families in Denmark, Norway and Sweden are popular (or even immensely popular) and that the monarchies as such seem to be safe from any republican challenges for the foreseeable future.

The presidents of Finland and Iceland are elected in general elections. In Iceland these are held every four years and in Finland every six years.

In order to be eligible for election, the Icelandic Constitution requires that the candidate must be 35 years of age and to otherwise fulfil the requirements to vote in elections for parliament. This includes in essence a requirement of Icelandic citizenship. To run for president, a backing of 1,500–3000 voters is required, there is no second round of voting and the candidate who receives to most votes will win the presidential election. If there is only one candidate, no vote will take place and he or she will be considered to be duly elected. There is no limitation on the number of times a person can be elected president, and several presidents have held the position for three to five terms or more.

In Finland, the only formal requirement for running for president is to be a born Finnish citizen. In order to run for president, a registered party that is represented in the Parliament must nominate the candidate. However, a minimum of 20,000 voters may also make a nomination in a procedure that is regulated in law. The candidate with more than half the votes will win the election, but if no one reaches this threshold, a second round will take place between the two candidates with the most votes. In this case the candidate with the most votes will win. Since the introduction of this two-step procedure in 1991, every presidential election has had a second round before a winner could be declared, except in 2018 when the sitting President got over 60% of the votes. The same person can only be elected for president two consecutive times.

i. Powers and Function

When you study the constitutional texts of Denmark and Norway, you may be excused for thinking that the king or queen is very influential. For example, Article 3 of the Norwegian Constitution states that the executive power rests with the king or queen in Council, Article 12 states that he or she elects a council with a prime minister and, according to article 21, the king or queen appoints all civil and military personnel of the state. The Danish Constitution has similar rules in Articles 3, 12, 14 and 27. However, this is not the whole truth, as the 'King' or 'Queen' in these articles really refers to the government under the leadership of the prime minister and in practice it is the government that holds all those important powers mentioned above. This is also reflected in the explicit rule on contra-signature in Article 31 of the Norwegian Constitution, but is considered to follow from the above-mentioned articles of the Danish Constitution.[1]

The norms on forming a government according to parliamentary principles are not found in the constitution, but rather in political practice that takes the form of 'constitutional conventions'. This was the case in Sweden until the Instrument of Government of 1974 came into force in 1975. In its regulation of the powers and function of the head of state, very few actual powers are attributed to the king or queen.

When it comes to political and formal functions, the king or queen in Denmark and Norway still have some constitutional roles in connection with the formation of a government, the adoption of legislation, etc. For example, according to Articles 78 and 79, the Norwegian king can refuse to sign a law that the Parliament has adopted and it is then sent back to Parliament, which cannot pass the law until two elections have been held and two identical decisions have been taken. The last decision does not need the signature of the king in order to be effective. The king thus holds a kind of suspensive veto that, depending upon the political situation, can be difficult to overcome. In practice, however, the king does not refuse adopted legislation. Furthermore, and not unlike the situation in the UK, the monarch

[1] See JP Christenssen, JA Jensen and MH Jensen, *Dansk Statsret* (Copenhagen, Jurist- og Økonomforbundets Forlag, 2016) 52.

in Norway and Denmark still formally appoints (or accepts as in the UK) a new government after a parliamentary election, but in reality it is the political situation in Parliament that dictates the monarch's 'choice'.

In Sweden, even this formal role in the formation of government has been abolished, as it is the speaker of the Parliament who leads the process of forming a new government after an election. The king or queen has no role in this procedure. This was an important result of the compromise reached before the adoption of the Instrument of Government of 1974, as the major political party as a matter of policy wanted to abolish the monarchy, but was able to accept a politically impotent monarch in exchange for getting its will through on some issues concerning the electoral system. The only instance in which the Instrument of Government gives the Swedish monarch a role of some importance is as chairman of the parliamentary Committee on Foreign Affairs, a constitutionally regulated organ for information and coordination between the government and the Parliament on issues of foreign policy (Chapter 10, § 12). As noted above, the Constitutions of Denmark and Norway in many instances give their monarchs a more formal and active role. However, a fair summary would be that the monarchs in the Nordic countries mainly have symbolic functions with very little or no political power as such and that this idea has been taken the furthest in Sweden, which could rather provocatively perhaps be called for a 'non-monarchy' in all but name.[2]

The monarchs of the Nordic countries all share a substantial immunity to legal claims, both criminal and civil. In the Danish (§ 13) and Norwegian (§ 5) Constitutions, this immunity is still almost absolute. There have been no constitutional amendments following the development in international law of the legal immunity of head of states and similar persons, particularly the rules in the Statute of the International Criminal Court in The Hague of 17 July 1998. Instead, a somewhat strained interpretation of the constitutions in question has been presented in order to harmonise international law with constitutional rules. In Sweden, a new provision was introduced in the Instrument of Government in connection with the reform of 2011, and Chapter 10, § 14 now makes a specific exception to the constitutional rules of immunity if this is necessary to fulfil obligations regarding international criminal tribunals. This difference in approach to constitutional problems is perhaps somewhat telling about the constitutional culture of the Nordic countries, where Sweden stands out as the most pragmatic of the three. Of course, this is closely connected to the issue of how easy or difficult it is to make constitutional changes, where Sweden, once again, stands out as the country where it is easiest to make such adjustments. The idea of keeping the Constitution 'fresh' in a descriptive and normative sense still prevails in Swedish constitutional thinking to a large degree.

[2] But this would of course be to pay more attention to the political realities than to the constitutional text, as according to Chapter 1, § 5 of the Instrument of Government, Sweden is undoubtedly a monarchy.

The presidents of Finland and Iceland also have symbolic functions as heads of state, but both are more politically involved in the running of government and legislation than their crowned counterparts.

Legislation that the Icelandic Parliament adopts must be signed by the Icelandic president. If this does not happen, the legislation becomes valid in any case, but a referendum must be held on its continuing validity as soon as possible. As can be imagined, this has not happened many times in practice and only one president has so far used this power (in 2004, 2010 and 2011). The Icelandic president can thus be said to have a weak form of 'veto' in relation to the Parliament's legislation. The president may introduce bills and draft proposals to the Parliament. Furthermore, the president may dissolve the Parliament and declare new elections, and can also adjourn parliamentary sessions for a short period of two weeks once a year. Formally, it is the president who concludes international treaties, but foreign policy is in practice handled by the government. All these, apart from signing legislation into law, are tasks of the president only in a formal sense, and must be proposed and executed by ministers of government. As a parallel to Norway and Denmark, the signature of the president validates a government measure when countersigned by a minister of government.

The Icelandic president formally appoints and discharges the ministers of government and presides over a State Council, which is composed of the ministers. Legislation and important governmental action should be submitted to the president in the State Council. All in all, the Icelandic president has some important functions besides the representative functions, but is still to a large extent in a position outside of everyday politics. The use of the presidential veto (Article 26) three times since the beginning of the 2000s (having never been applied before) can be seen as a step away from this traditional role, but it must be understood in context with a time of political and financial crises, and is thus an exception rather than a new trend. It has raised a new debate in constitutional law and political theory in Iceland on the role and powers of the president. The president has immunity for executive acts and against criminal charges (Article 11), but the latter may be lifted by the Parliament. A majority of three-quarters of the Parliament can instigate referenda on the removal of the president. If the result of the vote is in favour of the president, the Parliament must be dissolved and new elections held.

The Finnish president has more substantial power than his or her Icelandic counterpart, particularly in the field of foreign policy. However, a reduction of the president's powers has taken place through the new Constitution of 2000 in favour of a system closer to classical parliamentarism. According to the Constitution, the president appoints and discharges the ministers of government as well as certain senior public officials and judges. The president is also the formal commander of the military. Legislation should be approved by the president, who shall send it back to Parliament if approval is withheld. Parliament shall then vote on whether the law should enter into force without presidential approval. Foreign policy is made by the president in cooperation with the government, but important treaties that, for example, touch upon the Parliament's legislative powers must be approved by Parliament. Another important limitation on the president's power in this area is that issues relating to the European Union are dealt with by the government instead of the president. The president's criminal responsibility is reduced to crimes of treason and crimes against humanity; in such an event, a majority of three-quarters of the votes in Parliament will result in a prosecution against the president.

C. Summary

To summarise, the Nordic countries' institutional choice in relation to the function of head of state is divided between the old monarchies and the newer republics, but as we have seen, this division is more of a historical coincidence and is by no means guided by constitutional principles or based on clear political ideology. The function of the head of state in the Nordic countries is mostly symbolic, with the possible exception of the Finnish president, who has been a very important political figure in Finland and even after constitutional reforms in the 2000s remains particularly influential in the area of foreign policy. The Icelandic president has had increased political impact in the rather turbulent political climate of the state since around 2010, but this is perhaps not something that follows from the Constitution, but rather as a response to national political developments.

III. Parliament

A. The Basics

The Nordic countries are all parliamentary democracies in which the parliament, in addition to its classical legislative and controlling functions, is also the basis for governmental power. All Nordic countries have old traditions when it comes to representative organs with consultative and legislative powers, and the Icelandic Parliament, the Alþingi, is often said to be the oldest functioning parliament in the world with its 1,000-year history.

All members of parliament in the Nordic parliaments are elected for a period of four years and are protected by some basic rules on immunity as elected representatives of the people. These days, the parliaments are all one-chamber houses, but several of the countries have had dual-chamber systems previously, with Norway changing its rules as late as 2007 (which came into effect in 2009). The Icelandic Parliament is the smallest with only 63 members, and the Swedish Parliament is the largest with 349. Between these are Norway (169), Denmark (175 + 4 extra members of parliament for the Faroe Islands and Greenland) and Finland (200).

Considering the relative smallness of the population in all the Nordic countries, the size of the parliaments is somewhat out of proportion compared to large countries such as the UK (650) or France (577), and even compared to more similar-sized states, the Nordic parliaments are quite large.[3] One explanation for this is, at least regarding Sweden, Finland and Norway, that these countries are large in geographical terms and that a fair representation of all parts of the land leads to a high number of seats in parliament. But of course historical explanations are also relevant, such as the Swedish abolishment of the dual-chamber system in the early 1970s without a simultaneous reduction in the number of seats in parliament. It should be mentioned that the number of seats in the Swedish Parliament at the time of the aforementioned reform was actually 350, but after the election in 1974, both 'sides' of Swedish politics had 175 seats each. Quite a few issues in Parliament had to be decided by a lottery, an embarrassing state of affairs that was fixed by reducing the number of seats by one in 1976.

It should also be mentioned that the Faroe Islands, Greenland and the Åland Islands have special constitutional status with a certain level of independence from central government and with local parliaments.[4] The indigenous Sami people of Finland, Sweden and Norway also have some special representative fora in which issues specific to the more traditional way of life of the Sami are dealt with.[5]

B. National Elections

The basic rules on national elections are more or less similar in all the Nordic countries. All citizens aged 18 or over have the right to vote and non-citizens cannot participate in national elections.[6] Elections are held every fourth year and the electoral system is proportional (as opposed to majoritarian systems, where only one candidate in each constituency can be elected). The details of how this is accomplished vary according to different mathematical formulae, but one common method used in the Nordic countries is the so-called *adjustment seats*. These seats in parliament are distributed in addition to the normal distribution of seats to members directly elected in each constituency. This is done in order to ensure that each party's share of the total seats in parliament is more proportional in relation to its overall shares of votes at the national level. The number

[3] Some countries with around 10 million inhabitants all have relatively smaller parliaments: Portugal (230), the Czech Republic (200 + 80), Austria (183 + 61) and Belgium (150 + 71). The Netherlands with 16 million inhabitants has 150 + 75. The second set refers to a second chamber.

[4] Local parliaments have 33 members in the Faroe Islands, 31 in Greenland and 30 in the Åland Islands.

[5] There are also Sami people in Russia. It should be mentioned that the degree of self-government allowed to the Sami varies between the Nordic countries and that the status of the Sami is a sometimes hotly debated issue.

[6] However, they can participate in regional and local elections under certain restrictions.

of adjustments seats varies—for example, in Sweden, there are 39 and in Norway there are 19. The more such seats there are, the greater the national proportionality is ensured. The share of more than 10 per cent of the adjustment seats in the Swedish Parliament is rather unusual and reflects the importance given to political proportionality nationwide.[7]

The political parties are not extensively regulated in the Nordic constitutions, and in the Icelandic Constitution, for instance, they are not even mentioned. But their importance is clear from the rules on elections and from the more detailed provisions found in ordinary legislation on elections and the electorate system, so the constitutional texts do not provide the whole picture. In this regard, Finland and Iceland stand out as the countries with the weakest constitutional entrenchment of the electoral system, as those constitutions only stipulate that elections should be secret and proportional. In Denmark, the Constitution includes some more details, and in Sweden and Norway, some of the more specific rules on how the seats should be distributed are also included in the constitutional text.

A common method in modern democracies to reduce the risk of a very diverse and thus potentially ineffective parliament (and, as a consequence, a weak government) is to have an election threshold in the electoral system. A political party that does not achieve a certain level of support from the electorate will in such a system not be given any seats in parliament. Most countries in Europe have this kind of limit and it is usually around 3–5 per cent of the votes cast. In the Nordic countries, Sweden has a 4 per cent limit and Denmark a limit of only 2 per cent. Finland lacks a general election threshold altogether, and in Norway and Iceland, the established limit only applies to the adjustment seats, so its effect on the electoral result is somewhat limited, but it does allow for parties with strong local support to access parliament even if they lack national entrenchment.[8]

Most of the Nordic parliaments have the rule that parliament itself decides issues relating to the election of a candidate. This is the case in Denmark (§ 33), Iceland (§ 46) and Norway (§§ 55, 64). In Finland, the Constitution stipulates that the issue of the legality of elections is decided by an organ prescribed by law and the electoral law provides a possibility to appeal an election result to an administrative court and thus put the issue of the legality of elections in the hands of the judiciary. In Sweden, the Constitution confers the task of handling complaint versus elections to a special Election Review Board. The president of the Board should be a person who is or has been a judge and cannot be a member of parliament. The other six positions are elected by Parliament and are usually members (or former members) of parliament.

[7] It should be noted that issues of proportionality in electoral systems can assume a legal character in certain countries—in Germany, the Constitutional Court found that the electoral system of how mandates were distributed came into conflict with constitutional law on proportional representation; see Case 2 BvF 3/11 decided on 25 July 2012.

[8] In the 2017 election, two Norwegian parties, 'the reds' and 'the greens', received fewer than 100.000 votes and came below the 4 per cent limit, ending up with one seat each in the Parliament.

i. Organisation

The parliaments of the Nordic countries all have an internal organisation in which members of parliament may also be members of one of the several committees that works on preparing different issues for plenary sessions. These committees usually adhere to the organisation of the government in different ministries such as finance, defence and education. Issues dealt with by the ministry of education will thus be handled by the committee of education when they arrive in parliament, and so forth. Representation in committees is proportionate to the representation in parliament as a whole; thus, in cases of majority government, the parties supporting the government will normally also have a majority in the committees.[9] Due to the large size of the Swedish Parliament, not all members can have a seat on a committee, so there are a number of MPs who have no such appointments.[10]

The constitutional texts differ quite considerably in terms of the details of the organisation of parliamentary work. First of all, the establishment of a number of standing committees is not mentioned in all the Nordic constitutions. Thus, some of these very common committees are not based on a clear constitutional mandate, as in Norway, where the only regulation of the parliamentary committees is found in the standing orders of Parliament, which can be changed by an ordinary decision by Parliament. The same goes for Iceland and Denmark.

Finland and Sweden have a much more detailed constitutional entrenchment of the organisation of parliamentary work. The constitutional texts in these countries name certain standing committees that parliament should elect and leaves it open to have other committees besides those mentioned. The function of the specifically named committees are dealt with in further detail; for example, the Swedish and Finnish Constitutional Committees are mentioned in several separate rules concerning such different issues as legislation, parliamentary control of government and the prosecution of members of government.

In the context of constitutional regulation of parliamentary organisation, the traditional separation of the Nordic countries between West and East seems to hold true. The Eastern countries have a more detailed constitutional regulation and have some committees to which the constitution gives rather unusual tasks for a standing committee of a parliament. This might also seem like a division between more flexible (West) and more rigid (East) systems, but this conclusion would be too hasty. As the Swedish and Finnish Constitutions are much easier to

[9] However, many of the Nordic countries have more experience with minority government.

[10] There has been some criticism of this, as it means that there is a certain 'career' to be made for a member of parliament, from being a 'backbencher' to the position of chairperson of an important parliamentary committee. The prospects of such an internal career might undermine the relationship between the elected and their constituency, and give the political party of the MP a role that is difficult to square with the idea of representing his or her voters. The German Constitutional Court has repeatedly examined whether the way in which parliamentary work is organised is compatible with the ideas of a free mandate for MPs and with the equal position of MPs within the Parliament; see, eg, BVerGE 80, 188 and 140, 115.

change, the detailed constitutional regulation of the organisation of parliament is to some extent an illusion rather than a true safety net.

ii. Functions and Powers

a. Changing the Constitution

As already mentioned above, the parliaments of the Nordic countries all have constitutional functions typical of modern democracies, such as those relating to *legislation*, *control* of government, deciding on the *state budget* and *representation* of the electorate. Some of these will be discussed in more detail below, but before that, there is one further power that should be mentioned especially here: that of *constitutional change* itself.[11]

The rules on constitutional amendments or changes are quite different in the Nordic countries, from the very easily applied rules of the Swedish Constitution to the harsh demands of the Danish Constitution. However, all Nordic constitutions place some of the power to change the constitution itself in the hands of parliament, even if this is sometimes combined with other demands. A common feature is also a mechanism for some time for reflection and debate, in that the process for constitutional change demands that such a revision must be decided by two parliamentary decisions, with an election in between.

In Sweden and Iceland, the system for constitutional change is the easiest and only two decisions by a simple majority in parliament are required. Many smaller—and some not so small—alterations to the Swedish Constitution have been adopted since 1974 and the election of 2014 was the first since then in which no constitutional amendment was waiting for a second vote after the election. This could lead a casual observer to believe that constitutional change is part of the political struggle in society. However, this is not so in political practice, where consensus between all (or almost all) parties of the Parliament has been an entrenched tradition and historically the political majority would rather drop an issue that does not receive wide approval than force it through.[12] Whether this tradition will survive a more diverse Parliament, in which new political parties—which have not been part of this tradition—have emerged during the last 20 years, remains to be seen.

[11] It should be noted that the role of parliaments in financial matters is not dealt with below, even if it is a central part of the tasks of parliament to decide on the state budget. The constitutional rules in the Nordic countries on these issues are not extensive, as most details are dealt with in financial or budgetary laws that are quite technical, and therefore it is not possible to do justice to them within the scope of this short chapter. One common feature on the income side of the state budget is that taxes in the Nordic countries can only be decided by parliament; see, eg, Article 75 of the Norwegian Constitution, Article 81 of the Finnish Constitution and Article 43 of the Danish Constitution.

[12] The unwritten rule until the 1990s was that all of the five or six parties in Parliament (except the communists) had to accept the change. Since then, the communist party has had a 'makeover' into a more general 'leftish' party that has made it both larger and more included in constitutional affairs. A small 'green' party and a growing right-wing nationalist party have also entered the scene and have put some strain on the idea of a general consensus.

Since its adoption in 1944, amendments have been made to important parts of the Icelandic Constitution, such as the revision of the human rights chapter in 1995. However, the general revision of the Constitution promised in 1944 has never taken place. Following the collapse of the banks in 2008 and the ensuing economic crisis, a process was finally started to write a new constitution. A proposal for a new constitution was approved by a consultative referendum in 2012 with 67 per cent in favour, but the Parliament did not even vote on the issue as the bill on a new constitution was blocked in the Alþingi. Following the 2013 elections, it seems to have fallen off the political agenda for the time being.

The Norwegian and Finnish Constitutions adds a requirement of a two-thirds majority in parliamentary decision making as a way of ensuring a broad consensus. Both countries share a history of a relatively 'untouched' constitutional text for most of the time after the Second World War, but more substantial constitutional reforms were passed around the millennium or even more recently.[13] In Denmark, the continuity of the constitutional text is even stronger, as Article 88 of the Constitution of 1953 makes it very difficult to change the Danish Constitution.[14] After the Parliament has taken its second decision on the change, following an election and with no special rules on qualified majority, the proposal must be put to the people in a referendum within six months. The change is adopted only if approved by a majority in the vote and this majority must also be at least 40 per cent of those entitled to vote. In practice, this has made it very difficult indeed to get constitutional changes approved, as either they are very controversial and therefore not easy to get past a referendum or they are more technical and therefore are not very appealing for the voters, thus resulting in a turnout that will not be sufficiently high enough to satisfy the formal requirement.

Most Nordic countries do not have the kind of constitutional constraint on constitutional change that, for example, the German Constitution contains in its Article 79, so that certain changes are not possible within the constitutional system itself. The Constitutional Court of Germany is the last guardian of that provision. Norway however has just such a substantial rule on constitutional change in Article 121 of its Constitution, holding that changes in the Constitution must not contravene the constitutional principles or purposes.[15] However, the consensus seems to be that this constitutional rule may not be adjudicated in the courts, so

[13] In Finland a constitutional makeover took place in the late 1990s, culminating in a totally new constitution in 2000. In Norway several constitutional reforms have been passed during the last 20 years or so, the latest being the major expansion of the protection of constitutional rights in 2014 and a new provision on the courts' power of judicial review in 2015 (Article 89).

[14] It is often said that it is the constitution in the world that is the second hardest to change, coming after only the US Constitution.

[15] Actually, Chapter 1, § 1 of the Swedish Freedom of Press Act also contains such a substantial limit to changes in the Act (which are allowed only for the protection of individual rights and public safety); however, this passage has never been considered as legally or even politically binding, but rather as a gentle reminder of things that future constitutional legislators should consider.

it has little if any legal significance.[16] In that sense, the constitutional systems of the Nordic countries are flexible and open to whatever change the political system brings forth. However, the Danish Constitution is one of the hardest to change in the world, so any idea of a common Nordic constitutional heritage does not hold up to scrutiny here.

b. Legislation

When it comes to the legislative process, the Nordic parliaments have roles and functions comparable to most parliaments in modern democracies. In other words, they are formally the legislator, in that a normative act cannot constitutionally be 'a law' unless the parliament has adopted it as such. However, as in all modern democratic countries—and particularly in systems with parliamentarism in one form or another—the 'real' legislator is the government. Usually it will have the support of its members of parliament and/or coalition parties, and will thus be able to 'dominate' the proceedings in parliament. In common cases of minority government, the Nordic countries have the experience that the government is still the 'engine' of the legislative process, even if the role of parliament is more important in such cases. It is the government that has the practical resources to initiate legislation of a more general character, so even if parliament would want certain legislative results, it would often be difficult to achieve them without extensive involvement of the government.[17] Even so, the members of parliament in all Nordic states have an individual right to propose legislation and take specific initiatives in parliament, so it quite frequently happens that proposed legislation is modified or even fully introduced in parliament without governmental involvement. However, the latter is an exception to the rule that legislation in a parliament in a system of constitutional parliamentarism is mostly an affair for the government. For example, a stable political majority in the Swedish Parliament between 1920 and 1970 eventually led to the Parliament being given the nickname of a 'transit-zone' for governmental policy.[18]

A common feature of legislation in the Nordic countries is the use of a rather structured approach to legislative issues before they reach the parliament, which to some degree contributes to the well-known attitude of consensus instead of conflict in Nordic politics. The main characteristic is a chain of publicly available proposals that in a step-by-step process gets closer to the parliament. In short, this may include a first public report by experts and/or politicians, a number of

[16] See E Smith, *Konstitusjonelt demokrati* (Bergen, Fagbokforlaget, 2017) 299.

[17] In Sweden, the Parliament will often proclaim its will on a certain issue and expect the (minority) government to act accordingly, which is not always the case and in any event takes some time if it is considered to be of a lower priority than other things before the government.

[18] 'Riksdagen är regeringens transportkompani' (the Parliament is but a transport company for the government) was a generally held opinion on the relationship between these institutions in the period after the Second World War and it still, persists even though the situation has changed radically since then.

comments from civil society as well as political actors on the report, a revised version of the proposal made by the government—sometimes involving further discussions with stakeholders—and at last a parliamentary treatment of the proposal.[19] The constitutionally important aspect of this rather elaborate and time-consuming system is that to a large extent, it ensures that members of parliament have a full understanding and a wide range of facts and opinions available to them when it comes to voting on the government's proposed legislation. In particular, the formal inclusion of stakeholders as commentators/reviewers in the process is worth noting. Thus, the ideal of rational legislation, supported by facts and with full disclosure of alternatives, can to a large degree be fulfilled in the Nordic countries. A further effect of this way of handling legislative initiatives is that its first steps allow for a 'relaxed' and quite open search for viable solutions to societal problems between experts and politicians. This can in itself facilitate consensus on factual issues and agreement on policy in a topically limited and pragmatic atmosphere. The Nordic experience of being able to reach pragmatic political solutions across ideological differences can probably to some extent be attributed to this institutionalised way of bringing knowledge (science) and will (politics) together.

One specific remark on this vast topic of legislative process is the institution of the Law Council in Sweden. This is somewhat similar to the functions of Councils of State in many continental jurisdictions, as it is an institution that the government can consult on legislative issues.[20] However, there are also important differences. The Law Council consists of current and former justices of the two Supreme Courts.[21] One or two currently active justices are, according to seniority, temporarily moved to the Law Council for a period of one year. They do not participate in the courts' usual activities during this time. Usually the Council operates in two sections, with one current member from each of the highest courts and one retired member from any of them in each section. The Instrument of Government makes it obligatory to consult the Law Council on legislative issues before a bill is introduced into the Parliament in many cases and such referrals are often made even when they are not constitutionally mandated.[22] According to the Constitution, the Law Council should scrutinise the proposal from a legal (constitutional) perspective, as well as from legal/technical and linguistic points of view, and—this has been somewhat controversial—should also give its opinion on the estimated effectiveness of the proposal.[23]

[19] Of course, this procedure is not always followed, as many minor (and some major) legislative initiatives are dealt with internally within the ministries, but it is still the 'ideal' and in Sweden it is to some extent constitutionally prescribed by Chapter 7, § 2 of the Instrument of Government.

[20] It also has some functions that are similar to the Finnish Constitutional Committee of Parliament, which is examined below.

[21] See below on the court systems in the Nordic countries.

[22] See Chapter 8, § 21. A special law regulates the details of both the appointment of members and the inner workings of the Council.

[23] For examples of when the Council has been very critical, see the opinion on a proposal for a temporary stop for migration (7 December 2015) and the proposal for making the Convention of the Child into Swedish law (9 May 2017) (both available at www.lagradet.se).

As three of the Nordic countries (Denmark, Finland and Sweden) are members of the European Union (EU) and both Iceland and Norway are closely associated with the EU through their participation in the European Economic Area (EEA), the issue of how to nationally handle the legislative process in connection with the formation of policy at the EU level is dealt with extensively in Chapter 7 and therefore will not be discussed here.

c. Control

When it comes to the function of control over the government, this topic is dealt with more extensively in Chapter 4, so here it may suffice to say that all the Nordic parliaments have that function and may, for example, topple the government with a vote of no confidence. The institutions of parliamentary Ombudsmen and audit—controlling the government's activities in certain areas—are also present in the Nordic systems, the former having its historical roots in the Nordic countries.

A special institutional issue might, however, be worth more direct attention in this context, as some Nordic parliaments have a special committee on constitutional issues that is quite unique as an institutional design for constitutional control over legislation and governmental actions. It is the Finnish and Swedish Constitutions—which stipulate some obligatory committees—that give a committee on constitutional affairs some important tasks in the relationship between parliament and government.[24] Similar committees are established by law in Norway and Iceland, while Denmark lacks a parliamentary committee dedicated to constitutional issues.

The constitutional committees of the Parliaments in Finland and Sweden are not as alike as one might think, given the countries' constitutional history. However, they both have a central role in legal procedures against members of the government. Such procedures are very unusual indeed and are not of much practical interest, so we will not go into detail on this topic. Suffice to say that the committees have a role in evaluating the alleged fault before any prosecution can be brought against a minister.

Apart from that issue, the committees differ substantially in terms of their tasks and practical functions, even if the basic idea of scrutinising legislation of constitutional importance is a common baseline. Regarding the evaluation of proposed legislation and other actions of constitutional relevance,[25] the Finnish committee has established a practice of close cooperation with leading academics in the area of constitutional law and political science, who are consulted on a regular basis by

[24] The Swedish Instrument of Government also makes a financial committee obligatory. The Finnish Constitution stipulates no fewer than five committees, among them finance and foreign affairs. Likewise, the Danish Constitution requires a committee on foreign affairs. The control functions of these committees towards the executive are discussed further in Chapter 4.

[25] The entering into important international treaties might be an example.

the committee in the areas of their expertise. As such, the committee can be said to 'pool' expert competence in advance of its opinions and recommendations to the plenary sessions of the Parliament.[26]

The Swedish committee does not work in the same comprehensive way in relation to proposed legislation with constitutional impact, even if external experts are sometimes consulted on an ad hoc basis. To some degree, this may be explained by the legal expertise involved in the scrutiny by the Law Council, but even together with the committee's own work, the scrutiny by the Swedish committee is not equivalent to that of the Finnish committee regarding both the topics and method of work.[27] The Swedish committee has more focus on control of governmental action besides legislation. As such, the committee usually splits its attention and deals with legal/technical questions such as the correct registration of public acts, the way in which the government handles the promulgation and publication of laws etc in the autumn. More politically 'hot' issues, such as alleged legal mistakes by ministers or their close co-workers, are handled in the spring. In the line of this work, the committee (and its highly competent administrative office) makes investigations, holds hearings and makes official reports to the Parliament. Unsurprisingly, the spring reports are often characterised by the political attitude towards the government, as the members of the committee that are drawn from the opposition are generally more critical than members from the parties that support the government.

C. Summary

Of the Nordic countries, the Danish and the Icelandic Constitutions stand out as the ones that regulates the workings of parliament the least, while the Swedish Constitution perhaps gives the most detailed system of rules for its parliament. There is a sense of East/West division, as Finland and Sweden have some common features that we do not find elsewhere. The major explanation for the differences is perhaps not the 'constitutional culture' of the Eastern or Western sphere, but rather the rigidity or flexibility of the constitution in question. And, as we have shown, the Danish Constitution is very difficult indeed to change, so it therefore seems wise not to burden it with details that might become a problem in the future. The same does not apply to constitutions such as the Swedish or Finnish Constitutions, which can be adapted to changed circumstances quite easily.

[26] See, for example, the extensive opinion on the government's bill on regional reform, GrUU 26/2017 rd, in which no less than 70 experts, of which 25 or so were professors or researchers, were heard by the committee.

[27] The rather deep involvement of academics in the committee's work might, on the other hand, raise some questions on academic independence.

IV. Government

A. Formation of Government

As already mentioned above, the governments of the Nordic countries are all dependent upon the acceptance or at least tolerance of their respective parliaments. In Denmark, Iceland and Norway, however, this is not obvious from the constitutional text, but rather is based on long-standing political practice.[28] All these countries use a form of 'negative parliamentarism', in that a government will be able to function as long as a majority of the parliament does not go against it. However, this is not something that the Constitutions of Denmark and Norway regulate, and the same goes for the Icelandic Constitution. This does not mean that there is no constitutional foundation for the formation of governments in these countries, as the constitutional rules on votes of non-confidence against the prime minister have the function of structuring how a government may be formed in the first place. In Finland, the Constitution can be said to give a certain preference for positive parliamentarism if it is possible to form a government based on a majority in Parliament, but with an option for mere tolerance if no majority can be reached. The Swedish Constitution explicitly states that if more than half of the members of parliament vote against a candidate for prime minister, the proposal fails.

The chosen form of parliamentary base for governmental power leads to a risk of 'weak' governments, even if it does make the process of forming a government easier than a more demanding standard of explicit support by the parliament. However, the Nordic countries' experience of this form of government is not as troublesome as one might think. Governments based on parliamentary minorities, and on varying degrees of formal cooperation with some parties outside those forming the basis of government, have been common and generally functional. Perhaps a Nordic tradition of pragmatism and compromise has an important role to play in making this formally weak form of government into something quite acceptable from the perspectives of effectiveness and resolve.

B. Powers

The powers of a government classically consist of such actions as use of the states' financial resources, leading and controlling the public administration, and

[28] For instance, the parliamentary rule is not explicitly mentioned or referred to in the text of the Icelandic Constitution, but is based on an unwritten rule, which was developed outside the constitutional text.

conducting foreign policy, including decisions on war and peace. As will be made clear in Chapter 7 on the EU/EEA, the latter does not hold completely true in some areas, but the Nordic countries still conform to the standardised norm of constitutional powers and functions for a government as mentioned above. There are not so many remarkable or noteworthy issues to present here; the Nordic governments will present budgets and introduce legislation to their parliaments, they will conduct international diplomacy, and they will lead and direct the public administration within boundaries that are very similar to most constitutional democracies.

One issue that warrants some special attention concerns the last-mentioned relationship: the 'steering powers' of government in relation to the public authorities.[29] The 'normal' solution is that the state authorities are an integral part of government, with each authority sorting under a specific governmental ministry, such as the national police under the Justice Ministry and the Environmental Agency under the Ministry for the Environment. As such, the agencies are more or less parts—or rather extensions—of the government and take orders from their respective minister. Of course, there is no way a single minister can lead and direct all the public authorities under his or her department in any detail, so in practice the authorities have a lot of leeway in terms of handling their missions.[30] But formally the decision-making powers of the authority are part of the minister's powers and are only delegated to the public servants. This means that the minister is formally responsible for all decisions taken by authorities under his or her ministry, and he or she may at any time step in and revoke the delegation in order to make a certain decision himself or herself.[31]

All Nordic countries apart from Sweden conform to the picture painted above. In Sweden, the public authorities are constitutionally separated from the government by a special rule that forbids the government from interfering with a public authority in its decisions concerning individuals, as long as the decisions are based on the authority's exercise of public power. Furthermore, Swedish government ministers do not hold individual powers; instead, all formal governmental decisions are collective. This unusual limitation of the powers of individual ministers is based partly on the idea that the acts of government are so intimately connected with each other that no minister should have sole responsibility over a specific area of policy. In addition, the constitutionally protected independence of the public authorities from direct governmental orders or interference in their decisions is designed to act as protection for the

[29] By 'public authorities' in this context, we only refer to national authorities, not to regional and/or local authorities that can have a less direct relationship with the government.

[30] These missions include tasks that are created by law, governmental instructions and by way of financial decisions.

[31] A further exception must be mentioned, as sometimes the Parliament has given an authority more independence towards the government by law and of course in such cases the minister is also bound by the law.

citizens against political influence and discretion in specific cases. In a way, it is viewed as a logical consequence of the principle of legality—as the exercise of public power must be based on law, no other consideration than the law should govern the decisions of the authorities.[32]

C. Balancing the Parliament

One of the ways in which the government can influence the parliament, aside from party politics and other obvious means, is if it has the power to initiate new elections, thus threatening to change the composition of the parliament. Constitutionally, this is both an issue of principle of balancing the power between parliament and government and a pragmatic issue of giving the government the tools it need to actually govern.

In the Nordic countries, governments (or the head of state at the request of the government)[33] hold this power over the Parliament in Denmark, Finland, Iceland and Sweden. In Norway, by contrast, this common feature is lacking, thus enhancing the need for consensus and rationality, as a rigid attitude could lead to the collapse of important state functions. The Norwegian Constitution resembles the US Constitution in this area, but so far it has functioned without the 'deadlocks' that we sometimes see in American politics.

The models of governmental influence over the parliament in the other Nordic countries are quite different. The Danish solution is close to the British model, in that the government can choose a time for new elections within the four-year term and the new Parliament has a new full term from the date of the election. Finland and Iceland also fall within this tradition, even if the president in those countries must be involved as well as the government. The Swedish Parliament has a constitutionally fixed term.[34] This means that a new term following an election outside the fixed terms only lasts until the time when elections ordinarily would have been held. In such a system, the threat of new elections can result in more costs than benefits after only a short time and will seldom be an attractive solution to a political problem when less than two years remain until ordinary elections. Thus, the experience is that new, 'extra' elections are very seldom held between regular elections.

[32] In Sweden this already follows from the rule in Chapter 1, § 1 of the Instrument of Government that the exercise of all public powers must be based on law.

[33] In Finland the president can also act on his or her own initiative. In Iceland the president may only dissolve the Parliament at the request of the prime minister. In recent years, it has been debated whether the president can under certain circumstances reject such a request.

[34] A reason for this rather rigid regulation is the important connection in Swedish politics between national and local elections. As local elections are to be held at the same time as national elections, the latter cannot be allowed to vary.

D. Summary

Nordic governments do not stand out in general from democratic governments around the world. No clear division in East/West traditions can be found, but two rather exceptional peculiarities do catch the attention of a constitutional internationalist. The first is the Norwegian lack of a governmental 'weapon' against a parliament that no longer supports its policies, such as dissolving the parliament and initiating elections. This strong entrenchment of the parliament's power over government is unusual. The second is the Swedish Constitution's limiting of the powers of the government in relation to the executive authorities and the related limitation on the powers of individual ministers as members of government. Here, strong ideals of legality and a fear of undue political involvement in administrative issues have led to a unique solution.

V. The Courts

A. Organisation

A first—and striking—similarity between the Nordic countries is that they all lack a constitutional court with special competence regarding judicial review etc.[35] The explanation for this institutional choice is certainly not a simple one, but an important factor has been (and still is) the prevailing view that courts should not ordinarily deal with issues that in essence are 'political', and that a constitutional court would or could 'politicise' the courts and the judiciary to an undesirable extent. As the historical experience of the Nordic countries is not one of recent totalitarian regimes, the need for a judicial 'check' on political power has been more of a theoretical problem than an urgent issue in practice. In addition, Norway's 200 years of experience with judicial review by ordinary courts has to a certain extent served as a bulwark against proposals for a constitutional court in that country.

In relation to the general organisation of the courts, the Nordic countries do in fact align according to the 'East/West' dichotomy discussed earlier in this book. Denmark, Iceland and Norway all have a single court system consisting of general courts at different levels, headed by a Supreme Court. Aside from some specialised courts with specific jurisdictions, these courts deal with most types of issues, such as criminal law, civil law, administrative law and constitutional issues. Finland and Sweden instead follow a more continental tradition of having both general

[35] The subject of judicial review is dealt with extensively in Chapter 5, so it will only be briefly touched upon here and below.

courts and administrative courts in two court systems with a Supreme Court at the top of each. Of course, special courts exist here as well, outside of the ordinary systems.[36] Another common feature is that the Nordic countries abide by the usual 'three-level' organisation of: (1) local courts, (2) courts of appeal; and (3) a Supreme Court.[37]

The degree of constitutional entrenchment of the court system differs substantially between the Nordic countries. In Sweden and Finland, the structure of the court system is regulated in the Constitution, so that no major reforms can be made without constitutional change. The Norwegian Constitution mentions the Supreme Court, while the Danish and Icelandic Constitutions do not explicitly provide for a specific Supreme Court in the constitutional text. Here again, we see the differences between modern constitutional texts and constitutional documents that have been partially reformed or have remained almost untouched, a difference that in this case follows the East/West dichotomy of the Nordic judicial heritage.

The constitutions of all the Nordic states provide for a special Court of Impeachment (Rigsretten/Landsdómur), except in Sweden, where such a court was not included in the 1974 Constitution, as it had not been convened for 120 years. Criminal prosecutions to hold ministers accountable for their conduct in office are still subject to special procedure in all Nordic states, which will be explored further in Chapter 4.

B. Constitutional Protection of Judicial Independence

The legitimacy of the judicial branch of government can be said to rest on three separate ways of ensuring the independence of judges: in the procedure of appointment, in the actual judging of individual cases and in the way in which a judge may be dismissed from his or her position.

Judges in the Nordic states are all appointed by the executive power, by the president in the republics and by the government in the other states. As mentioned in Chapter 5, the procedure has become more open and transparent in recent years in several of the countries, even if the basic prerogative of the executive has not changed in principle. In Norway and Sweden, for example, the office of judge for a supreme court is applied for in the same way as other seats in the court system and

[36] The most interesting of these special courts from an institutional point of view are perhaps the Labour Courts, which exist in all Nordic countries and are specially designed to deal with issues on the labour market, including representatives of the parties (unions and employers) as judges together with professional judges.

[37] This could be said to be only half-true, as in Finland, the general courts conform to the picture of three levels, but where the administrative courts only have two levels (local courts and a Supreme Administrative Court). Furthermore, the Icelandic court system used to be a 'two-level' system, but on 1 January 2018, new legislation on the judiciary came into force, establishing a Court of Appeals, in line with the other Nordic countries.

the evaluation of candidates is similar as well. However, these important changes have not been accomplished by constitutional provisions, but rather by changes in ordinary legislation.

The Danish system includes a feature of more principal interest, as a candidate for a position as judge on the Supreme Court will have to 'test-vote' in four cases in the court before being confirmed as a judge there. In practice, this gives the court a 'veto' on candidates who do not live up to the standards of the highest court, a rare instance of judicial power in the executive area of appointments of public servants. Another point of interest is that since 2010, the Icelandic system provides for the involvement of the Parliament. If the minister of justice decides not to follow the proposal of a special assessment committee, he or she must seek the approval of the Parliament in order to appoint another candidate.[38]

The constitutional protection of independence in the act of judging itself is quite similar in the constitutional texts of the Nordic countries, even if the context and history of these provisions differ quite substantially. Such provision can, for example, be found in Article 95 of the Norwegian Constitution, Chapter 11, § 3 of the Swedish Instrument of Government, Article 64 of the Danish Constitution and (an identical provision to the Danish one) in Article 61 of the Icelandic Constitution (largely unchanged since 1874). Together with both national and international provisions on the right to a fair trial, national Ombudsmen in Sweden and Finland who investigate complaints against the courts in this regard and a free and critical press, the guarantees against political or other types of pressure against judges are strong in the Nordic countries. This does not mean that judges are immune to shifts in public debate or 'outrage' of the media, but there is little or no evidence that the courts in the Nordic countries are unduly sensitive to political pressure of any kind.

A factor that should be mentioned here is that judicial independence does not relate to the legal safeguards against outside pressure as such, but also concerns issues such as salaries, promotion and everyday working conditions. There are more subtle ways of influencing a judge or a group of judges than direct orders and such structural issues must also be given attention. This chapter cannot go into any depth on this topic in this context, but it should be mentioned that in Sweden, for example, the salary of the individual judge is decided by the Chief Judge of his or her respective court and that the criteria for such decisions are quite vague and open to interpretation.[39] Principled criticism of this still rather new (and management-influenced) system has so far been met with little understanding from the government, as the idea of individual salaries was part of a reform of the whole public sector, but without special consideration of the special role played by the courts.

[38] This became a practical issue in 2017 when the Minister of Justice did not follow the conclusion of such a committee. This decision was highly controversial and highlighted the vagueness of the rules on the involvement of Parliament in such cases.

[39] This does not include the judges of the two Supreme Courts for reasons of protecting their independence.

The appointment of judges lasts until they reach retirement age. There are a limited number of ways in which a judge can lose his or her position, a common feature being that a court must be involved. However, the details of the different constitutions are actually quite different in this respect. In Denmark and Iceland, the Constitutions stop at demanding that a court decide on the issue of 'sacking' a judge and do not explicitly deal with any specific demands on this court procedure. The Swedish Constitution contains four provisions on these issues, one dealing specifically with the judges of the Supreme Courts and the others with the procedure concerning other judges.

C. Courts as Loyal Interpreters of Laws

In Chapter 5, we examine the judicial powers of courts in more detail, especially in the context of judicial review of legislative and administrative acts. The impact of membership of the EU is dealt with in Chapter 7. Here it might therefore suffice to briefly introduce some reflections on legal interpretation in the courts.

As mentioned above, the legislative procedure in the Nordic countries is often an elaborate and time-consuming affair. It leaves several written documents on the intended purpose and function of legislation, often written by legal experts and indirectly approved by the government and the parliament in the process of adopting the rules in question. Some of these legal experts are even judges temporarily functioning as experts for a particular legislative project. The views expressed in such documentation are generally regarded as guidance for the practical application of the rules in question. Such preparatory works are therefore used extensively by the courts in the Nordic countries as interpretive tools when facing legal uncertainties. The fact that judges both participate in the making of new laws and as the practical users of those laws can to some degree explain the willingness of courts to follow such interpretive sources without feeling unduly influenced by politics.[40] It might be said as a general observation that the courts in the Nordic countries try to stay loyal to legislative intent.

D. Summary

When it comes to the courts, there is some ground for an East/West division between the Nordic countries. The Eastern states of Finland and Sweden have dual court systems (administrative/general courts), while the Western states of Denmark, Iceland and Norway have one general court system. This has some wider implications, for example, regarding the position of administrative law

[40] As a contrast, see *Pepper v Hart* [1992] 3 WLR 1032, in which the British House of Lords (nowadays the Supreme Court) allowed for a rare consultation of political statements regarding the purpose of a tax law.

as a separate legal field, the possible tension between the two 'highest' courts in relation to interpretation of legal sources that to some degree affect all courts (ie, constitutional rules and EU law) and for the formation of a distinct judicial 'culture' within a national legal system.

VI. Concluding Observations

Following the discussion in this chapter, there is time to point out some common threads of the Nordic constitutional institutions. From an international perspective, the parliaments of the Nordic countries have a strong constitutional and factual position, quite like the British Parliament, but with written constitutions as some kind of legal limit to their sovereignty. Lately—and under the influence of international law, such as the European Convention on Human Rights and EU law—this traditional division of powers has shifted to some degree in favour of the courts, but not to the extent that the basic idea of parliament as the legitimate source of public power has been undermined as such. Beside the constitutional institutions dealt with here, it should be noted that the Nordic states also share an experience with strong non-governmental organisations in general and labour unions in particular. This is a factor outside the constitutional design that has probably contributed to the stability and functionality of the political systems in the Nordic countries. Likewise, entrenched ideas on openness and transparency in government are a common feature among the Nordic states. In Sweden it is constitutionally regulated in great detail, while some of the other Nordic countries have opted for less restraining rules on that level, but with more or less the same end result.

As we have seen, it is not easy to find strong support for the idea of grouping the Nordic countries into an East and West constellation as a tool for comparative analysis when it comes to the basic institutional issues dealt with in this chapter. Instead, we have several important differences between the institutional set-ups in the Nordic countries that do not conform to such a handy division. The picture is much more complicated. While the Western countries (Denmark, Iceland and Norway) share both a common history and some institutional features, the differences are many in central areas such as the head of state, the electoral system and the relation between parliament and government. The same goes for the Eastern countries (Finland and Sweden), which also share a long history and important institutional features, but have also made significantly divergent choices in those same areas. And while Denmark and Sweden are the oldest states as such, and therefore share some historical experience, they are perhaps also the most different when it comes to constitutional attitudes, such as the choice between flexibility and rigidity.

A concluding remark would be that even in societies that are fairly similar when it comes to historical experience, the economy, social and religious factors, and political structure, many other factors outside the legal sphere seem to influence the choices of constitutional institutions and their detailed function. It is necessary to know the particular history of each country in order to be able to understand its constitution. In that sense, history and law are forever intertwined in a way that is a challenge to all comparative legal studies. We hope that this study will bring forward some of those particularities as a way of helping us all reach a more general understanding of the functions of constitutional law.

4

Mechanisms for Parliamentary Control of the Executive

BJÖRG THORARENSEN

I. Introduction

This chapter will address how the Nordic constitutional systems provide for parliamentary control mechanisms to supervise the actions of the executive branch, and the various means and methods that have developed for holding governments and ministers to account. The legislature prescribes the rules governing the executive power and that the executive is subordinate and accountable to parliament.[1] In recent decades it has nevertheless been asked in all the Nordic countries whether national parliaments are losing power and how the relationship between the three branches of government is changing. It has been argued that the 'fall of parliamentary sovereignty', particularly with respect to the judiciary, was perhaps the most significant political trend of the twentieth century.[2]

The classical Nordic doctrine of the supremacy of the legislature has come under challenge. This is partly explained by the growing impact of European legislation, with legislative powers being transferred to supranational institutions of the European Union (EU). Thus, Nordic national parliaments have increasingly been challenged by the internationalisation of politics and, in particular, by the ongoing process of European integration.[3] The trend regarding parliamentary decline can also partly be explained by the increased powers of the judicial branch in the exercise of judicial review, which is placing greater restraints on the legislator. It has been suggested that Nordic judicial systems have great respect for their national parliaments as democratically chosen legislators.[4] Nevertheless, there are

[1] H Yamamoto, *Tools for Parliamentary Oversight: A Comparative Study of 88 Parliaments* (Geneva, Inter-Parliamentary Union 2007) 9.

[2] B Bricker, *Visions of Judicial Review: A Comparative Examination of Courts and Policy in Democracies* (Colchester, ECPR Press 2016) 3.

[3] T Persson, 'The Parliaments of the Scandinavian Countries' in P Nedergaard and A Wivel (eds), *The Routledge Handbook of Scandinavian Politics* (New York, Routledge, 2018) 103.

[4] J Husa, *Nordic Reflections on Constitutional Law: A Comparative Nordic Perspective* (Frankfurt am Main, Peter Lang, 2002) 173.

clear signs that judicial control over the legislator has been growing, particularly in Norway and Iceland, as will be discussed further in Chapters 5 and 6 in this volume.

The de facto influence of the parliaments in the Nordic countries varies according to the parliamentary base of the government at any given time. Minority governments may result in stronger parliamentary oversight, while a tradition of strong majority governments may both weaken political accountability and affect the likelihood that parliament will apply the available procedures for parliamentary control to supervise the actions of both ministers and the administration.[5] Each country has developed its own distinctive parliamentary model. Whereas Denmark, Norway and Sweden, all parliamentary monarchies, have relied extensively on minority governments, Finland and Iceland, both semi-presidential systems, have relied more on majority coalition governments.[6]

In the Nordic context, parliamentary oversight over the actions of the government administration is considered to be an important function of the national parliaments. All the Nordic constitutional systems have certain features in common in this area, while in other areas they are completely different, and some examples of this will be studied and compared. The main elements of parliamentary control to be explored in this chapter include the constitutional basis for such control, such as interpellations and requests for information, the control mechanisms of parliamentary standing committees, the appointment of special investigation commissions, special control institutions such as Parliamentary Ombudsmen and finally the relationship between the political and legal (criminal) responsibility of ministers. Finally, an assessment will be made as to whether amendments of laws related to parliamentary oversight have resulted in more efficient control, and particularly whether the codification of rules into constitutional texts results in strengthened control.

II. Ideas Underlying Parliamentary Control and New Challenges

Traditionally, the main functions and powers of the Nordic parliaments as in other parliamentary democracies are considered to be threefold: (1) *law-making powers*, which means the competence to legislate on all matters within the boundaries of the constitution; (2) *financial powers*, which include the power to impose taxes, decide the budget for the state and the oversight and management of the state budget; and (3) *control powers over the executive*, which is the subject that

[5] F Sejersted, *Kontroll og konstitution. Statsrettlige studier av Stortingets kontrollvirksomhet* (Oslo, Cappelen Akademisk Forlag, 2002) 26.
[6] Persson (n 3) 104.

will be explored further in this chapter. However, this will not include scrutiny of bills in parliamentary committees which fall within the scope of the parliaments' law-making powers.

The role of parliament in controlling the executive in Nordic constitutional law derives from its position; as a body representing the people, it is to ensure that the administration of public policy and the execution of law are in accordance with law and that they meet the people's needs.[7] Traditionally, the concept of *control* means the right of parliament to request information and clarification from the individual ministers and the government through interpellations in debates or by requesting reports on ministers' conduct and their administration, the oversight of the legality of ministers' actions in the performance of their duties and political oversight. In a wider sense, it also covers responses to situations in which there is a loss of confidence in ministers, such as declarations to the effect that an individual minister, or the government, no longer enjoys parliament's confidence, and possibly the power to prosecute ministers for criminal conduct in office.

Supervision of public accounts and state monetary affairs traditionally falls under the supervisory role as part of the financial powers of Nordic parliaments, either through the election of special auditors or through special institutions acting on behalf of parliament. Being connected to parliament, these institutions have undeniable democratic legitimacy in protecting citizens' and taxpayers' interests by auditing the collection of state revenues, the use of state funds and the general management of state property. The idea is to promote economy, efficiency and general effectiveness in state administration by conducting audits and other expert tasks relating to the control of financial management. In a broad sense, such institutions protect an important dimension of the constitution.[8]

In spite of the fact that the supervisory role has been acknowledged as an integral part of the Nordic constitutional systems since the nineteenth century, it was rarely mentioned in the first constitutions. Accordingly, it was not defined explicitly as a formal role, though some aspects of it were reflected in scattered constitutional provisions.[9] In the absence of political accountability of ministers towards parliament, the first Nordic constitutions focused solely on their legal responsibility. Hence, the Swedish Instrument of Government of 1809[10] and the Norwegian Constitution of 1814 provided for a system where the ministers, who were accountable solely to the crown, were legally responsible to the parliaments in a special court of impeachment (*Riksretten*). This model was later followed in the other Nordic constitutions: in Denmark in 1849, in Iceland in 1903 and in Finland in 1919. As regards other aspects of means to control the executive, the

[7] Yamamoto (n 1) 9.

[8] J Husa, *The Constitution of Finland. A Contextual Analysis* (Oxford, Hart Publishing, 2011) 71.

[9] Sejersted (n 5) 26–28. On the situation in Sweden in the Instrument of Government in 1809, see F Sterzel, *Riksdagens Kontrollmakt* (Stockholm, PA Norstedt & Söners Förlag, 1969) 12–14 and 26.

[10] Hereinafter, the Swedish Instrument of Government will be referred to as 'the Swedish Constitution'.

initial constitutions were mainly silent, although under separate provisions, individual MPs could, with parliament's permission, request information regarding a public matter.[11]

There has clearly been a growing demand in the Nordic countries since the latter part of the twentieth century to strengthen means to control their governments' activities. Partly, this can be seen as a reaction to the growing Europeanisation of politics. Nordic parliaments have sought to compensate for their alleged decline in legislative activity by developing their oversight and control mechanisms with respect to EU affairs.

New patterns of parliamentary practices have emerged in order to secure the ability of Nordic parliaments to control national governments.[12] One aspect of this is how parliaments react to situations which have aroused vociferous requests for the investigation of events that have had a serious impact on the public and assign responsibility for the situation or identify a possible abuse of power.[13] There has been a growing trend in appointing independent special investigation bodies for this purpose. Examples of this are the Special Investigation Commission set up in Iceland in 2009 to investigate the events that led to the collapse of the three main banks in the country in 2008[14] and the Special Investigation Commission in Sweden, appointed in 2005 following severe criticism of the government's slowness in responding to the deaths of or injuries to large numbers of Swedish holidaymakers in Thailand in the tsunami catastrophe in 2004.[15]

III. The Constitutional Basis of Parliamentary Control

A. The Explicit Provisions in the Constitutions of Finland and Sweden

Codification in constitutional texts of parliament's role and the tools available to it to supervise the executive has developed along different lines in the individual Nordic states. The provisions of the current East Nordic constitutions, those of Sweden and Finland, which are the most recent instruments, both having been

[11] Such provisions were found, eg, in Article 66 of the Danish Constitution of 1849 and Article 37 of the Icelandic Constitution of 1874.

[12] Persson (n 3) 103.

[13] J Nergelius, *Svensk statsrätt* (Malmö, Studentlitteratur, 2016) 301.

[14] 'Report of the Special Investigation Commission to Investigate and Analyse the Processes Leading to the Collapse of the Three Main Banks in Iceland', submitted to the Alþingi on 12 April 2010.

[15] SOU 2005:106. *Sverige och tsunamin—granskning och förslag* (Finansdepartementet, 1 December 2005).

adopted in the latter part of the twentieth century, have undergone a comprehensive revision with respect to the supervisory role of their parliaments vis-a-vis the executive branch. In the Swedish Constitution, adopted in 1974 and largely reformed in 2010,[16] Chapter 13 is devoted to parliamentary control (*kontrollmakten*). It lists the means of control available to the Parliament (*Riksdagen*), such as examination by the Committee on the Constitution, the prosecution of ministers, declarations of no confidence, interpellations and questions, and the control institutions: the Parliamentary Ombudsman and the National Audit Office.

The most comprehensive provisions on parliamentary control are to be found in the Finnish Constitution (Act No 731/1999), which came into force in 2000. This sets out in considerable detail the means available to either committees or individual MPs of the Parliament, the (*Eduskunta/Riksdagen*), for exercising oversight of the government or of individual ministers, through interpellations, statements and reports, questions and debates, and Parliament's right to demand information. These provisions are to be found in Chapter 4 of the Constitution on parliamentary activity (Articles 43–49). In addition, a special chapter, Chapter 10, under the heading 'Supervision of Legality', is devoted to the supervisory role of special organs, such as the Parliamentary Ombudsman and the Chancellor of Justice, over the executive power and the prosecution power available to Parliament, which is able to bring charges against ministers to hold them to criminal accountability for their conduct in office.

B. Links to the Government's Special Control Organ, the Chancellor of Justice

As an institution with a constitutional basis in Finland and Sweden, the Chancellor of Justice is a special feature of these East Nordic states, where it has strong historical roots in the constitutional systems; there is no similar tradition in the West Nordic states. In Finland it developed in the latter part of the eighteenth century in the context of a struggle for supremacy between the aristocracy and the monarch. The Chancellor of Justice of the Council of State, under Article 108 of the Constitution, is an independent supervisor of legality with the duty to monitor the legality of the operations of the government and other public authorities or agencies. The chancellor also monitors the activities of the members of the Finnish Bar Association. It has been suggested that from a constitutional point of view, the office of the chancellor is a somewhat puzzling institution, being not merely an organ to monitor the lawfulness of the official acts of the executive, but also a sort of 'High Jurist of the Crown'. This means that the chancellor must, if requested, provide information and opinions on legal issues for the president

[16] SFS 2010:1408; see J Nergelius, 'Constitutional Reform in Sweden: Some Important Remarks' (2013) 2013(4) *Tijdschrift voor Constitutioneel Recht* 372.

and the government, as well as for individual ministers. The institution has a number of parallels in various countries where such historical institutions exist, for instance, the UK.[17]

The closest parallel and, as one might expect, the model for the Finnish office of chancellor is to be found in Sweden. Under Article 12:1 of the Swedish Constitution, the Chancellor of Justice (*Justitieskansler*) is defined as one of the administrative authorities under the government. Despite many similarities, there are nevertheless also many differences. The Swedish Chancellor of Justice is given various supervisory tasks in constitutional provisions, mostly in Chapter 9. One of the principal tasks is monitoring to ensure that the limits of the freedom of the press are not transgressed; the chancellor has investigatory and prosecution powers in relation to offences against press freedom (Articles 9:1 and 9:2). As in Finland, the Chancellor of Justice also supervises the activities of the members of the Swedish bar.[18]

C. The Limited Constitutional Provisions in the West Nordic Systems

The Norwegian, Danish and Icelandic Constitutions contain far fewer and scattered provisions regarding the tools for supervision, and they are still largely based on the nineteenth-century constitutions. Article 75 of the Norwegian Constitution lists the supervisory functions together with the other main tasks of the Parliament (*Storting*). Among them is the supervision of monetary affairs, and a paragraph regarding the Ombudsman's office was added in 1995. Its wording, which is still based on its original version, stipulates in parts (f) and (g) that it devolves upon the Storting to have submitted to it the records of the Council of State and all public reports and documents, and the conventions and treaties which the monarch has concluded with foreign powers. On this basis, the Storting can request such documents from the government.[19] Further amendments were made in 2007 to strengthen Parliament's right to obtain information from the government and the government's duty to provide it. The Danish Constitution of 1953 (Article 53) and the Icelandic Constitution of 1944 (Article 54) contain almost identical provisions, with common roots in the Danish Constitution of 1849 stating that, subject to the permission of the Parliaments (*Folketing/ Alþingi*), any Member of Parliament may, by tabling a question or requesting a report, request information, or an answer to a question regarding a public matter, from

[17] Husa (n 8) 153.
[18] Nergelius (n 13) 309.
[19] E Smith, *Konstitutionelt demokrati. Statsforfatningsretten in principielt og komparativt lys*, 4th edn (Bergen, Fagbokforlaget, 2017) 250.

a minister. They also both state that Parliament may appoint committees from among its members to investigate matters of general importance. Such committees are entitled to demand written or oral information both from private citizens and from public authorities (Article 51 of the Danish Constitution and Article 39 of the Icelandic Constitution).

Notwithstanding limited references in the Constitutions of Norway, Iceland and Denmark, there is increased emphasis on the assumption that parliament's controlling role over the executive, including the right to take the initiative on investigations and hold open hearings, is a key element in strengthening parliamentary power in the constitutional system.[20] This is reflected in numerous amendments made in the parliaments' standing orders/rules of procedure on the issue. For instance, a new organisation of the supervisory system in Norway in the 1990s and in Iceland in 2011 provided for the establishment of special supervisory committees in the Storting and the Alþingi; these are the main bodies among the standing committees responsible for controlling the executive and they also function as coordinating bodies on supervision, with powers to take the initiative on certain control measures. Moreover, the minority of committee members are given certain tools to exercise control.

Finally, it is common to both to the West and East Nordic systems that they all have rather detailed provisions regarding supervisory functions in the standing orders of the parliaments, or in special acts on certain external controllers, such as the parliamentary Ombudsman, or on measures available in certain fields of parliamentary control.[21] It is neither possible here, nor is it the objective of this chapter, to analyse in detail this extensive set of rules. In the following, issues related to separate control mechanisms will be addressed, and their efficiency and impact will be compared and assessed in the light of the different political landscapes and traditions in the Nordic countries.

D. The Different Constitutional Basis for the Supervision of State Finances

An area in which great differences can be found in terms of how explicitly the Nordic constitutions provide for supervisory tasks is in the mechanisms they lay down regarding state finances. Historically, the prime financial monitoring organs are special National Audit Offices, which play a significant role in the parliamentary supervision of the government and have constitutional bases in the various

[20] J Thorsvik, 'Hva har skjedd med Stortingets makt?' (2016) 93(3) *Nordisk Administrativt Tidsskrift* 17.

[21] An example of such legislation is Iceland's Act on Investigation Commissions, No 68/2011, which provides that the Alþingi can appoint an investigation commission to investigate issues which concern important public interests.

national constitutions, with some differences between them.[22] Again, the East Nordic constitutions contain more detailed provisions on the issue and in addition they stipulate specifically the monitoring role of their committees on finance. The Swedish Constitution states that there shall exist a committee on finance (Article 4:3), and lists the committees on finance and on taxation among the 15 standing committees of the Parliament. Section VI below deals with the responsibilities of these committees. A similar structure can be found in the Finnish Constitution (Article 35), which lists the finance and the audit committees among the standing committees of the Parliament; Chapter 7, on state finances, includes a special provision in Article 90 on the supervision and auditing of state finances.

Furthermore, both the Finnish and Swedish Constitutions contain a constitutional basis for these countries' central banks, which are under the authority of their parliaments and whose roles and main functions are described in the constitutions.

The West Nordic constitutions, by contrast, contain minimal references to the supervision of state finances and do not mention it as the special task of a standing committee on finance; nevertheless, standing committees on finance do operate under the parliamentary standing orders. The constitutions say merely that the financial accounts of the state are to be subject to parliamentary supervision. Under Article 47 of the Danish Constitution and Article 75 (k) of the Norwegian Constitution, Parliament is to appoint a number of auditors, whose roles are further defined in these provisions. The Icelandic Constitution, as amended in 1995, provides a more open frame for the supervision of state finances, stipulating that the financial accounts of the state, its institutions and administrative bodies, are to be subject to an audit by, or under the supervision of, the Alþingi, as provided by law.

IV. Interpellations and Questions

The term 'interpellation' traditionally means a formal request for information on, or clarification of, the government's policy. The procedure has developed through practice in each of the Nordic parliaments and may be understood differently with respect to each of them. As an independent procedure, interpellations take

[22] The history of the National Audit Office in Finland can be traced back to 1695, when it was set up as an independent body to monitor financial administration under the Swedish crown. See Husa (n 8) 70. In Sweden, the system for supervising state finances underwent a complete revision and a new National Audit Office under the Riksdag was established in 2002; this is now provided for in Article 13:7. Previously, there were two revision authorities, one under the government and the other (less influential) under the Riksdag. Accordingly, Sweden was one of the very few countries in the world which did not have an independent authority for the revision of state finances. See Nergelius (n 13) 310.

the form of a written request for information with the intention of launching a debate. Although the procedure for issuing an interpellation is similar to that for written questions, different rules concerning the government's reply may apply to interpellations, and parliamentary political groups generally play a more prominent role than do individual MPs.[23]

A. The Significance Attached to Interpellations in the East Nordic Systems

In this respect, different traditions prevail in the East Nordic systems as compared to the West. The Constitutions of Finland and Sweden contain special references to interpellations. The purpose of an interpellation is usually to debate an important issue on which the opposition believes that the government's measures are misdirected or inadequate. However, there are differences between Finland and Sweden in terms of the application of interpellations. In Finland, they are applied in more serious matters than are oral or written questions from MPs, usually in connection with confidence in the government. Article 43 of the Constitution stipulates that a minimum of 20 MPs may submit an interpellation in order to gauge confidence in the government or a particular minister. The government must reply to an interpellation in plenary session within 15 days. Interpellations are generally answered by the prime minister or the minister whose administrative sector the question concerns. An interpellation, together with the ensuing debate and vote, is a significant parliamentary event. In Finland, interpellation is considered a powerful means to ensure the functioning of the parliamentary system. Parliament may also test the degree of confidence enjoyed by the government by making an interpellation. The result of the subsequent vote of confidence decides whether or not the government may continue in office. Generally, the publicity attracted by such a move is greater than the risk to the government. The risk last arose in the late 1950s, but this has not reduced the use of interpellation.

Meanwhile, the Swedish system of interpellation follows a different procedure and has a different impact. Under Article 13:5 of the Constitution, no minimum number of MPs is required in order to submit interpellations. Furthermore, this constitutional provision applies both to interpellations and questions from individual MPs, actions concerning the performance by ministers of their duties. In Sweden, interpellations are usually related to issues of greater importance than are other questions from MPs.[24] The Riksdag can also organise regular times for interpellations, and these are held at least once a week.[25] Apart from interpellations, the Swedish and Finnish Parliaments submit hundreds of written or oral questions to

[23] Yamamoto (n 1) 60.
[24] Nergelius (n 13) 303.
[25] Yamamoto (n 1) 60.

the government or its individual ministers every year. MPs may submit written questions to the minister responsible for further information on a particular matter, and the minister must reply within certain time limits. Further rules regarding both oral and written questions are laid down in the standing orders.

B. Questions Requiring Written or Oral Answers

No distinction is made between interpellations and written questions put by individual MPs to the government or its individual ministers in the constitutions in the West Nordic states.[26] What the Nordic constitutions, except in Norway, have in common that they enshrine the right of MPs to question government ministers, and this is generally acknowledged, even though this is not always expressly stipulated as a legal obligation that the ministers are obliged to reply. MPs' questions, both oral and written, are an important tool for the opposition parties in exercising restraint on the government, and are regulated in detail in the parliaments' standing orders. There are usually fixed question times each week when MPs present brief oral questions to the appropriate ministers and hear their replies. Ministers do not receive the questions in advance, so question time is a test of their command of current issues in their administrative sectors. Question time is one of the media highlights of the parliamentary agenda.

Written questions are usually subject to a formal procedure, which is stipulated in detail in the rules of procedure. The Icelandic procedure for written questions is a classic example in this respect. It presupposes that an MP who wishes to call for information, or a response from a minister, concerning a matter of public interest is to submit a written question to the speaker. The question must be clear, confined to a limited topic or single matter for which the minister is responsible, and phrased so that it can be answered in brief terms. The speaker is to decide promptly whether a question should be allowed. If a written response is requested, the speaker is to send it to the questioner and it must be printed and distributed. If a minister is unable to respond to the question within the time limit, he or she is to notify the speaker of this, stating the reason and indicating when a response may be expected. More detailed rules on the process are set out in Article 57 of the Parliament's standing orders.

Generally speaking, there are many similarities between the Nordic parliaments in this respect, although there are also important differences in relation to how the parliamentary control is exercised with questions in interpellations. For instance, it has been suggested that Denmark stands out from the other countries in terms of a great number of oral questions and Sweden with written interpellations.[27]

[26] Such a distinction is made, however, in the standing orders of the Norwegian Storting. Interpellations are considered to be a more elaborate way of presenting questions. Compared to other questions, interpellations generally deal with matters of greater scope and political importance, and generally lead to debates.

[27] Persson (n 3) 103.

As stated before, interpellations have a special status under Article 43 of the Finnish Constitution. For comparison, according to Article 45, which deals with other questions, announcements and debates, paragraph 4 explicitly provides that the Parliament makes no decisions on matters referred to in this section. This means that no decision on confidence in the government or its member can be made; this is only possible under the interpellation provision in Article 43.

V. Parliament's Right to Obtain Information and Ministers' Duty to Provide it

The system of oral or written questions, requests for reports and the supervisory functions of the parliaments in general would be futile if ministers were not obligated to answer them. The right of MPs to demand information and duty of ministers to provide it are generally considered to be deeply rooted in all the Nordic constitutional systems. However, they are manifested in different ways from one country to another, not necessarily in constitutional provisions but also in standing orders or even in legislation on the criminal accountability of ministers regarding their conduct in office.[28] The most detailed constitutional provision, imposing the broadest obligations on the government and individual ministers, is to be found in Article 47 of the Finnish Constitution, which stipulates the general right of the Parliament to demand the information it needs for the deliberation of matters. It also states in greater detail the right of parliamentary committees and individual MPs to request information. Special provisions in Articles 96 and 97 cover the parliamentary right to receive information in relation EU matters and international affairs. Further discussion on the latter-mentioned provisions is to be found in Chapter 7 of this volume.

The approaches to the ministers' duty may differ. The *positive obligation* of ministers is reflected, for instance, in the Finnish provision referred to above, which states that the appropriate minister *shall ensure* that committees and other parliamentary organs receive, without delay, the necessary documents and other information in the possession of the authorities. Similarly, in the standing orders of the Icelandic Alþingi, a new provision, added in 2011 (Article 50), states that ministers

[28] In Norway, the duty of ministers and the government to provide information to parliament developed through extensive parliamentary practice and was finally codified in the Norwegian Constitution in 2007, now to be found in its Article 82. See E Smith, *Regjeringens opplysningsplikt over for Stortinget* (Oslo, Universitetsforlaget, 1997). In Danish constitutional literature, it has been considered that ministers are not under a legal obligation to answer questions and requests from MPs, and no such obligation is laid down in the Constitution, for instance. However, in political reality and practice, a minister will always answer questions, and invoking the fact of not being legally obliged would elicit a strong reaction from parliament. More importantly, it constitutes a punishable offence under the Act on Ministerial Responsibilities if a minister, in his answer, gives parliament wrong or misleading information, if such information is of great significance for a handling for the case. See L Busck, *Folketingets kontrol med forvaltningen* (Copenhagen, Gads Forlag, 1988) 57.

shall provide the information to which they have access and which is of significance for the evaluation by the Alþingi of a matter that is being processed by Parliament. In the Danish system, on the other hand, the *negative obligation* is set forth by defining it as punishable conduct under the Act on Ministerial Accountability if a minister gives the Parliament wrong or misleading information, if such information is of great significance for the matter under discussion. A new provision, added into Article 82 of the Norwegian Constitution, combines both approaches, by declaring both the government's duty to provide the Storting with all information that is necessary for proceedings on the matter in question and, furthermore, that no minister may submit incorrect or misleading information to the Storting or its bodies.

The constitutional and legal amendments made in Finland, Norway and Iceland over the last two decades reflect a trend in the Nordic constitutional systems to place more emphasis on the duty of ministers to provide relevant and correct information to parliament and, furthermore, to make it clear that certain requirements apply regarding circumstances and procedure. First, the obligation to give relevant information applies regarding matters pending before the parliaments. Second, it is usually specified that the information requested must be necessary, or of great significance, for the discussion of the issue in question. Usually, constitutional and legal provisions allow for the exercise of some discretion by ministers; they are able to assess what materials are necessary for a particular matter. However, if a minister gives wrong or misleading information, or intentionally decides not to submit information of great relevance to a matter, this could constitute grounds for holding the minister concerned to political or legal accountability. Further means and methods of invoking ministerial accountability will be discussed below.

VI. Control Mechanisms of Parliamentary Committees

Parliamentary committees play an important role in the Nordic parliaments, each of which has its own committee system with its own characteristics. The structure of the committees reflects parliamentary history and traditions, and they differ in the way in which they have evolved from one parliament to another, though certain main features are common for all the parliaments. In all the parliaments, the committees have been identified as a necessary condition for effective parliamentary influence and there is a system of standing committees that broadly corresponds to government ministries. Apart from the control purpose, the committees are important arenas for negotiations, bargaining and compromise between parties in government and opposition in relation to the legislative functions of the parliament.

Again, the East Nordic constitutions contain more detailed provisions on parliamentary committees and their functions than those of the West Nordic countries. Some examples are given below to illustrate this, and cast some light on what is unique to each country or trace recent steps taken to increase the oversight role.

A. The Special Preventive Control of the Constitutional Law Committee in Finland

It is unique to Finland that a Constitutional Law Committee (*Grundlagsutskottet*), acting under Article 74 of the Constitution, has the principal function to exercise particular abstract *ex ante* supervision that legislative proposals and other matters brought for its consideration are in accordance with the Constitution and international human rights treaties (see further Chapters 5 and 6 in this volume in relation how this system impacts on the judicial review exercised by the courts). The Constitutional Law Committee consists solely of MPs, representing both government and opposition parties, many of whom are lawyers by education. There is also a strong tradition that the Committee should seek expert advice from professors and scholars of constitutional law in assessing the constitutionality of legislative proposals and other matters brought for its consideration.[29] The Committee can also review proposals for EU directives or other EU measures, that are dealt with by Parliament in accordance with Article 96 of the Constitution for their compatibility with the Constitution and human rights obligations binding upon Finland. This *ex ante* review of European legislation is without parallel elsewhere and will be discussed further in the Nordic context in Chapter 7 of this volume.

Opinions issued by the Constitutional Law Committee serve two important functions. *First*, they provide authoritative interpretations of the Constitution and determine the proper legislative procedure, such as whether the government bill may be adopted as on ordinary law through a single majority or whether it has to be enacted through a qualified procedure for constitutional enactments due to its conflict with the Constitution. *Second*, as the doctrine is practised so as to guarantee the appropriate protection of rights, the Committee is currently in the habit of demanding amendments to the government bill so as to achieve harmony with the Constitution and human rights obligations that are binding upon Finland.

The threshold of sending a matter to the Constitutional Law Committee is quite low, as is the threshold of finding constitutional problems in matters brought to the Committee. For instance, in 2014 the Committee gave 75 opinions out of 367 government bills and demanded changes in 24 opinions for the purpose of

[29] J Lavapuro, T Ojanen and M Scheinin, 'Rights-Based Constitutionalism in Finland and the Development of Pluralist Constitutional Review' (2011) 9(2) *ICON* 511.

achieving harmony with the Constitution and/or human rights treaties. From a purely quantitative perspective, therefore, political pre-enactment review of rights by the Committee does have a real impact on legislative proceedings. However, this does not necessarily imply constitutional activism by the Committee. The opinions of the Committee are usually strikingly dogmatic and apolitical, as well as unanimous without involving any genuine discussion and reflection of moral principles, political values or party lines.

The Constitutional Law Committee comes relatively close to the French Constitutional Council with respect to the emphasis on preventive control of legislation. It should be noted that certain other actors, such as the Chancellor of Justice, the Speaker of Parliament and the President of the Republic, have certain competences to review the constitutionality of legislative proposals during various stages of the legislative process. However, their roles are clearly secondary to that of the Constitutional Law Committee, which, as a matter of constitutional law, had the last word insofar as the constitutionality of legislative proposals was concerned. Apart from its preventive control, the Committee deals with matters relating to allegations of malfeasance by ministers, the reports of the Chancellor of Justice and the Parliamentary Ombudsman and the Government Annual Report. The impact of its control function vis-a-vis the executive seems to be less important than its main role of monitoring the constitutionality of legislative bills.

B. The Historical Role of Sweden's Committee on the Constitution

The Swedish system also provides, in Article 13:1 of the Constitution, for a Committee on the Constitution (*Konstitutionsutskottet*). This has its own characteristics that are different from those of its Finnish counterpart. It is one of 15 standing committees of the Riksdag. Also with strong historical roots, dating back to 1809, it focuses less on preventive control, but has as its main task the examination of ministers' performance of their official duties and handling of government business. Accordingly, it is the main organ of control over the government of the Swedish Riksdag. In order to exercise its functions, it is entitled to have access to the records of decisions taken on government matters and to the documents pertaining to such matters, as well as any other government materials that it deems necessary. Moreover, the Committee is required, at least once a year and more often if appropriate, to inform the Riksdag of any observations it has made and considers worthy of further attention in connection with its examination (Article13:2). Certain traditions have evolved regarding the making of reports.

Criticism has been levelled at the fact that as the composition of MPs in the Committee on the Constitution reflects the proportional representation of parties in Parliament. Therefore, the Committee is politically biased in line with the majority parties in government and unable to assess objectively, or adopt a critical position on, the performance of the government or of individual ministers.[30] This is a classical concern when it comes to the efficiency of parliamentary control over the government in the Nordic parliaments and illustrates in a nutshell that strong majority governments are likely to weaken parliament's will to supervise the actions of ministers and the administration. The polarisation between the government and the opposition parties is inevitably reflected in the majorities within the parliamentary committees. One way of reacting to this is to organise the committee work with the aim of boosting the status of the opposition parties, eg, by allowing the minority within a committee to initiate inquiries. In Sweden, for instance, the chairmanship of the Committee on the Constitution has been allocated to the opposition since 1991. The same applies with respect to key control committees in the Norwegian and Icelandic Parliaments.

C. The Special Status Granted to the Foreign Affairs Committee in Denmark and the Changed Landscape in European Integration

An interesting example of a model that was unique for Denmark when it was adopted in the 1953 Constitution is the special constitutional status granted to the Foreign Affairs Committee. The objective was to clarify the division of powers over foreign affairs between the government and Parliament, an area which traditionally had been acknowledged as falling under the royal prerogative in the Danish constitutional system.[31] Under Article 19(3) of the Constitution, the Committee is appointed by the Folketing from among its members and the government has an obligation to consult it prior to taking any decision of major importance on foreign policy. The Danish model, creating a constitutional basis of parliamentary control over the executive in the field of foreign affairs, was without clear parallels elsewhere in Nordic constitutional law in 1953. Since then, there have been great developments in constitutional theory and practice regarding consultation and parliamentary participation in foreign affairs, not only in the Nordic countries but also in Europe generally.

Today there is a drastically changed landscape with respect to relations between states and foreign policy in the light of European integration and the unprecedented cooperation between states within the EU. The EU Member States have

[30] Nergelius (n 13) 305. Historically, there was a large proportion of single-party minority government in Sweden, almost all led by the Social Democrats. Since 2005, this has changed and coalition governments have been the norm. See ME Hansen, 'Cabinets and Ministerial Turnover in the Scandinavia Countries' in P Nedergaard and A Wivel (eds), *The Routledge Handbook of Scandinavian Politics* (New York, Routledge, 2018) 93.

[31] H Krunke, *Den Udenrikspolitiske Kompetence—Udenrigspolitik og magtforelding ved overgangen til det 21. århundrede* (Copenhagen, Jurist- og Økonomforbundets Forlag, 2003) 368.

created a strong EU oversight system in which the most important bodies are parliamentary committees of European affairs. Their powers vary, but their main task is to be responsible for coordinating the parliamentary scrutiny of European affairs and monitoring the activities of government representatives in the Council of Ministers and the European Council.[32]

This is now clearly reflected in the East Nordic constitutions, which, following recent substantial amendments (to Sweden's in 2010 and Finland's in 2011) explicitly set forth processes on how the national constitutional system involves important aspects of that of the EU and the inter-relationship between the two constitutional orders.[33] This includes procedures on how the national parliaments participate in the preparation of matters involving the EU and the parliamentary right to demand information, for instance, on matters handled by the European Council. Both constitutions contain special chapters on international relations, guaranteeing the right of parliament to receive information, stipulating the role of the Foreign Affairs Committee and monitoring the government in its work on foreign affairs.

Meanwhile, as non-members of the EU, Iceland and Norway, as members of the European Economic Area (EEA), are under an obligation to follow developments in the EU closely since they are affected by EU legislation. However, their parliamentary oversight of EU affairs has generally been considered weak.[34]

D. Different Means of Strengthening the Oversight Role of Standing Committees in the West

Discussions regarding parliamentary committees in the West Nordic constitutional systems initially focused on the legislative output of standing committees. When the regular standing committees were established, they were usually each responsible for certain affairs and had an important role in the preparation of bills falling under their mandate. In the latter part of the twentieth century, the emphasis on the role of the committees has developed. For instance, in 1972, the committee system in the Danish Folketing was revised to improve the committees' ability to affect legislation. As a consequence, individual MPs were able to specialise in certain policy areas and accumulate significant expertise within their particular field of responsibility. Meanwhile, the Folketing could, through the 'common part' of the committees—which was not involved in legislative work—gain a far more detailed insight into the work of the ministries than it had before. Accordingly, the

[32] Persson (n 3) 110.

[33] B Thorarensen, 'The Nordic Constitutions in a Multilevel Constitutional Order' in *Rettens Magt, Magtens Ret. Festskrift til Henning Koch* (Copenhagen, Jurist- og Økonomforbundets Forlag, 2014) 409–11. See further discussion regarding the impact of EU on Nordic constitutional systems in Chapter 7 of this volume.

[34] Persson (n 3) 110. Further references regarding the role of Nordic parliaments in the increasing Europeanisation are made to Chapter 7 of this volume.

ability of the Folketing to exercise more stringent control over the government and the administration was improved; this was reflected in a great increase in the number of inquiries and questions from MPs about the use of these improved control measures.[35] Under the present standing orders of the Danish Folketing, there are a high number of committees, or 23 specialised standing committees, two of which are devoted to certain internal affairs (standing orders and the outcome of general elections).[36]

In the Nordic West, more emphasis has been put on the oversight roles of parliamentary committees along the lines of the system in Sweden and Finland. General oversight committees have been established, which are responsible for supervisory measures and/or coordination of the oversight work of standing committees.[37] While the Norwegian Storting and the Icelandic Alþingi have taken measures in this direction, the Danish Folketing remains the only Nordic parliament not to have established such a general oversight committee. It appears that after the comprehensive revision of the committees in the 1970s, it has not been a particular point of concern in Denmark that Parliament is losing power, calling for reorganisation. On the contrary, the conclusions of a special study of power and democracy, published in 2003, revealed that the Folketing had not only strengthened its control over the government, and hence the central administration, but also increased its influence on legislation. One issue which attracted special attention in the study was that a sporadic and largely unregulated phenomenon in the 1970s, the hiring of special advisors to assist ministers, had been clarified, regulated and become subject to intense political scrutiny. Effective control of the ministers is now considered to include the Folketing being aware of the premises on which it receives advice from civil servants. One of the contributory factors in the power relationship was the development in the parliamentary base of the government. Accordingly, the numerous minority governments in Denmark in the 1970s resulted in the strengthened position of the Folketing in relation to the government. But even without regard to the parliamentary base of the government, the Folketing was considered to have stepped up its use of various procedures for parliamentary control over the years. In addition, a trend over the past 25 years had given political accountability a more judicial touch through the use of tribunals of inquiry and the court of impeachment, as will be discussed below.[38]

[35] L Togeby, JG Andersen, PM Christiansen and S Vallgårda, *Power and Democracy in Denmark: Conclusions* (Aarhus, Magtutredningen 2004) 22.

[36] Forretningsorden for Folketinget (published 2016), Article 7.

[37] Yamamoto (n 1) 10 and 16.

[38] Togeby et al (n 35) 22. The conclusions of a study in Norway on power and democracy, also published in 2003, cast some light on the advantages and disadvantages of minority parliamentarism. In Norway, where there is a long tradition of minority governments, parliament is indeed in a stronger position to control the government's actions, but at the cost of a certain long-term political stability, and this may eventually result in a blurred line between the legislator and the executive, where the Storting interferes with matters falling within the realm of executive power. See *Makt og demokrati. Sluttrapport fra Makt- og demokratiutredningen* (Oslo, NOU 2003:19, 2003) 19.

As mentioned above, the revision of the standing orders in Norway and Iceland provided for the establishment of special control committees in both parliaments. These are now the main bodies among the standing committees responsible for supervising the executive, and they also have the power to take certain initiatives on control measures which may result in the prosecution of ministers.

The Committee on Scrutiny and Constitutional Affairs in Norway (*Kontroll- og konstitusjonkomiteen*), reorganised in 1992, is one of the Storting's 12 standing committees. Its mandate is defined in Article 12 (8) of the Standing Orders, but its main role is the monitoring and supervision of government administration. It is the only one of the Storting's committees that is not responsible for a particular subject matter other than this, apart from bills of amendments of the Constitution. This special focus on the monitoring of all areas of administration is intended to increase the effectiveness of its control. Experience has shown that despite the fact that other standing committees may exercise supervision related to their particular subject areas, control has generally moved to the Committee on Scrutiny and Constitutional Affairs. This is distinguished from the other standing committees by the fact that it is able to deal not only with business matters referred to it by the Parliament, but also to act on its own initiative when exercising supervision. It has applied measures such as open hearings, which have drawn more public attention to the issue at stake than hearings in the regular standing committees. However, it does not have independent resources, which would enable it to investigate or deal with complicated or extensive issues. Other measures may apply for such purposes, such as appointing parliamentary committees of inquiry with external experts.[39] The Committee on Scrutiny and Constitutional Affairs also deals with matters concerning constitutional responsibility. It is empowered to initiate inquiries that may lead to an impeachment process against members of the Storting, ministers and Supreme Court judges. Such procedures will be discussed further below in section IX.

The Norwegian parliamentary committee system was used as the main model for a comprehensive revision of the committee system in the Standing Orders of the Icelandic Alþingi in 2011. The main purpose of the amendments was to strengthen the Alþingi's position vis-a-vis the executive, and to that end to redefine the role of parliamentary committees, adopt clearer rules regarding the duty of ministers to provide information in the handling of matters and concurrently to strengthen the role of the opposition in the control mechanism. One of the factors that precipitated the revision was the criticism set forth in the extensive report of the Special Investigation Commission appointed in 2009 to investigate the events that led to the collapse of the three main banks in Iceland.

The Constitutional and Supervisory Committee (*Stjórnskipunar- og eftirlitsnefnd*) was established as one of the Alþingi's eight standing committees. It is responsible for constitutional affairs, the affairs of the President of the Republic,

[39] Sejersted (n 5) 153–57.

the Alþingi and its institutions, elections, the affairs of the government ministries in general and other matters relating to the supreme government of the state. In addition, the Committee is to discuss reports from the National Audit Office and the annual report and notices from the Parliamentary Ombudsman.

The Committee was given a new task not previously assigned to any specific body in Parliament: to take the initiative on investigating any decisions taken by individual ministers, or their procedure in handling matters, that may warrant an enquiry. It is noteworthy that it is sufficient that one-quarter of the members of the Committee request such an inquiry. The Committee shall submit a report to the Alþingi on the conclusions of its inquiry. It shall also conduct assessments and submit recommendations to the Alþingi concerning appropriate times to appoint an investigation commission, as provided for in the Act on Investigation Commissions. The Committee is to examine reports by investigation commissions and submit to the Alþingi its report and recommendations on further action to be taken by the Alþingi. Such action could take the form of a proposal for a parliamentary resolution to initiate legal proceedings against a minister before the Court of Impeachment.

Experience to date has shown that the Constitutional and Supervisory Committee has been active in its work and enhanced the monitoring role of Parliament. It has held open hearings and initiated the appointment of special investigation commissions. The right of one-quarter of the members of the Committee to request an inquiry into the actions of individual ministers or their procedure in a certain matter, or to request information, has turned out to be an important tool in drawing attention to possible flaws in the conduct of ministers and in the administration. Nevertheless, the decision to act on the outcome of such an inquiry must be backed by the majority of the Committee. In the light of the fact that the Icelandic political system has for a long time been characterised by strong majority governments, at the end of the day there has generally been a lack of political support in the government parties for taking action against the government.

VII. Special Investigation Commissions

All the Nordic constitutional systems provide for the possibility of setting up special commissions to investigate a certain matter or particular problem of public concern. An investigation initiated by the parliament is considered a reflection of the parliament's constitutional role in overseeing the government.[40] As the main objective of such investigation commissions is usually to reveal facts in a certain case, they may facilitate the work of parliament to react and take further measures based on the finding of such a commission. Special investigation commissions

[40] Yamamoto (n 1) 39.

may be of various types and are not necessarily always appointed directly by the parliaments: frequently they are appointed by the government following a resolution from the parliament. Accordingly, the initiative and request to appoint them may come from the parliament following a debate and a certain preparatory steps within a parliamentary committee.

A. Differences in the Nature, Composition and Appointment of Investigation Commissions

The composition of investigation commissions may vary. Some of the Nordic constitutions stipulate that parliament may appoint commissions of MPs to investigate matters of general interest; they are entitled to demand written or oral information from both private citizens and public authorities. Identical provisions on such commissions are to be found in the Danish Constitution (Article 51) and the Icelandic Constitution (Article 39). However, such commissions have rarely been appointed and never since the mid-twentieth century; the last occasions were in 1945 in Denmark and in Norway, and in 1955 in Iceland. No further laws have been enacted or regulations elaborated in the standing orders of the parliaments on the issue. It has been a controversial issue in constitutional theory, particularly in Denmark, whether such commissions should have a role in the preparation of the prosecution of ministers before the Court of Impeachment.[41] More recent legislative amendments in Denmark and Iceland on independent investigation commissions, which will be discussed below, have resolved such speculations.

In the Nordic context, special investigation commissions created at the initiative of and appointed by the parliaments, usually by a parliamentary resolution, generally share certain features, regardless of which procedure is used to appoint them. They usually consist of external experts and are frequently chaired by a legal expert (a law professor or a judge) to secure their neutrality and independence. They have special powers of investigation, including the right to call witnesses and to have access to government papers. Their powers may be defined in legislation: either in a specific act on a concrete investigation or, as in Denmark and Iceland, in a general act on investigation commissions.[42] They are appointed ad hoc to examine a particular issue of public concern with a fixed time allocated for the task. They may conduct intensive investigations over a relatively short period and

[41] JP Christensen, *Minsteransvar* (Copenhagen, Jurist- og Økonomforbundets Forlag, 1997) 543; and B Thorarensen, *Stjórnskipunarréttur. Undirstöður og handhafar ríkisvalds* (Reykjavik, Codex Publishers, 2015) 582.

[42] An example of the former model can be seen in Act No 142/2008 on a Special Investigation Commission to investigate and analyse the processes leading to the collapse of the three main banks in Iceland. The great debate concerning the findings of this committee initiated a comprehensive revision of rules concerning parliamentary control, including the adoption of a new general Act on Investigation Commissions in Iceland (Act No 68/2011). Such legislation had already been in force in Denmark since 1999 (Act No 357/1999).

be able to reveal facts that are embarrassing for the government. In the parliamentary resolutions, the commission's mandate is usually limited to matters specified in the terms of reference.[43]

B. Some Examples from West Nordic Practice

There appears to be a stronger tradition in the West Nordic states for the appointment of ad hoc external investigation commissions on the basis of parliamentary resolutions. In Denmark, the Act on Investigation Commissions, No 357/1999, was adopted following broad debate and criticism of the lack of an appropriate process to investigate particular serious problems of public concern. Under the Act, the Minister of Justice appoints an investigation commission to investigate particular problems of public concern if the Folketing so requests. The Act contains detailed provisions on matters including the qualification of members, the commission's independence and its powers. Since the adoption of the Act in 1999, nine investigation commissions have been appointed,[44] the most recent in October 2015 in the 'Tibet case', on the interference by the police in a public demonstration against an official visit from China.

In Iceland, before the adoption of Act No 68/2011, on Investigation Commissions, special acts were passed providing for the appointment of ad hoc commissions in four instances between 1985 and 2008 to investigate matters of public concern.[45] A certain turning point was reached with the appointment and the findings of the Special Investigation Commission, established by Act No 142/2008, with the mandate of investigating and analysing the processes leading to the collapse of the three main banks in Iceland in October 2008. The collapse of the banks and the ensuing deep economic crisis set off a heated debate in Icelandic society and also widespread protests, particularly against the government and the Parliament, but also against other state institutions responsible for control in the financial market, in addition to great public anger against the banks and their directors.[46] The commission's extensive report, submitted to the Alþingi in the spring of 2010, contained a detailed analysis of how the situation in the three largest commercial banks deteriorated steadily from 2007 onwards. This revealed various flaws in the handling of the situation by the government and individual ministers, and also by the administration, in the course of events leading to the collapse and their failure to take action regarding the banks, which had grown very

[43] Yamamoto (n 1) 39.

[44] C Dethlefsen 'Om Folketingetsopfølgning på beretninger fra undersøgelseskommissioner' in *Festskrift til Jens Peter Christensen* (Copenhagen, Jurist- og Økonomforbundets Forlag 2016) 406–10.

[45] B Hlöðversdóttir, 'Sérskipaðar rannsóknarnefndir' (2011) 3 *Tímarit lögfræðinga* 290.

[46] B Thorarensen, 'The Impact of the Financial Crisis on Icelandic Constitutional Law: Legislative Reforms, Judicial Review and Revision of the Constitution' in X Contiades (ed), *Constitutions in the Global Financial Crisis: A Comparative Analysis* (Farnham, Ashgate 2013) 263.

rapidly in the preceding years. It also revealed how poorly equipped the supervisory bodies had been to monitor the financial institutions, as well as other serious weaknesses in the system.[47]

This report gave rise to a call for the comprehensive revision of control mechanisms and action on accountability in the administration and the supervisory role of the Alþingi. This resulted, *first*, in a complete reorganisation of the system of parliamentary standing committees in 2011 (discussed in section VI.D above), in which the Alþingi's oversight function was highlighted. *Second*, the aforementioned 2011 Act on Investigation Commissions was adopted. *Third*, for the first time in Icelandic constitutional history, impeachment proceedings were initiated against the former Prime Minister, partly on the basis of the commission's conclusions. These proceedings will be discussed further below.

Three commissions have since been appointed on the basis of the Act, their tasks being related, directly or indirectly, to the collapse of the banks. The most recent commission, appointed in 2016, was charged with investigating certain aspects of the privatisation of the Agricultural Bank of Iceland (*Búnaðarbankinn*) in 2003. Its report, released in May 2017, found that the Icelandic government had been systematically deceived both before and after the alleged purchase of a share in the Agricultural Bank by a German bank, Hauck & Aufhäuser. In fact, the German bank did not purchase any of the state's share in the bank when it was sold in January 2003, contrary to what was announced publicly.

In Norway, at least seven investigation committees have been appointed by the Storting in the last few decades.[48] A number of ad hoc committees have also been appointed by the government or individual ministries; these will not be discussed further here. As in the case of Denmark and Iceland, the majority of the Storting must approve a motion to appoint an investigation committee following preparation of the matter and, in Iceland, a proposal from the Committee on Scrutiny and Constitutional Affairs.

Among the Nordic countries, it is unique in Norway that the Storting appoints an external and permanent Parliamentary Intelligence Oversight Committee consisting of seven members. This operates on the basis of Act No 7/1995, and its role is to monitor the Police Security Service, the Defence Security Service and Military Intelligence. Its members are usually selected on the basis of expert knowledge. It is unusual that a parliament is so directly involved in monitoring security affairs, due to the very delicate information and secrecy this involves, but the existence of the Norwegian committee can partly be explained by certain events in Norway and the findings of a special investigation committee in the 1990s on the illegitimate security surveillance of citizens.[49]

[47] See English excerpts of the report's findings at www.rna.is/media/skjol/RNAvefKafli2Enska.pdf.

[48] In 2009, some proposals were made in Norway regarding a comprehensive legislative act on investigation commissions; however, no such act has been adopted. See NOU (2009):9 Lov om offentlige undersøkelseskommisjoner. Særskilt offentlige kommisjoner. Utredning fra utvalget oppnevnt av Justis- og politidepartementet, 4 May 2009.

[49] Sejersted (n 5) 166. See Dokument nr 15 (1995–96) *Rapport til Stortinget fra komm-isjonen som ble oppnevnt av Stortinget for å granske påstander om ulovlig overvåking av norske borgere* (Lund-rapporten).

The question whether ad hoc investigation commissions should have a mandate to assess the possible criminal accountability of ministers has been subject to some discussion in Denmark, Norway and Iceland. Under the Nordic constitutions, a decision to prosecute a minister rests with parliament. It would therefore not be generally appropriate if the investigation and assessment of the possible legal accountability of ministers could be delegated to external bodies outside parliament. In Denmark this is reflected in a special provision in Article 4(4) of the 1999 Act on Investigation Commissions, which states that they cannot be commissioned to make an assessment of legal accountability. This is controversial and has been criticised in light of the fact that there may be a blurred line between the establishment of facts and the assessment of conduct of ministers involving their legal accountability.[50] At least there is a consensus that such commissions can play an important role in establishing the facts of events or situations which may possibly entail the legal responsibility of ministers, and thus facilitate the work of the Folketing. After that, the case will be prepared by the Committee on Standing Orders. The adoption of the 1999 Act in Denmark was closely linked to a heated debate concerning the preparation and investigation of the 'Tamil case', in which the former Minister of Justice was prosecuted before the Court of Impeachment and convicted in 1995, as will be discussed below.

In Sweden and Finland, there are fewer examples of investigation commissions appointed by the parliaments in recent decades. The Finnish Constitution provides, in Article 35(1), for Parliament to appoint ad hoc committees for the preparation of, or inquiry into, a given matter; until now, none has been appointed. In a number of instances, the government or ministries in Sweden have appointed ad hoc investigation commissions for issues of public concern that have been debated in Parliament where the government or the administration has come under scrutiny and has been the subject of severe criticism. Examples of this are the commissions appointed in the 1990s to investigate the murder of Olof Palme and an investigation commission appointed by the Minister of Justice to examine police operations during the riots in protest against the EU summit in Gothenburg in 2001.[51] In 2005, a commission was appointed in response to serious criticism of the slow reaction of the Swedish government to the death and injury of large numbers of Swedish holidaymakers in Thailand in the tsunami catastrophe in 2004. It managed to finalise an extensive report on the issue in less than a year. It has been suggested that this illustrates the advantage of appointing ad hoc commissions with experts for such tasks, which may finalise a task even within a few months, instead of permanent institutions which would be less likely to be as efficient.[52]

[50] Christensen (n 41) 380 and H Gammeltoft-Hansen 'Kommissionsundersøgelser og ministeransvar' in *Festskrift til Jens Peter Christensen* (n 44) 390.

[51] *Göteborg 2001*. SOU 2002:122.

[52] Nergelius (n 13) 312. See also SOU 2005:106. *Sverige och tsunamin—granskning och förslag* (Finansdepartementet, 1 December 2005).

VIII. The Role of Parliamentary Ombudsmen

A. Origins of the Office of Ombudsman and its 'Exportation' from Sweden

It has been maintained that the office of Parliamentary Ombudsman is Sweden's most significant 'constitutional export product'.[53] Indeed, the creation of a special organ acting on behalf of Parliament in monitoring the administration has become a successful control tool, particularly in ensuring respect for individual rights vis-a-vis public power. It has spread continuously throughout the world during the course of the twentieth century and is now firmly linked to the principles of democracy and the rule of law.[54] The origins of the first independent Ombudsman in Sweden can be traced back to 1766; the institution was formally established there in the 1809 Constitution. More than a century later, it was established in Finland with the 1919 republican Constitution, and the Ombudsman became a common feature of the East Nordic constitutional systems. The creation of the office of Ombudsman in these countries has strong historical ties with the office of the Chancellors of Justice (discussed above in section III.B). Thus, there is an historical explanation for these two high supervisors of legality, the Ombudsman having originally been intended as a kind of parliamentary-spirited counterweight to the Chancellor of Justice, the appointee on the government side. Today, there are no visible traces of the conflict-embedded origin of the Ombudsman's office.[55]

The provisions on the Ombudsmen in the present Constitutions of Sweden and Finland have been elaborated further and are now placed in the relevant chapters on parliamentary control and supervision of legality. Article 13:3 of the Swedish Constitution is devoted to parliamentary Ombudsmen in the plural, as it states that the Riksdag elects one or more parliamentary Ombudsmen who are to supervise the application of laws and other regulations in public activities, under terms of reference drawn up by the Riksdag. Accordingly, the Office of the Ombudsmen (*Justieombudsmän*) is a body to which the Riksdag appoints four Ombudsmen individually, one of them as Chief Parliamentary Ombudsman. In Finland, the Parliamentary Ombudsman operates under Articles 38 and 109 of the Constitution. The Eduskunta appoints the Ombudsman, and two deputies, for a term of four years. The Ombudsman is to ensure that the courts of law,

[53] Nergelius (n 13) 307.

[54] Currently 26 out of 28 EU Member States have established national Ombudsman institutions; most of them were formed in the latter part of the twentieth century. See G Kucsko-Stadlmayer, 'The Legal Structures of Ombudsman-Institutions in Europe' in G Kucsko-Stadlmayer (ed), *European Ombudsman Institutions: A Comparative Legal Analysis Regarding the Multifaceted Realisation of an Idea* (New York, Springer, 2008) 2.

[55] Husa (n 8) 155.

other authorities and civil servants, public employees and other persons, when the latter are performing a public function, obey the law and fulfil their obligations. The Ombudsman monitors the implementation of basic rights and liberties and human rights.

B. Common and Distinguishing Features of the Ombudsmen in the Nordic Countries

The Parliamentary Ombudsmen in all the Nordic countries have the common objective of monitoring that those who exercise public authority obey the laws and fulfil their obligations in other respects. In addition, they are expected to ensure that the fundamental rights and freedoms of the citizens are not encroached upon in the course of public administration. Still, there are great differences between the East and West Nordic models of the Ombudsman and the scope of their control. Notwithstanding the fact that the position of Ombudsman is of Nordic origin, it is clear that no archetypal Scandinavian model exists. Nevertheless, the separate Ombudsmen have a common basic objective, are all appointed by the parliaments, report regularly to the parliaments on their work and make observations on the state of the administration and possible shortcomings in legislation.

The West Nordic parliamentary Ombudsmen have certain features in common. They have their roots the Danish institution, the first Ombudsman in Denmark having taken office in 1955 on the basis of the 1953 Constitution with the aim of giving the Danish Parliament tools to bring public administration under stronger parliamentary control and reinforce the means of protecting the legal position of the individual. This was considered important in the light of circumstances at the time: the executive branch had developed a life of its own after the emergency regulations of the 1930s and the economic reconstruction during the post-war years.[56] Article 55 of the Danish Constitution prescribes that a statute shall provide for the appointment by the Folketing of one or two persons, who shall not be members of the Folketing, to control the civil and military administration of the state.

The Norwegian office of the Ombudsman, established a few years later in 1962 by statute, was given a constitutional basis in Article 75(l) in 1995. Accordingly, the Storting shall appoint a person, who is not a member of the Storting, in a manner prescribed by law, to supervise the public administration and all who work in its service, to ensure that no injustice is perpetrated against individual citizens. Iceland's parliamentary Ombudsman, established in 1988, is unique among these offices in the Nordic countries in the sense of not having an explicit constitutional basis for its operation. As in the other Nordic countries, his or her role and functions are regulated in a comprehensive act of law—the current Act is No 85/1997.

[56] J Stern, 'Denmark' in Kucsko-Stadlmayer (ed) (n 54) 154.

The Icelandic Ombudsman is elected by the Alþingi for a period of four years, with the role of ensuring that individuals do not suffer injustice at the hands of the administrative sector. He or she is also to ensure that the principle of equality is observed and that administration is conducted in conformity with the law and good administrative practice in other respects.

The main difference between the West and East Nordic traditions, in terms of roles and jurisdiction, is that the Danish, Norwegian and Icelandic institutions have more limited authority. They can therefore only control the administration through 'soft' sanctions such as opinions, recommendations and reports, whereas their powers in the East are wider. In Sweden, for instance, the Ombudsmen in the role of extraordinary prosecutor may initiate legal proceedings against an official who, disregarding the obligations of his or her office or mandate, has committed a criminal offence other than an offence against the Freedom of the Press Act and the right to freedom of expression.

The main function of the Ombudsman system is to deal with individual complaints from those who claim to have been unfairly or illegally treated by the authorities in either the state or municipal branches of the administration. The Ombudsman examines the case and makes a statement as to whether the administrative action or decision was in violation of the law or was manifestly unreasonable. In legal systems without specialised administrative courts, like the three West Nordic states, a court action is costly and time-consuming; by taking a complaint to the Ombudsman, an aggrieved person can obtain a decision through a much easier process. Accordingly, even though they are not legally binding on the authorities, the soft sanctions such as opinions on individual complaints are primarily intended to provide quick, flexible and affordable remedies in order to minimise the individual's feeling of 'paralysis' vis-a-vis bureaucratic state institutions.[57] They have developed to become an efficient remedy for individuals and private entities, as the administrative body or official in question will normally reconsider the matter and comply with the Ombudsman's recommendations; this has clearly enhanced the quality of administrative practice. An investigation initiated by the Ombudsman can also disclose such flaws in the administrative actions of a minister as to lead to the minister concerned being called to account by parliament.[58]

The jurisdiction of the Ombudsman in the West Nordic model does not usually cover proceedings or decisions within parliament, proceedings by the courts of law or decisions by the authorities which are open to review by the courts,

[57] Kucsko-Stadlmayer (n 54) 2.

[58] An example of this can be seen in decision of the Danish Folketing to institute proceedings against Erik Ninn-Hansen, former Minister of Justice, before the Danish Court of Impeachment in 1993. One of the starting points leading to the prosecution was the report of the Parliamentary Ombudsman in Denmark of 1989, where his investigation into the Ministry of Justice's administration of cases concerning Tamil refugees' applications for family reunification disclosed various flaws.

according to law. The administration of the court system would also traditionally be excluded from the supervision by the Ombudsman.[59]

Dealing with individuals' complaints is also an important part of the Ombudsman's functions in the East Nordic model. However, the jurisdictions of the Swedish and Finnish Ombudsmen are broader and are intended to control not only the entire executive branch, but also the organs of the judiciary. In Finland, the Ombudsman (as well as the Chancellor of Justice) may decide to bring charges against a judge for unlawful conduct in office (under Article 110 of the Constitution), and in Sweden, the Ombudsmen have similar powers in relation to judges as in relation to other public officials. Despite the wide powers in the East Nordic countries, the decisions of the Ombudsmen are legally administrative decisions; they are not judgments and are neither legally equivalent to nor capable of amending judgments of the courts. They are not subject to appeal to any other higher authority.[60]

IX. Legal and Political Accountability of the Government and Individual Ministers

The means available to a parliament to react to malfeasance by ministers, and disaffection in relation to the work of the government and individual ministers is traditionally a part of the control powers over the executive. The sanctions which the Nordic parliaments apply in this context are of a similar nature, have related historical roots and have evolved in a similar manner. Before parliamentary rule asserted itself in the Nordic countries in the early twentieth century, parliaments enforced legal responsibility by prosecuting ministers for criminal conduct in office before special courts of impeachment. This was the only means available to parliament to hold ministers to account.

Four of the Nordic constitutions (with the exception of that of Sweden) still provide for special courts of impeachment for the prosecution of ministers for certain defined forms of conduct in office. The rationale for having special processes dealing with criminal charges against ministers has become more controversial in modern times, especially the idea of granting the prosecuting power to the parliaments. The provisions have rarely been exercised in recent decades, though there have been examples in Finland (1993), Denmark (1995) and most recently in Iceland (2012). Even though all the Nordic countries provide for specific processes to investigate alleged mismanagement by ministers, for instance, by

[59] H Zahle, *Dansk forfatningsret 2. Regering, forvaltning og dom* (Copenhagen, Christian Ejlers' Forlag, 2001) 149.

[60] Husa (n 8) 156.

entrusting the task of investigating and assessing their legal responsibility to special committees or ad hoc committees and making actual use of these investigative prerogatives, such decisions are often highly politicised.[61]

Ministers' and governments' legal responsibility has largely been replaced by political accountability, this being derived from systems of parliamentary rule now expressly enshrined in all the Nordic constitutions except that of Iceland. However, the effectiveness of this accountability appears differently in the Nordic countries depending on different traditions in the relevant political systems. A short analysis follows below, starting with the initial purpose and practice of applying the legal accountability of ministers.

A. Legal Responsibility of Ministers

i. Prosecution Power, Courts of Impeachment and Their Exclusive Jurisdiction

Under all the Nordic constitutions, the decision to prosecute ministers for unlawful conduct in office rests with parliament. Here, as in most other areas, the Swedish and Finnish Constitutions contain elaborate provisions regarding the procedure; in both instances, the standing committees on constitutional affairs play a special role. The Swedish Constitution stipulates that this decision is taken by the Committee on the Constitution; in the case of a minister, the conduct in question is defined further as 'a criminal act committed in the performance of his or her ministerial duties only if he or she has grossly neglected his or her official duty by committing the criminal act' (Article 13:3). In Finland, the Constitutional Law Committee gives its opinion concerning the minister's unlawful conduct before Parliament can decide to bring charges (Article 114). Further details of the circumstances under which the Constitutional Law Committee may initiate an inquiry into the lawfulness of the official acts of ministers are set out in Article 115.

Finland's High Court of Impeachment deals with charges against ministers and also other high officials such as the Chancellor of Justice, the Parliamentary Ombudsman and the judges in the highest levels of the judiciary (Article 101). It has been convened four times: in 1933, 1953, 1961 and 1993. The last occasion was when Kauku Juhantalo, Minister of Trade and Industry, was convicted by the Court for demanding illegal advantage in his capacity as a minister and was given a suspended sentence of a year's imprisonment.[62]

There is one, more recent, example of an inquiry by the Finnish Constitutional Law Committee concerning alleged unlawful conduct of a minister in office. In

[61] T Bergman, WC Müller, K Strøm and M Blomgren, 'Democratic Delegation and Accountability: Cross-national Patterns' in *Delegation and Accountability in Parliamentary Democracies* (Oxford, Oxford University Press, 2003) 173.

[62] Husa (n 8) 147.

the autumn of 2010, the Committee initiated an inquiry against the former Prime Minister, Matti Vanhanen, in relation to a possible conflict of interest stemming from campaign contributions. However, after its investigation and questioning of the former minister, the Committee concluded that no unlawful conduct had taken place and no proceedings were initiated.

The system of a special court of impeachment was abandoned in Sweden in 1974 after it had not been convened for 120 years. Today, criminal prosecutions to hold ministers accountable for their conduct in office are still subject to special procedure. Such cases are tried directly by the Supreme Court of Sweden, the judgment of which in the case is final. No prosecutions of ministers have taken place since the adoption of the 1974 Constitution.

The Norwegian system of legal responsibility of ministers is a hybrid one in the Nordic context. Since the adoption of the 1814 Constitution, there has been a special Court of Impeachment (*Riksretten*) under Article 86; in common with its Finnish counterpart, its jurisdiction covers not only criminal proceedings brought by the Storting against ministers, but also proceedings against judges of the Supreme Court and Members of Parliament. Article 86(1), as amended in 2007, further states that proceedings are to be brought against ministers for 'criminal or other conduct in cases where they have breached their constitutional obligations'. Further conditions for criminal liability are elaborated in the Act on Accountability for Conduct Prosecuted before the Court of Impeachment of 5 February 1932 (*Ansvarlighetsloven*). The Court of Impeachment in Norway has been convened eight times, always in proceedings against ministers; the last occasion was in 1927.[63] The basis for the accountability of ministers when acting in the Council of State when they have failed to oppose an unlawful decision by the Council is stipulated in Article 30. The conditions for such responsibility were amended in 2007, the aim being to make their scope narrower.[64]

The means of enforcing legal responsibility of ministers in Denmark and Iceland are the two most similar systems within the Nordic states. Denmark's Court of Impeachment (*Rigsretten*) was established under the 1849 Constitution; the relevant provision is now in Article 59; this is linked to Article 16, which defines ministers' criminal liability and stipulates that ministers may be impeached by the crown or the Folketing for maladministration of office. The Icelandic Constitution of 1944 similarly states, in Article 14, that ministers are accountable for all executive acts and that the Alþingi may impeach them on account of their official acts. Such cases are to be tried by the Court of Impeachment (*Landsdómur*). This arrangement was imported from Denmark in 1904, when Iceland had a year earlier been granted supreme executive power and its own minister with a new government ministry located in Iceland.

[63] A Fliflet, *Grunnloven. Kommentarutgave* (Oslo, Universitetsforlaget, 2005) 352.
[64] Smith (n 19) 258.

In Denmark and Iceland, the conditions for the criminal liability of ministers are further elaborated in special acts on ministerial accountability; these are Act No 117/1964 in Denmark and Act No 4/1963 in Iceland. They define in further detail the subjective and objective conditions for criminal responsibility of ministers and for their liability to pay compensation. It is also clear that the courts of impeachment have exclusive jurisdiction over criminal offences committed by ministers in office. This means that the regular prosecuting authorities are not able to prosecute ministers for such conduct before the regular courts.

The four Nordic courts of impeachment have in common their special composition, which is explicitly provided for in the constitution, except in Iceland, where this is provided for in a special act on the court, Act No 3/1963. A certain number of the judges in these courts are elected by parliament for a fixed term, while the others are the presidents of the Supreme Court or its equivalent and the most senior-ranking justices. In Iceland and Norway, the elected judges form the majority of the court (8 out of 15 judges in Iceland; 6 out of 11 in Norway), whereas in Denmark and Finland, the numbers are equal. The practice of electing the judges regularly for fixed terms, even though there are no cases, is intended to guarantee their impartiality; when and if proceedings are initiated, there will be no link between their appointment and any individual case. The purpose of the appointment of external judges has been explained by the need to ensure, in the light of the special nature of such cases with their political overtones, that judges will have a certain 'political insight'.[65] This original objective of the special composition of the court has become more controversial in modern times. Thus, it can be questioned whether it is acceptable, with regard to modern notions of a fair trial, that both the decision to prosecute ministers and the position of judges may be coloured by political elements instead of being subject solely to legal considerations. These were among the questions addressed in two of the most recent proceedings before the courts of impeachment in Denmark and Iceland, discussed here below. Furthermore, these questions were addressed in subsequent proceedings against Denmark and Iceland in the European Court of Human Rights.

Denmark's Court of Impeachment in has pronounced judgment in five cases: in 1856, in two cases in 1877, in 1910 and in 1995, whereas the Icelandic court has pronounced only one judgment, in 2012.

ii. The 'Tamil Case' in Denmark

The decision of the Danish Folketing to prosecute Erik Ninn-Hansen, the former Minister of Justice, in the autumn of 1993 was the first of its kind for more than 70 years. It had a long prelude, with a certain starting point in a report by the parliamentary Ombudsman in 1989, which criticised the Ministry of Justice's administration in processing Tamil refugees' applications for family reunification. This initiated a broad public debate and media coverage. Despite initial reluctance

[65] Christensen (n 41) 481–89.

on the part of the government to react to the allegations of unlawful conduct by the minister, as requested by some MPs, the majority of the Folketing approved a special act in 1990 under which a special Court of Inquiry was appointed to investigate the case.

Following the investigation and the questioning of a number of witnesses, the Court of Inquiry published an extensive report in 1993 which contained serious criticism of the ex-minister's discharge of his official duties in his capacity as Minister of Justice in respect of the handling of the Tamil refugees' family reunification case. On the basis of the report, the Folketing decided on 11 June 1993 to institute proceedings against Ninn-Hansen before the Court of Impeachment. Under an indictment on 14 June 1993, the prosecutors, appointed by Parliament, charged Ninn-Hansen with a violation of section 5 of Act No 117/1964 on Ministerial Accountability. Under this provision, a minister is liable to punishment if, wilfully or through gross negligence, he neglects the duties which fall to him under the Constitution, or other laws, or due to the nature of his office. In its judgment of 22 June 1995, the Court of Impeachment convicted the accused and sentenced him to four months' imprisonment, suspended for one year.

Ninn-Hansen contested the legality of the Court of Impeachment and the procedure in his case, filing a complaint to the European Court of Human Rights in Strasbourg. He claimed that a number of flaws in the procedure had resulted in his not having received a fair trial and that his rights under Article 6 of the European Convention on Human Rights had been violated. He pointed out, inter alia, that the proceedings in the Court of Inquiry had been conducted in an inquisitorial manner, without a proper separation between the functions of the judge and those of the prosecutor. Furthermore, he claimed that the composition of the Court of Impeachment violated the independence and impartiality requirement of Article 6 of the Convention, both with respect to the participation of the judges elected by the Folketing and the participation of the Supreme Court judges. In its decision of 18 May 1999, the European Court of Human Rights rejected all his claims and declared his application inadmissible, with detailed reasoning.[66] The Strasbourg Court recalled that the 15 lay judges in the case were appointed for a period of six years and, during that time, it was not possible for any authority, including Parliament, to change the composition or in any other way influence the lay judges. The Court accepted the purpose of their appointment, ie, that the case before the Court of Impeachment required a certain level of insight into political matters. It also noted that the mere appointment of these judges by the Folketing could not be seen as casting doubt on the independence or impartiality of the Court of Impeachment. It was not found that any of the judges in question actually received any instructions or was biased. Although political sympathies could play a part in the process of appointment of lay judges to the Court of Impeachment, the

[66] See Application No 28972/95 in *Erik Ninn-Hansen v Denmark*, Decision of the European Court of Human Rights of 18 May 1999.

Strasbourg Court did not consider that this alone gave grounds for legitimate doubts as to their independence and impartiality. Nor was it established that they had been appointed with a view to adjudicating this particular case or had declared political affiliations concerning the subject matter at issue. Thus, having had regard to all the particular circumstances of the case and the special character of the Court of Impeachment, as well as the guarantees which existed in order to protect it against outside pressures, the Strasbourg Court did not consider that the participation of judges appointed by Parliament revealed any evidence of a violation of the independence and impartiality requirement in Article 6 of the Convention.

iii. The 'Bank Collapse Case' in Iceland

The criminal accountability of a minister was put to the test for the first time in Iceland's history by a judgment of the Court of Impeachment in 2012. The basis for the prosecution was the report of the Special Investigation Commission (SIC), described in section VII above, which investigated the processes leading to the collapse of the three main banks in Iceland in October 2008. One of its objectives was to assess whether mistakes or negligence had occurred in the course of implementing laws and rules applying to activities in Iceland, and, if so, who might be responsible. The report, released in 2010, disclosed various flaws and failures to react in the handling by the government and individual ministers of the situation which culminated in the collapse of the banks. At the time of the collapse, Geir Haarde was serving as Prime Minister of the government, which was formed in 2007 by the Independence Party, of which he was a member, and the Social Democratic Alliance. He resigned in 2009 and a new government was formed, consisting of a coalition between the Social Democratic Alliance and the Left Green Movement. These two parties gained a majority of seats in Parliament in the subsequent elections in April 2009. In 2009, the Alþingi elected an ad hoc review committee of MPs which was given the task of responding to the forthcoming report of the SIC on the collapse of the banks. This included the adoption of a position on ministerial accountability and assessing whether there were grounds for impeachment proceedings before the Court of Impeachment. In the autumn of 2010, the ad hoc committee submitted a proposal to initiate impeachment proceedings against four ex-ministers: Haarde and those who had held the portfolios of finance, business and foreign affairs in his government. The last of these had headed the junior party in the coalition, the Social Democratic Alliance. The conclusion of the vote was to indict only Haarde, and the Alþingi appointed a prosecutor to handle the case on its behalf.

In the spring of 2011, Haarde was indicted on various charges of negligence of his duties as prime minister in the period leading up to the crisis, including gross negligence in relation to the government's failure to take measures to avert the impending disaster. In its judgment of 23 April 2012, the Court of Impeachment acquitted him of all the charges except one. Accordingly, by nine votes to six, he was convicted of having grossly neglected his duties under Article 17 of the Constitution to hold ministerial meetings on 'important governmental affairs' in order to discuss and formulate a government policy to respond to the serious problems confronting Iceland's banking system and the national economy in 2008. This was deemed to fall under section 8(c) of the Act on Ministerial Responsibilities, regarding the duties of ministers under the Constitution. However, Haarde was not sentenced to any punishment and the Icelandic state was ordered to bear all legal costs, including fees to his counsel.

Just as in the Danish case of Ninn-Hansen, Haarde decided to take his case to Strasbourg, where he claimed that various flaws in the prosecution and court procedure had violated his right to a fair trial in a criminal case under Articles 6 and 7 of the European Convention on Human Rights. He complained that he had not been given the opportunity to testify during the pre-trial stage of the proceedings and that the indictment lacked clarity. Furthermore, he claimed that the composition of the Court of Impeachment, and Parliament's involvement in determining its composition, constituted a violation of the requirement regarding an independent and impartial court. The European Court of Human Rights pronounced a judgment in the case on 23 November 2017, where all of his claims were rejected.[67]

The Strasbourg Court confirmed and elaborated upon its former position further with respect to the independence of the Court of Impeachment. It accepted generally that the participation of the lay judges in question could be seen as beneficial for the Court of Impeachment's understanding and examination of the issues in the case, since the lay judges contributed a certain level of insight on political matters. The requirement of Article 6(1) that the Court of Impeachment should be independent not only from the executive and the parties but also from Parliament did not entail that the mere appointment of judges by Parliament could as a result cast doubt on the independence or impartiality of the Court. And although political sympathies could play a part in the process of appointment of lay judges to the Court of Impeachment, the Strasbourg Court did not consider that this alone raised legitimate doubts as to their independence and impartiality. It had not been shown that the lay judges sitting in Haarde's case declared any political affiliations concerning the subject matter in issue or that there existed other links between them and Parliament which could give rise to misgivings as to their independence and impartiality.[68]

Furthermore, the Strasbourg Court gave detailed argumentation regarding the decision of the Alþingi to initiate proceedings against Haarde and its nature. It explored the existing rules on criminal liability of government ministers in the member states of the Council of Europe, which revealed a great variation in relation to both the applicable procedures and the substantive criminal provisions.

[67] *Haarde v Iceland*, Application No 66847/12, judgment of 23 November 2017.
[68] ibid § 105.

There is a clear trend that for offences committed during the exercise of official functions, the national parliament in European states is typically involved by taking the decision as to whether to initiate proceedings against a government minister.[69] As this decision rests with the parliament, the matter may, to some extent, involve considerations of a political nature. However, the Court did not consider in Haarde's case that this fact in itself was sufficient to raise an issue under Article 6. It had to be borne in mind that the charges brought by Parliament were eventually examined and adjudicated upon by a court of law. Accordingly, the Strasbourg Court came to the conclusion that the process leading to the applicant's indictment was not arbitrary or political to such an extent that the fairness of his trial was prejudiced.[70]

Ever since the proceedings were initiated against the former prime minister and in spite of the fact that no violations of his rights occurred according to the European Court of Human Rights, there has been an ongoing debate in the political arena in Iceland, with many arguing that Haarde's prosecution was a political mistake that should never be repeated. Particular attention has been given to the vote in the Alþingi in the autumn of 2010, in which Haarde was the only person selected out of the four ex-ministers whose prosecution had been proposed: it has been alleged that this illustrated the shortcomings of a situation where the power to embark on a prosecution is in the hands of a political body and therefore is more likely to be arbitrarily applied. It has been claimed that the Alþingi failed the test of taking an objective decision on the issue and that it decided to spare the other candidates prosecution from political motives. However, no suggestions have yet been made for a revision of the system and the procedure before the Court of Impeachment, even though such amendments would not necessarily require amendments to the Constitution.

B. The Relationship between Legal and Political Accountability of Ministers

The principle of parliamentary accountability, which became rooted in all five Nordic constitutional systems in the early twentieth century, implies the question whether the legal responsibility of ministers has become superfluous. Indeed, before parliamentary rule was introduced, the impeachment procedure was the only means that parliaments had to act in relation to malfeasance by ministers who executed the authority of the crown and were accountable only to the crown.

Parliamentary rule gradually became codified explicitly in four of the Nordic constitutions in the twentieth century, most recently in that of Norway in 2007.

[69] On the detailed comparative study on the subject, see European Commission for Democracy through Law, *Report on the Relationship between Political and Criminal Responsibility* (CDL-AD(2013)001, March 2013).

[70] *Haarde v Iceland* (n 67) §§ 86 and 88.

In Iceland it has been an unwritten constitutional principle since 1904 and is still practised as such. In four of the Nordic countries (all except Finland), negative parliamentarism is practised. This normally means that the government which wins the election will be in power, with or without one or more coalition partners, unless it becomes clear that there is no support for it in parliament. Constitutional provisions in Denmark (Article 15), Norway (Article 15) and Sweden (Article 13:4) reflect this in a similar manner by stating that the parliaments may pass a vote of no confidence, and the minister or the government in question will then be obliged to resign. Partly because of negative parliamentarism, minority governments have been relatively frequent in some of the Nordic countries, although excluding Iceland. In such a situation, parliament may be in a stronger position to exercise control, as has been discussed above.

In the Finnish system, there has been, since the early 1990s, the practice of positive parliamentarism. This was codified explicitly in the 2000 Constitution. Article 61 states that Parliament elects the prime minister, who is then appointed to the office by the president; other ministers are then elected according to nominations by the prime minister. This means in practice that a vote for the government is required at the time of its formation. In addition, the duty of the government, or individual ministers, to resign in the event of a vote of no confidence is stipulated in Article 64 of the Constitution.

The strongest reaction element in parliamentary rule in the Nordic countries lies in the fact that the possibility of passing motions of no confidence exists, and not necessarily in the frequent use of this tool. As a matter of fact, motions of no confidence against governments have rarely been approved in the history of the Nordic parliaments and even more seldom in relation to individual ministers. In Denmark such motions have been approved only three times against a government (1909, 1947 and 1945) and never against a minister; in Norway only twice against the government (1928 and 1963); in Iceland three times (against the minister in 1909 and 1911—at that time there was only one minister forming a government—and against the government in 1950); and in Finland four times against the government (1926, 1928, 1957 and 1958) and twice against individual ministers (1922 and 1948). In Sweden there have been five votes of no confidence under the current Constitution of 1974, but none of them was successful.

On the other hand, there have been many instances in the Nordic countries where the government has 'voluntarily' resigned in situations where it has obviously lost majority support in parliament and a motion of no confidence has been in preparation, or would clearly be approved if proposed, or where disagreement between coalition parties results in the government's resignation. There have been even more cases where individual ministers have voluntarily resigned for various reasons, including severe criticism of their conduct in office, or even outside office, before they would be forced to do so on the basis of a formal declaration of no confidence. In this way, accountability of the government and ministers towards parliament is indeed real and effective, and manifests itself in a similar manner in all the Nordic countries.

But the question regarding the link between legal and political responsibility has not been answered. First, it should be noted that these two types of responsibility, and the reasons for invoking them, are of entirely different natures. As a starting point in the comparison, it is clear that criminal liability can be enforced against individual ministers only and not against governments as such, not even in Finland and Sweden, where the government is recognised as an entity which takes formal administrative decisions. Accordingly, only political responsibility can be invoked against governments. The conduct of the ministers involved is also of a different nature. The threshold for applying political accountability is lower, whereas legal responsibility is subject to strict conditions, for instance, the demonstration of gross negligence on the part of the minister. As all public officials are subject to criminal liability for conduct in their work, it would be unacceptable to exclude ministers, as the highest executants in the administrative sector, from such liability. This should in itself suffice to clarify that the legal responsibility of ministers cannot be replaced with political accountability, and that political accountability should instead be supplementary. A situation in which a minister commits unlawful actions in office may only be revealed after his or her time in office; indeed, this would normally be the case. Obviously, political liability which requires a vote of no confidence could not be exercised (the events leading to impeachment proceedings may, however, have been the reason for his or her resignation at the outset).

It might be argued that the idea behind special criminal procedures against ministers is outdated. This could apply particularly in the light of the political element in the decision to prosecute, where the majority of the parliament at a given time may turn against a political opponent in a previous government. Also, the parliamentary appointment of judges based on the need for political insight into the issue may be questionable. Indeed, there may be concerns that the conditions for a fair trial are jeopardised; this was discussed in both the most recent impeachment proceedings in Denmark and Iceland.

These may be weighty arguments. However, this would not justify the abolition of the impeachment system rather than amending it to meet the concerns raised above. Abolition would mean, due to the exclusive jurisdiction of the courts of impeachment, that ministers would in practice be immune to prosecution for unlawful conduct in office if, for example, the majority parties made a tacit political agreement that parliament would refrain from exercising its prosecution powers. This would be unacceptable and would undermine both the powers of parliament and conditions for lawful administration, since the ministers, as the supreme holders of executive powers, would lack the necessary restraint in their work.

As the European Court of Human Right stated in the Haarde case, 'while the purpose of the relevant constitutional, legislative and procedural frameworks on this subject should be to seek a balance between political accountability and criminal liability, and to avoid both the risk of impunity and the risk of ill-founded recourse to criminal proceedings, there may be risks of abuse or dysfunctionalities involved, which must be avoided'.[71]

So, adequate solutions should be found to meet the demands of both the special circumstances when assessing allegations of criminal conduct by ministers in office and the fair trial elements. This must acknowledge the importance of ensuring that criminal proceedings are not misused for the purpose of harming political opponents or as instruments in political conflict.

X. Concluding Remarks

This chapter has outlined the main elements in parliamentary control mechanisms vis-a-vis the executive in the Nordic countries, has analysed and compared different means and methods, and has identified certain features that are unique to each constitutional system.

The first general conclusion regarding the Nordic constitutional systems is the clear difference between the East and the West Nordic states regarding the constitutional basis of parliamentary control and the main organs involved. This applies not only to how explicitly the control functions of the parliaments are elaborated in the written provisions of the constitution, but also the material structure and powers of the control organs. Sweden and Finland, with the most recent constitutions, have codified most explicitly the control of the executive as one of parliament's main tasks, defining the means of exercising control and the functions of the main committees and control bodies. They also share many common features which can be traced to common historical roots in their constitutional history. For instance, they have in common the long tradition, and constitutional status, of a special constitutional committee among the standing committees of parliament. Although there is some fundamental difference between the tasks of these two committees, they both play a key role in preparing impeachment proceedings against ministers.

It has been illustrated how the West Nordic constitutional systems furnish the parliaments with very similar main tools for controlling the executive. However, as the Constitutions of Norway, Denmark and Iceland are still largely based on their initial nineteenth-century constitutions, they are much less explicit on this issue. The supervisory role of parliament is not defined explicitly as one of their main tasks, except as regards the supervision of state finances. Separate tools for supervising the ministers in Denmark and Iceland are set forth in scattered provisions, mainly declaring the rights of individual MPs to pose questions or request reports from ministers. Out of the three West Nordic constitutions, Iceland's is by far the

[71] ibid § 85.

most reticent regarding the relationship between parliament and the executive. As important parts of the Icelandic Constitution have remained unchanged for a century, it reflects neither current reality regarding the executive branch and the work of the government nor the role of the Alþingi in supervising the executive.

Unlike those in the East, the West Nordic constitutions remain silent on the system of standing committees and their role in supervising the government. Detailed regulations on this are found only in the standing orders of the parliaments in Iceland, Denmark and Norway. As in Sweden and Finland, the organisation of the standing committees is highly sophisticated and has developed significantly during the last few decades.

It has been demonstrated that there is a trend in all the Nordic countries to take steps to strengthen the position of parliament vis-a-vis the executive. Examples from Norway and Iceland illustrate the reorganisation of the parliamentary standing committees, one of which has been given a special supervisory role. Moreover, external ad hoc investigation commissions appointed by parliament to investigate issues of great public concern appear to be more common in the West Nordic countries in recent years, and Denmark and Iceland have adopted special acts on the powers of such commissions.

The sanctioning of ministers for unlawful conduct in office through an impeachment procedure is regulated in a similar manner in all the Nordic countries, even though no court of impeachment exists in Sweden. The application of this tool in various ways in each of the countries has been examined. While the procedure appears to be outdated in Norway and Sweden, some impeachment proceedings have taken place since the 1990s in Finland, Denmark and Iceland. Controversial though it may seem, in modern times, for a political body to be deciding on the prosecution of individuals for alleged criminal acts, a lack of political willingness to revise the system seems to be a common problem in all the Nordic countries. Accordingly, political reluctance to exercise parliament's prosecution powers may result in the unfortunate situation that ministers will enjoy, in practice, immunity from prosecution for crimes committed in office.

It is difficult to conclude, from the analysis set out in this chapter, that the parliamentary control mechanism in any one Nordic country is either the most efficient or the most successful. This is impossible to measure since, notwithstanding similarities in the framework for control and many common features, each of the systems has different components that may be functioning well, but are not necessarily comparable with those found in another context. It can at least be maintained that even though the Swedish and Finnish written constitutions provide the most comprehensive and transparent picture of the role of the parliament in controlling the executive powers, there is no clear link between the codification of such mechanisms in constitutional texts and the effectiveness of the control.

Finally, the history of politics in the Nordic countries shows that the practice of negative parliamentarism is likely to produce minority governments and in some of them—for instance, in Denmark and Norway—such traditions have evolved. Meanwhile, in Iceland, for instance, there is no such tradition; on the contrary, there has been strong majority support for Icelandic governments in recent decades. This has changed the emphasis in Icelandic politics to polarisation between the government and the opposition parties, rather than between parliament and the executive. Strong majority governments may both weaken political accountability and affect the likelihood that parliament will apply the available procedures for parliamentary control to supervise the actions of ministers and the administration. Despite the steps taken, for example, in Sweden, Iceland and Norway to strengthen the status of the minorities in parliament within the standing committees, at the end of the day, it will always be in the hands of the political forces with a majority in parliament to take major decisions regarding the control of the executive. This is inherent in the idea of democratic government, but at the same time it reflects the limitations of parliamentary control. It is therefore of the utmost importance that the constitutional democracies of the Nordic states should share a strong commitment to acknowledge and respect the role of external organs to monitor the administration, such as the Parliamentary Ombudsman, and, more importantly, the effective judicial control over the executive.

5

Judicial Review of Legislation

EIVIND SMITH

I. Introduction

The five Nordic states appear to be relatively close when it comes to elements like history and cultural heritage, as well as prevailing political philosophies. In particular, commonly shared conceptions of democracy seem to be close to each other in a way inducing the idea that the role of judicial review of enactments by the highest directly elected body of the land—the judiciary—in constitutional matters is relatively uniform. One important element might then be the prevalence of majority government as opposed to constitutional restraints on political action as defined by courts; the qualification as 'judicial supremacy' may come to mind.

At a legal-technical level, today's existence of systems of judicial review of legislation in all five states (section II) confirms the idea of relative conformity. A closer look, however, reveals huge differences between them in the field of constitutional jurisprudence. This appears when it comes to the emergence of these systems (section III) as well as to the practice actually developed by the relevant courts (section IV).

Identifying exact empirical causes for such differences would be hazardous. To some extent, however, they might stem from differences in constitutional history as a reflection of that of the relevant state.[1] We may use two examples in support of this point.

The Norwegian system of judicial review is by far the oldest and remains probably the most active of the five. It emerged gradually after the adoption of the 1814 Constitution, a text that served not only as the genuinely constituent document of the modern state of Norway but also as the declaration of independence of that state (Article 1). Understanding the exceptionally early emergence of judicial

[1] For an account of the different historical developments in French, see E Smith, 'Pays scandinaves' in L Favoreu and JA Jolowitz (eds), *Le contrôle juridictionnel des lois: légitimité, effectivité et développements récents* (Paris, Economica, 1986) 223–82.

review in Norway seems to necessitate taking into account the strong status as a positive symbol that these features bestow upon the Constitution. In the other Nordic countries, no similar patterns paved the way for a similar position for the relevant constitutions.

The last country to join the club of countries with a minimum level of judicial review of legislation did so through the insertion of an explicit provision in the new 'millennium' Constitution for Finland (Act No 731 of 1999) that entered in force on 1 March 2000. But the absence of such review in the previous century as well as its still rather remote practical importance under the present Constitution must by necessity be understood in light of the particular abstract *ex ante* control mechanism managed by the Parliament's Constitutional Law Committee (see Chapter 4).[2] Quite a few seem willing to argue that this mechanism takes away most, if not all, of the need for active judicial review of legislation. But at present it is more important to point out that no similar mechanism exists in Finland's neighbour countries.

Other elements for explaining the differences between the Nordic states, notwithstanding a number of reasons for expecting the opposite to be the case (see Chapter 2), may include patterns of legal education and—not least—differences in the systems for selecting judges, namely members of the supreme courts.

Whatever the causes, the relatively recent relationship between the national Constitution, on the one hand, and key elements of international law, namely the European Union (EU), the European Economic Area (EEA) and the European Convention on Human Rights (ECHR) law, on the other hand, seems likely to reduce the gap (section V). However, such relationships hardly suffice for eliminating differences between the countries when it comes to current judicial attitudes towards the task of adjudicating on the basis of legal norms that are supposed to constrain the freedom of domestic political action one way or the other.

To some extent, the following remarks will be organised according to the divide that may be observed, regarding many aspects of public law, between the three Western and the two Eastern legal systems within the Nordic states. Historically, we speak about the system established in the 'imperial' capital (Copenhagen) and later on followed—in chronological order—by Oslo and Reykjavik, as opposed to the system established by Stockholm and later on by Helsinki. The divide is most apparent when it comes to institutions. If understood as a key to different patterns of legal-political thought, it is less easy to demonstrate and as a consequence less apparent.

[2] On this system and its relationship with judicial review, see further J Lavapuro, T Ojanen and M Scheinin, 'Intermediate Constitutional Review in Finland: Promising in Theory, Problematic in Practice' in J Bell and ML Paris (eds), *Rights-Based Constitutional Review: Constitutional Courts in a Changing Landscape* (Cheltenham, Edward Elgar, 2016) 218–43.

II. The Constitution as Positive Law

A. Introduction

Judicial review of administrative acts exists in all five countries, either in the hands of the ordinary courts (Denmark, Norway and Iceland) or in those of specialised administrative courts (Sweden and Finland). Administrative enactments may well be closely linked to parliamentary legislation in a way that is likely to raise some of the same questions about the legitimacy of the judge's role towards parliament as judicial review of legislation regularly does. In this chapter, we will nevertheless address judicial review of legislation only.

Constitutions may well have effects on the functioning of the political system without serving as positive law in the sense of being submitted to the appreciation of judges. However, under circumstances that are otherwise comparatively equal, the legislative power is likely to have more freedom of appreciation as to the limits to its own powers if the formal adoption of a piece of legislation represents the last word regarding the constitutionality of that piece than if that question—one way or the other—may depend on how judges construe constitutional limits for the powers of the ordinary law-making institutions.

Reviewing legislation presupposes the existence of legal norms of a superior rank by which the legislative power is bound. This way, the question of knowing how and when systems of judicial review have emerged or were established may be phrased as one regarding the very status of the relevant Constitution as positive law. It may gain the status of positive law by explicit constitutional provisions, along the lines traced, for instance, by Article 20(3) of the German *Grundgesetz* and followed by a number of more recent constitutions, or its status may at least be definitively confirmed in this way. But a similar status may emerge even by virtue of jurisprudence acting in concert with the legislative power itself, as well as with the contribution of law scholars and other actors in the public space. As we shall see, both kinds of tracks have been in use in the Nordic sphere.

Before embarking on the different national experiences at hand, it should be noted that the Constitution appears as positive law in the jurisprudence not only when pieces of legislation are set aside (by way of non-application) as unconstitutional, but even when the provision is upheld. Cases where application is denied are certainly those that are most likely to retain our attention. But this is precisely what makes it even more important to underscore that the same qualification may result from verdicts that make reference to constitutional norms at points of direct importance (ratio decidendi) for the outcome of the individual case, while nevertheless concluding that no violation of the constitution has occurred.

B. The Western States[3]

For 200 years, the Constitution of Norway was silent about the existence or not of a power for the judiciary to review legislation. But this silence did not stand in the way of the Supreme Court of Norway starting to apply the Constitution as positive law. According to the provisions of the new Constitution (1814), the Court's first session took place in 1815. Then one had to wait only a few years before finding cases where the Court used a constitutional provision (Article 97 on non-retroactivity) as a seemingly decisive argument about how to resolve the issue at stake; it seems as if the first example appears in the handwritten minutes from 1821. This would not have been possible, or it would at least have been meaningless, had the Constitution not been accepted as positive law.[4]

The following decades provide more examples. It is true that the number of examples is not high. But this fact needs to be understood in light of the development of Norwegian society during a phase where the state was a rather passive one; in combination with a well-established laissez-faire attitude, the legislative activity was sparse and therefore provided little room for constitutional litigation.

Understanding the further development requires knowing that the reasoning underpinning the conclusions of the Supreme Court was secret; only the formal conclusions (X shall serve Y years in prison or pay W in compensation) were published. This of course implies that our knowledge of the legal arguments actually used is most certainly incomplete. It even implies that the political community of that time was kept uninformed, at least in principle. But not knowing on which grounds sometimes controversial judgments were based was less and less supported by Parliament, which finally (1863) obtained the royal consent necessary for the entry into force of a statute forcing the members of the Supreme Court to vote and to give individual grounds in public.

A few years later (1866), the Supreme Court adjudicated another case on non-retroactivity (UfL 1866, p 165, Wedel Jarlsberg). The case may be noted because the majority ruled against the government. But the most interesting aspect of the case lies in the reasoning underpinning this outcome: speaking for the majority, the Court's President Lasson explained that according to established doctrine, it is eminently the obligation of the judge to give priority to the Constitution when constitutional and statutory norms could not be applied simultaneously. This clearly recognises the Constitution's character as positive law. And once this step was accomplished, the reasoning leaned heavily on a kind of hierarchical

[3] Interesting comparative developments in English, mainly on the three Western Nordic systems, may be found in R Helgadóttir, *The Influence of American Theories on Judicial Review in Nordic Constitutional Law* (The Hague, Martinus Nijhoff, 2005); and K à Rógvi, *West-Nordic Constitutional Judicial Review: A Comparative Study of Scandinavian Judicial Review and Judicial Reasoning* (Copenhagen, DJØF Publishing, 2013).

[4] On the Norwegian system, see, for instance, E Smith, *Konstitusjonelt demokrati*, 4th edn (Oslo, Fagbokforlaget, 2017).

argument that, in fact, was close to that expounded by US Chief Justice Marshall in the admittedly more well-known *Marbury v Madison* (1802) case, a case where the sub-constitutional piece of legislation was not set aside, as had happened in the Norwegian case.

After 1866, the state remained relatively passive in the sense of not intervening in the lives of its citizens. But once the politically toxic question of the personal union with Sweden had definitively been brought to its end by the unilateral breaking away of Norway (later confirmed by treaty) in 1905, the legislative power adopted a series of measures with the aim of regulating economic activities. This wave of new legislation was soon met by opposition from the judiciary through a series of Supreme Court judgments setting aside key measures on constitutional grounds. The political reaction grew strong, and in the much-commented-upon case reported in Rt 1918, p 401, a majority in the Court took a step back, without denying the existence of the power of judicial review. In a sense, then, we might speak about a Norwegian 'New Deal' battle almost two decades before the more well-known fight in the 1930s between US President Franklin D. Roosevelt and the Supreme Court.

Little by little, the period of what has often been regarded as judicial 'activism' of the Supreme Court of Norway during a number of years from 1909, evaporated. The Second World War and the German occupation (1940–45) came next, and the major social setting during the following years was about reconstructing the country by 'everyone together'. No major setting aside of legislation took place, whereas some cases occurred where the Supreme Court may be said to have given too much leeway to the majority will in Parliament.

Since a landmark decision in 1976 (Rt 1976, p 1; see further below), a gradual shift in the climate regarding constitutional jurisprudence has taken place. This part of the story is better told in a later sequence of this chapter (see sections IV–VI). In relation to Norway, it just remains to be said that a new constitutional provision was adopted in 2015 in order to finally make the nearly two centuries-old system of judicial review appear in the text of the fundamental law (Article 89). Unfortunately, the text of the provision is somewhat blurred compared to this aim. But because nothing indicates that a change in the system was envisaged, the established jurisprudence and the way it has been met by the other branches of government will continue to determine the real bearing of the system from time to time. In this respect, it is worthwhile noting that the legislative and executive powers have always, notwithstanding instances of political criticism, taken all the necessary consequences of the final outcomes reached by the judiciary.

Unlike in the Norwegian Constituent Assembly in 1814, the question of including a clause on judicial review in the Constitution to end absolute monarchy (1849) in Denmark was discussed. The Constituent Assembly rejected the idea, and the succeeding Constitutions (of 1866, 1915, and 1953) have not changed the situation; in fact, these texts are constitutional amendments adopted according to the procedure established by the preceding constitution rather than complete new documents, as their name might indicate. But the silence of the constitutional text has not been understood as completely excluding judicial review of legislation adopted by the elected Parliament and signed by the king.[5]

A series of Supreme Court judgments handed out in 1920–21 deals with legal aspects of the dismantling of the remaining fragments of the feudal system regarding farmland (U 1921.148 H, 1921.153 H and 1021.644 H). None of them concluded that the Constitution had been violated by the relevant pieces of legislation. As already pointed out, this does not stand in the way of regarding them as establishing the Constitution as positive law in a sense that would entail a power for the judiciary to assess the constitutionality of legislation. But in the last of the three cases, the outcome seems explicitly to result from a judge-made criterion inducing judicial self-restraint insofar as the unconstitutionality may not be established 'with the certainty required for the Courts to set aside legislation duly adopted according to the procedure set forth by the Constitution'. This restraint seems to have been observed for many years.

Whether a similar restraint was observed when the Supreme Court of Denmark for the first and, so far, only time set a legislative provision aside as unconstitutional has been the subject of some debate. A statute excluded seven enumerated, somewhat controversial 'folk high schools' (colleges that issue no formal diploma) from the financial support that they would otherwise have enjoyed under the statute's general clause. In the 'Tvind' case of 1999 (U 1999.841 H), however, the Court unanimously found that the exclusion violated Article 3 of the Constitution on the 'separation of powers' between the three branches of government. In a context of political controversy regarding the activities of the relevant group of schools, it was for the judiciary and not for the legislative power to determine whether given institutions satisfy the general criteria for subvention laid down by law.

In Iceland, a few cases from the local courts have been identified as being of a constitutional nature under the 1874 Constitution of Iceland given by the King of Denmark. The cases suggest that the 'constitution' was already regarded as positive law at that early stage. This idea was confirmed after the country finally became independent (under a kind of personal union with Denmark) in 1918 and almost immediately seized the ensuing opportunity to establish its own Supreme Court (1920). Most notably, this happened in a 1943 case (10 L&H 601), where the majority, based on a rather extensive substantive interpretation of the Constitution's freedom of the press clause, declined to sanction a clear violation of a nineteenth-century statute forbidding the publication of medieval sagas without retaining the original spelling.

Under the Constitution of the new Republic (1944), the Supreme Court, in a series of cases on property rights in the 1950s, adopted a review standard close to that established by the Danish Supreme Court around 1920 ('not sufficiently clear that the Constitution has been violated'; see H 1952:434). This fits well with the

[5] On the Danish system, see, eg, JP Christensen, JA Jensen and MH Jensen, *Dansk Statsret*, 2nd edn (Copenhagen, Jurist- og Økonomforbundets Forlag, 2016).

fact that Icelandic lawyers were still trained in Copenhagen and heavily influenced by Danish textbooks.

This standard was seemingly adhered to for some time. But in 1990 (H 1990:2), the Supreme Court deviated from its prior position regarding the Icelandic tradition on the impartiality and independence of police commissioners in small localities acting simultaneously as local judges, a system previously accepted by the judiciary. It did so while explicitly referring to a report by the European Commission of Human Rights of 8 March 1989 (*Kristinsson v Iceland*, no 12170/86) that the Icelandic practice at this point represented a violation of Article 6 of the Convention.

Soon afterwards (1995), the Constitution was amended by adding a number of important human rights in a text as discreet on such issues as the Constitution of Denmark. In a number of subsequent cases, the Supreme Court made active use of the new provisions (see further section IV). Arguably then, Iceland is one of the two Nordic states (along with Norway) where judicial review of legislation has been most active.

C. The Eastern States

When it comes to the story of the acceptation of the Constitution as positive law and of judicial review of legislation, the split between East and West fits well with reality. Before the adoption of the institutional part of the Swedish Constitution—Regeringsformen (the 'Instrument of Government')—in 1974, some discussion took place about the introduction of judicial review, namely in the field of rights. In a spirit of benevolence towards the introduction of judicial review, some authors even pinpointed a few cases where the relevant court had arguably, albeit in implicit ways, made reference to constitutional provisions in a manner that presupposed that the Instrument of Government had the status of positive law and—hence—the possibility of judicial review. It should be added that the possibility of upholding the two 'constitutional laws' regulating the freedom of the press and related matters according to particular rules of procedure has never been in doubt.

The growing interest for introducing judicial review in an era of growing interest in rights led to the inclusion of an explicit clause in the new Instrument of Government (1974). But the wording of the new provisions on judicial review eloquently testifies to the reluctance with which this step was taken.

First, the power not to apply legal norms whose application would contradict norms of a superior rank was not written into a constitution with effect for the courts alone, but was included in a chapter dealing with courts and other parts of the 'public administration' and enshrined in the same sentence for both. This still appeared as the consequence of the overall state apparatus as organised by the Instrument of Government: according to an age-old tradition, public administration enjoys a constitutionally guaranteed, relative independence in relation to the government, while no clear distinction was made between judicial and other bodies. This was all the more true for the administrative tribunals, where no clear distinction was made between tribunals and other parts of the public administration.

Second, the new clause explicitly addressed not only review of legislation, but review of any legal norm notwithstanding its formal rank. In this sense, we might actually talk about a clause concerning the hierarchy of legal norms as much as about (judicial and administrative) review or, in other words, the *lex superior* principle.

However, within this broad scope for action, third, the clause established a distinction between enactments by Parliament and the government, on the one hand, and by other public bodies, on the other hand. For the two first categories, non-application should only take place insofar as the violation of the superior norm (of constitutional or legislative rank respectively) was 'evident' (or 'manifest'). The bonds on the power of judicial review of acts adopted by the highest directly elected body of the land fit rather well with the concern for its legitimacy as a part of a democratic system of government influenced by widespread ideologies in the Nordic countries along the lines suggested above. Why the government should enjoy a similar form of protection to that of Parliament may only be explained by reference to the particularities in Swedish constitutional history.

The efficiency of the clause is quite another matter. After all, it is for the judges themselves to determine when and to what extent the unconstitutional character of (an application of) a given sub-constitutional enactment is 'evident'. The limitation clause hardly did more than confirm and possibly solidify an inherited attitude of deference to ordinary legislation or—in other words—of reluctance towards juridical review of legislation within the judiciary itself.

The new power of judicial review nevertheless provided some grounds for judicial activity. For instance, a court of appeals found a legislative ban on the use of uniforms to be in violation of the freedom of expression as guaranteed by the Instrument of Government (RH 1997:47). Soon afterwards (1999), the statute was amended accordingly. A Supreme Court case in 1981 on Sami rights regarding the clause on non-discrimination reflects a more reluctant attitude, although admittedly on a more sensitive point (NJA 1981, p 1, Skattefjällsmålet).

From the last years of the 'evident violation' clause, a Supreme Court case from 2005 deserves mention because it highlights the difference at this point between the Supreme Court's approach to the Instrument of Government and to the European Convention on Human Rights (NJA 2005, p 805, Pastor Green). Referring to the Constitution's clause on 'evident violation', the Court refused to set aside a lower judgment inflicting punishment on a pastor for denigrating homosexuals in violation of the penal code. By contrast, it found a violation of Article 10 of the European Convention on Human Rights, where no similar clause exists, and acquitted the pastor of the criminal charge.

After becoming the subject of growing criticism, the entire provision on judicial (and administrative) review was finally abolished as part of a major, albeit mostly technical reshuffling of the Instrument of Government in 2010. The new clause (Chapter 11, Article 14) must be understood in light of the systematic isolation of the provisions regarding the judiciary from those dealing with the public administration as such. From now on, enactments by the government no longer enjoy a different status from administrative acts in general, and judicial review of legislation is no longer submitted to the 'evidence' test.

But the power of the judiciary is not entirely left alone. Instead, the new constitutional clause states that 'particular attention shall be paid to the fact that Parliament (Riksdagen) is the foremost representative of the people and that fundamental law takes precedence over other law'. The somewhat blurred formulation eloquently testifies to another compromise; in fact, it simultaneously stresses that the will expressed by Parliament deserves particular consideration, thus inducing a measure of judicial self-restraint, and that Parliament is submitted to the limits laid down by the Constitution, thus rather speaking in the opposite direction. Thus, more than ever, it would be for the judges to find their way. It remains unlikely that it will rapidly depart from the country's well-established constitutional culture and political traditions, maintaining a strong vein of positivism and judicial self-restraint.

Finally, in the Republic of Finland (from 1917), it was commonly assumed that the judiciary had no say at all as to the constitutionality of legislation.[6] At the same time, the particular system of *ex ante* advance control by the Parliament's Constitutional Law Committee settled as a primordial feature of the Finnish constitutional system (see further Chapter 4).[7] The position of judicial review cannot be understood without taking this part of the system into account.

The exclusion of the judiciary from the field of constitutional law came to an end as a result of the present Constitution (from March 2000), which states that 'if, in a matter being tried by a court of law, the application of an Act would be in evident conflict with the Constitution, the court of law shall give primacy to the provision in the Constitution' (section 106). As to the clause on 'evident' violation, we are clearly—when it comes to statutory law—faced with a copy of Sweden's Instrument of Government adopted in a period when Sweden considered abolishing its similar clause (which finally happened in 2010).[8]

[6] The assumption was based on an *a contrario* argument from Article 92.2 of the Finnish 1919 Constitution prohibiting courts and other authorities from implementing government decrees that were in conflict with the Constitution or Acts of Parliament, while remaining silent on judicial review of parliamentary legislation.

[7] It is worth mentioning that even some other state actors, including the Chancellor of Justice, the speaker of the Parliament, and the President of the republic, are bestowed with certain powers to review the constitutionality of legislative proposals at various stages of the legislative process.

[8] At the same time, the question of abolishing the 'evident' criterion was considered by the Finnish authorities, but was eventually left aside when some amendments were adopted in 2010; *cf* Lavapuro et al (n 2) 529.

III. Legal-Technical Characteristics

Across huge differences in history and constitutional basis, judicial review of legislation in the five Nordic states shares a number of legal-technical characteristics that should be kept in mind when approaching recent trends in constitutional jurisprudence (section IV). For a reason that will be explained later, we concentrate on the supreme instances.

At some points, however, there are noteworthy differences across the East-West divide. We start with the structure of the judiciary.

In each of the three Western Nordic states, we find a single-tier judicial system with a single supreme instance encompassing all the main parts of the legal system (civil, criminal and administrative law) and with the power to review legislation insofar as necessary in order to resolve the individual case. This implies that no conflict of competencies may occur when it comes to the final word on the meaning of the Constitution.

Each of the two Eastern Nordic states, on the other hand, has two supreme instances: one for civil and criminal cases, and another for administrative law. Within their respective fields of action, each of them may even review legislation according to the constitutional clauses already mentioned. For a long time, however, the possibility of conflicting answers to identical or comparable constitutional questions entailed by this duality did not lead to the establishment of a mechanism of conflict resolution. This situation seems to reflect a state of constitutional reflection where the eventuality of active judicial review seemed sufficiently farfetched as to make conflicting outcomes in the two supreme instances unlikely.

This absence is also striking because comparative law clearly demonstrates that the solution did not necessarily have to take the form of a separate judicial instance (like a 'constitutional court'). Even something like a joint chamber with members from both Supreme Courts and mandated to lead the way when incommensurable interpretations of the Constitution have appeared or might result from cases on their way to the courtroom would easily do. And this is precisely what is envisaged by a reform that is pending in 2018: in cases concerning constitutional interpretation and some other matters, a 'grand chamber' composed of five members of the court to which the relevant case belongs and four from the other supreme instance may be convoked in order to give the consensual answer.

The fact that no institutional answer to the existence of two supreme instances, both vested with the power of having the last word on constitutional matters exists, probably testifies to an expectation that a mechanism for harmonising possibly conflicting answers would not strictly be needed. One reason likely to underpin a similar expectation might be a presumption that the judicial activity in the field of judicial review of legislation will remain low. So far, the experience seems to confirm this expectation, although there are some examples of tensions provided by Finnish jurisprudence (see further section IV).

As to the recruitment of Supreme Court judges, they are all appointed by the head of the executive (the King in Council, the president or the government). But the traditions and selection procedures vary historically as well as today. During most of their modern constitutional history, the systems in Denmark and Sweden have been deeply influenced by their formal career systems, supplemented with ministerial intervention (Sweden and Finland) or a wide discretion for the Supreme Court itself to select its new members (Denmark). In all these countries, however, modifications implemented during the course of the last few decades have made the basis for recruitment significantly more open. It remains to be seen whether such changes will entail consequences when it comes to the styles of adjudication.

In Norway as well as in Iceland, the systems for selecting new members of the apex courts have always been more open. In the absence of formal career systems, they have even, in parts of the history of these systems, allowed for a strong presence of former high-profile political figures within the relevant court. This openness has certainly provided some clues for understanding the most different developments of judicial review in Norway and Iceland as compared to the other Nordic countries; for Norway, this pattern appears most clearly in the system's formative period (the nineteenth and early twentieth centuries).

More recently, however, the tendency in all these countries has been to select judges on more or less purely legal-technical grounds. In relation to the Supreme Court of Norway, for instance, the last judge with a past as a member of government left the Court in 1990. More importantly, none of the systems includes elements of an openly 'political' character similar to those prevailing for courts with important constitutional functions in almost any other non-Nordic legal system (discretion given to the bodies nominating or appointing new judges, a distinctive role for Parliament etc). In Norway, however, discussions about the need for introducing such elements into a situation where the Supreme Court seems to adopt an increasingly outspoken profile in relation to constitutional matters have just started. In Iceland, there has been a growing debate about the role of Parliament in the appointment of judges under certain circumstances, a system that was applied for the first time in 2017 and immediately became controversial.

Beyond such more or less pronounced particularities, the five systems of judicial review share a number of fundamental legal-technical characteristics distinguishing them from such specialised constitutional courts that have emerged in many countries around the world since the end of the Second World War (with their Kelsen-inspired precedents in Central Europe after the first World War).

A first key element has already been established by our previous remarks: no specialised court for constitutional affairs exists in the Nordic states. No recruitment procedures have been established with the aim of selecting some of, or all, the judges among people with expertise in and/or experience of constitutional issues. Moreover, no general procedure applies for dealing with constitutional affairs. Instead, questions regarding the constitutionality of legislative enactments appear as integral parts of ordinary civil or penal litigation (in all five Nordic states) or according to administrative law procedures (in Sweden and Finland).

In this way, constitutional questions appearing in a case that they have to adjudicate upon will need to be tackled by any judge to which that case is presented. In fact, the supreme instance available does not have a monopoly to adjudicate on such matters; in opposition to systems with specialised constitutional courts, then, we may talk about decentralised systems of judicial review. But any question related to constitutional law that appears to be a serious one (or where the lower instance rules against the state) is likely to be adjudicated by the relevant Supreme Court by way of appeal. In itself, this fact suffices as a justification for concentrating on the role of the Supreme Courts in the way we do in this chapter.

In order to understand the functioning of these systems, it is important to see that the control exercised by Nordic courts is by necessity concrete: it is activated when a point of constitutional law is called upon in support of or against the position of the parties in a court case. The constitution counting as positive law, the relevant question must be answered to the extent and insofar as necessary to resolve the case. But in cases where the court finds one or more provisions unconstitutional as actually applied, the formal validity of those provisions is not affected, as is the case in systems of abstract review (which is normally vested in specialised constitutional courts).

By virtue of the comparatively weak doctrine of precedent applicable in the different Nordic countries, a clear ratio decidendi issued by a supreme court regarding the constitutionality of a statutory norm is likely to have a bearing not only between the parties to the case, but also regarding future cases. In fact, a statute deemed to be unconstitutional would normally be amended according to ordinary legislative procedure insofar as necessary in order to give the court's understanding of the Constitution effect beyond the individual case that is formally resolved. In systems of concrete control, however, it is perfectly conceivable that no such follow-up is needed. This may be so in cases where the situation of the party who has been found to be a victim of unconstitutional acts or omissions deviates from what might be seen as the 'normal' situation according to the relevant piece of legislation. In such situations, the statute may remain unaltered insofar as it is interpreted in conformity with the judicial dictum.

Unlike in most systems with specialised constitutional courts and/or procedures, judicial review in the Nordic legal systems is possible only when a statute has been applied in a manner presumed to be unconstitutional or when a similar situation may be imminent (*ex post*). Formally, it is not the constitutionality of the legislative norm as such, but of the way in which it has been applied in the individual case that is at stake. Only legal persons with a sufficient interest (standing) related to the relevant case may sue (or defend themselves in cases of criminal law).

In situations where the facts of the case seem to be situated at the core of the contested provisions, the real issue might nevertheless be about the fate of the legislative provision itself. If applying it to these parties would be unconstitutional, it is hard to see how it could be upheld as a part of the country's legislation at all. But even in such situations, a Nordic court could never declare a piece of parliamentary legislation null and void. In systems of concrete review *ex post*, the conclusions remain formally binding only for the parties to the case.

In systems of concrete *ex post* review, court cases are most likely to raise questions about the presumed violation of constitutional rights. Most of the jurisprudence actually reflects this observation. But insofar as basic requirements of standing are fulfilled, even questions of an institutional or procedural nature may be brought up.

A number of examples not directly related to rights may be mentioned, including the only case where the Supreme Court of Denmark has refused to apply statutory provisions due to unconstitutionality (U 1999.841 H, Tvind); this case dealt with the legislative power's violation of the tripartite separation of powers under Article 3 of the Constitution. In Iceland, the Supreme Court equally found that granting the power to annul final judgments to an administrative committee on the reopening of cases violated an identical provision in Article 2 on the constitutional separation of powers (H 628/2015). One of the Norwegian signal cases from 2010 (Rt 2010, p 535) was really about the legislative power to dispose of historically determined church property for purposes other than those covered by the (admittedly somewhat archaic) purposes laid down by a constitutional clause that had remained unaltered since 1814, whereas previous cases have dealt with private parties' obligations to pay taxes fixed by the executive power in situations where it was argued that the relevant power belonged to Parliament alone (see, for instance, Rt 1952, p 1089).

In the same direction, it is even worth mentioning that the frequent adjudication on the basis of a presumed lack of a statutory basis for given executive actions is necessarily of a procedural nature. The constitutional problem that might occur in this sense could be remedied through proper legislative action insofar as no substantive right is threatened.

So far, we have only addressed the question of whether the judiciary enjoys the power to review the constitutionality of ordinary legislation. The question of whether they even have an obligation to do so is a different one. In a certain sense, a positive answer might appear to be self-evident once the status of the constitution as positive law is established.

Today all the five Nordic judiciaries are supposed to be obliged, and not only empowered, to carry out such a review. The existence of an obligation to review has been made explicit by Article 89 of the Constitution of Norway (2015), whereas Article 70 of the Constitution of Iceland, read in conjunction with Article 6 ECHR (without the limitation to 'civil' law cases), is understood as having a similar meaning. Without explicit support in the constitutional texts, the answer now seems to be the same in the three other states as well. But this point of departure does not stand in the way of judges being more or less keen to uncover problems of a constitutional nature not bought forward by the relevant parties.

Historically, however, the answer has sometimes been controversial, at least to the extent that it has been linked to the slightly different question of knowing whether the judge should limit himself to review on the basis of constitutional arguments set forth by the parties or should even review on the ground of constitutional intricacies discovered by the court itself. In Sweden, first of all, the tendency used to be to insist on the necessity of the courts to proceed on constitutional grounds only insofar as required by the relevant parties.

IV. Recent Developments

A. Introduction

In combination with the generalised recourse to ordinary judicial procedures, the complete absence of judicial recruitment with a particular eye on the function of adjudicating issues related to constitutional law would normally induce the adoption of a relative discrete role for Nordic judges when acting as constitutional judges compared to the role often played by specialised constitutional courts in many countries. Such observations go hand in hand with the general pattern that the constitutional history of the Nordic countries reflects widespread scepticism towards the role of the courts in constitutional matters. Even in Norway, the idea about majority rule by Parliament as more 'democratic' than judicial review has prevailed during important periods of modern history.

Globally, this state of mind is reflected in the way in which systems of judicial review of legislation have emerged or are introduced by constitutional amendment. In general, this assumption also seems to fit well with the reality as shown by the jurisprudence of the seven supreme judicial instances empowered to review the constitutionality of legislation.

However, during the last few decades, a change in judicial attitudes towards the task of reviewing legislation seems to have occurred. At least partly, this change may be understood as domestic adjustments in response to the growing influence of international instruments of human rights, primarily the ECHR and the Strasbourg Court (see section V). In fact, parts of the jurisprudence of the Supreme Courts regarding the constitutionality of legislative enactments seem to reflect a move towards more self-confidence within the judiciary. Sooner or later, all of them may have asked themselves why they should be so reluctant when reviewing the constitutionality of political action in an era when reviewing legislation on behalf of international public law, namely EU and ECHR law, has become increasingly frequent.

Historically as well as today, important differences nevertheless exist between the five states in the field of constitutional jurisprudence. But before embarking on the different national experiences, a few remarks of a more general character may be useful. First, it should be recalled that a high number of judicial interventions in the field of constitutional law do not necessarily indicate that the relevant constitution is successful. In fact, it may even point in the opposite direction: in stable and well-governed societies like the five Nordic states, it might be better to avoid litigation about constitutional items through mechanisms for the proper preparation of legislative bills. The comparatively successful Nordic societies were not created by the judiciary acting as constitutional judges, but by genuine political action that primarily has had recourse to measures of a legislative and administrative nature.

When it comes to the preparation of legislation, however, there are important differences between the Eastern and Western Nordic countries. The existence or not of systems of *ex ante* review independent of the executive power is particularly striking.

In Finland, it is not possible to understand the system for avoiding unconstitutional legislation or legislation that unduly infringes upon rights without taking into account the abstract *ex ante* review carried out under the responsibility of the Constitutional Law Committee of Parliament, which is regularly assisted by external experts in the field of law and other matters in a way that is likely to ensure that narrow partisan political considerations are kept at a distance (see further Chapter 4). In Sweden, the independent 'Legislative Council', staffed with members (or retired members) of the two Supreme Courts, plays an important role in reviewing upcoming legislation.

No similar institutions exist in the three Western Nordic states. This does not in itself signify that legislative bills are necessarily of a low quality when it comes to their relationship with possibly conflicting and/or overarching legal norms; on the contrary, the quality of the relevant legislative departments is generally acknowledged. In given situations, however, both their closeness to the political leadership and their position within the ministerial administration may influence the degree of attention paid by the legislative departments to the strictly legal, as opposed to political, aspects of upcoming legislative bills. This contributes to explaining why discussion about institutional reform at this point reappears from time to time. But it remains the case that such discussions have never taken solid root.

In a different direction, it may be worthwhile noting that systems of concrete judicial review—ie, review of how the relevant legislation is applied in individual cases, not of the legislation itself—do not produce formal conclusions about the presence or otherwise of unconstitutional conduct. The view of the relevant court about the constitutional questions at stake only appears in the reasoning underpinning the formal conclusion. The answer may nevertheless appear with all possible clarity (some of the recent Norwegian cases provide examples), but this is not always so. A court may find its way between 'yes' and 'no' by preferring different techniques of 'interpretation'. On the one hand, it may prefer a restrictive interpretation of the legislation in such a way as to create harmony while ensuring respect for the constitution; the Norwegian case reported in Rt 1976, p 1 (see below) provides a clear example. But harmony may even be obtained by a restrictive interpretation of the constitution in such a way as to ensure increased leeway for the legislative power without openly disregarding the constitution; such examples may be found from all the five Nordic legal systems.

B. The Eastern States

In Sweden, the general system of judicial review of public enactments on behalf of superior law at several levels now enshrined in the text of the Instrument of Government seems firmly established in the jurisprudence of the Supreme Courts. Jurisprudence reviewing administrative enactments is frequent and such acts are sometimes set aside because they conflict with legal norms of a higher formal mark. When it comes to judicial review of legislation, the situation is quite different,[9] and there are few such examples. In fact, what seems to be the first example of clear non-application of a statutory provision by the Supreme Court took place well before the judiciary was enfranchised from the constitutional clause on 'evident' violation (since 2010): A tax law could not be applied during a short transitional period (NJA 2000, p 132, Falk). But the case is far from being spectacular; the provision itself was not found unconstitutional, and it seems as if the outcome of the individual case could reasonably have been achieved through interpretation of the relevant provision in light of the constitutional ban on retroactivity.

The revised clause does not seem to have produced any kind of explosion in the number of Supreme Court cases on legislation being unconstitutional. In fact, the only case where a court has refused to apply a statutory provision on the ground of it being unconstitutional seems to be a judgment handed out by an administrative court of appeals in a case concerning sterilisation as a mandatory requirement for a sex change (judgment of 19 December 2012, unreported); the constitutional provision at stake (Article 6 in Chapter 2 on rights) was read in junction with Article 8 ECHR.

This state of affairs may be seen as a reflection of judicial self-restraint on behalf of ideology or tradition. But it might also reflect the generally high quality of legislation. In this respect, the well-established *ex ante* review by the 'Legislative Council' deserves mention as a mechanism that is likely to contribute to enhancing the quality of draft legislation.

After the introduction of judicial review of legislation by the explicit provision in the new Constitution of Finland, the development in this field for the two-tiered judiciary has not been dramatic.[10] When we notice both the Constitution's rather restrictive formula and the traditional absence of the judiciary in constitutional matters, this does not appear to be surprising.

First of all, however, the situation must be understood in light of the importance of the system of *ex ante* review of legislation carried out under the auspices of Parliament's Constitutional Law Committee (see section IV) within the Finnish

[9] On recent jurisprudence in the Swedish system, see, eg, K Åhman, *Normprövning: Domstols kontroll av svensk lags förenlighet med regeringsformen och europarätten 2000–2010* (Stockholm, Norstedts Juridik, 2011).

[10] On the Finnish system, see, eg, Lavapuro et al (n 2).

system of government. To the extent that this system contributes to enhancing the quality of current legislation vis-a-vis the Constitution and Finland's international obligations, it may in itself reduce the space for litigation. But there seems to be more to it than just a causal effect: when judicial review was introduced, Parliament made it clear that the courts, when handling pieces of legislation that have already been dealt with by the Constitutional Law Committee, shall take due notice of its opinion and shall normally presume that provisions having passed the *ex ante* test are within the limits of the Constitution. In other words, the review by the parliamentary committee should remain the primary review mechanism, in the sense that courts should intervene only in concrete cases where the legislation is applied in a way that is in evident conflict with the Constitution.

This point of departure fits well with a few cases where the two apex courts have nevertheless found unconstitutionality. Most of them deal with questions regarding double jeopardy (*ne bis in idem*) at points where the Constitutional Law Committee had expressed itself in ways that were found to be inconsistent, in one instance by even explicitly referring the solution to the judiciary. In 2010–11, the two supreme courts of the land adopted different conclusions in a way that did not immediately clarify the law in a field that has admittedly caused some headaches among judges in several countries struggling to follow (or to predict) the jurisprudence of the European Court of Human Rights.[11]

The only case that seems to deviate from this pattern is a plenary judgment by the Supreme Court of Finland on the right to private life under Article 10 of the Constitution understood in light of ECtHR jurisprudence under Article 8 (KKO 2012:11). The relevant act was found to be in manifest conflict with the Constitution.[12]

C. The Western States

In Denmark, the assumption that the Supreme Court remains relatively discrete regarding the constitutionality of legislation seems to be confirmed when it comes to rulings on substantive issues. As a matter of fact, the 'Tvind' case (1999; see above) on the separation of powers remains the only one where the Supreme Court has found statutory provisions unconstitutional.

However, this does not imply that the Constitution's status as positive law or the existence of judicial review has been seriously questioned. If need be, a Supreme Court case from 2008 provides eloquent testimony (U 2008.278H): whereas a minority of four judges found that the contested legislation contradicted the Constitution's provision on property (Article 73), the majority (five out of nine)—leaning towards the Court's own jurisprudence from the 1920s—concluded that

[11] See further ibid 233f.
[12] See further ibid 523–24.

the claim of unconstitutionality was not established to the degree of certainty required for similar conclusions.

When it comes to the conditions for obtaining judicial review, on the other hand, recent years have produced some interesting, rather bold cases. The jurisprudence at this point deserves attention even if the relevant cases do not directly regard legislation, but rather acts of government on issues that have been the subject of much discussion in national politics.

The leading case appeared when 11 'ordinary citizens' sought standing against the Prime Minister for having violated the Constitution when deciding upon Danish acceptance of the Maastricht Treaty on the European Union (U 1996.1300H). The claimants were not concerned by the governmental action in any other way than any Danish citizen, but were nevertheless granted standing. For the Supreme Court, the key argument in favour of opening up the courtroom was the treaty's strong general impact on the lives of the Danes. In this way, the Court clearly deviated from the precondition for litigation normally in use.

Fifteen years later, the Maastricht precedent was followed in a case on the constitutionality of the Danish accession to the Lisbon Treaty (U 2011.984H). Opening up access to the court in this way, the Supreme Court acted in a manner closer to a constitutional court accustomed to cases of abstract review of legislation than to a court operating within a judicial system focusing on concrete review of the application of the relevant statutory provision.

In the meantime, the Supreme Court had refused to follow the same path regarding the conditions for standing in a case on the Schengen Agreement (U 2001.2065H). The underlying argument was nevertheless confirmed, as the substantive reasoning was similar to that already adopted in the Maastricht case. The difference was only that the impact of the Schengen Agreement on the Danish population in general was not significant enough to justify a similar deviation from the ordinary criteria of standing.

Standing was refused even in 2010 in a case concerning abstract review of the decision to engage Denmark in the war on Iraq. This time, the Supreme Court used the fact that the war had no particular bearing on the litigants as compared to other citizens as the main argument for refusing to hear the case (U 2010.1547H). But the purity of the argument was somewhat blurred by the inclusion of remarks on the constitutional questions at stake, actually concluding that no violation had occurred. In this way, the 2010 case may be read in support both of the conventional 'legal interest' doctrine on standing and of the opposite.

When the Maastricht decision was handed down (1996), the Supreme Court had already deviated from the normal requirements for standing (U 1994.29H), but in a different way: two MPs had lost a parliamentary vote on the privatisation of a state-owned insurance institute to which they were opposed on the ground that the measure would contradict a constitutional provision. They then sued the government, but did not claim that they were affected by the privatisation in ways that were different from any other Danish citizen. In its justification for allowing the case to be heard by the judiciary, the Supreme Court, interestingly enough, called upon the minority's interest in having the constitutional question tested as the main argument for granting standing. In this way, a jurisprudential norm was established according to which a parliamentary minority has the right to have its constitutional concern during the legislative process investigated by the judiciary (although the possibility has not been used since 1994). How could one avoid comparing with the right enjoyed by parliamentary minorities to having the constitutionality of majority legislation tested in systems where a specialised constitutional court is the apex instance in constitutional matters?

The striking boldness manifested by the Danish Supreme Court regarding the conditions for standing in a few cases spreading over nearly 20 years certainly merits attention. But so does even the fact that in none of these cases has the judiciary found in favour of the litigants on the merits of the case.

Further to the West, Icelandic constitutional jurisprudence confirms a level of activity far beyond what is typical among the Nordic states—activity uncontestably sparked by the adoption of an extended bill of constitutional rights (1995). However, applying the regular strict criteria of standing, in 1994 the Supreme Court rejected (H 1994:1451) the claims of an individual who requested that the Convention on the European Economic Area (the EEA Agreement) should be declared unconstitutional due to a lack of standing on the issue.

According to Icelandic observers, the Supreme Court has found the application of pieces of legislation to be materially in conflict with a human rights provision in the Constitution in 12 cases between 1995 and 2015.[13] In addition, the Court has concluded several times that a piece of legislation violated the principle of separation of powers in Article 2 (as discussed above in section III).

The jurisprudence covers a number of issues, including the freedom of expression, equality and criminal procedure. In most of them, the constitutional provisions at stake are read in conjunction with the corresponding provisions in the ECHR. In a case regarding social security (H 2000:4480), for instance, the majority in the Supreme Court explicitly referred to the need to evaluate the contested pieces of legislation in light of the Constitution and concluded on their unconstitutionality on the grounds of equality and the right to social assistance. Shortly afterwards, it called upon the Constitution's provision on the freedom of information when ordering that an association of pensioners should have access to a governmental memo on the consequences to be drawn from a previous case (H 2002:1024).

In a case relating to a presumed father's right to have his status as the father of a child born out of wedlock decided by a court against the will of the mother, the Supreme Court leaned towards the Constitution when accepting the father's

[13] For an oversight, see B Thorarensen, 'Judicial Control over the Legislature: Different Trends in Icelandic and Danish Practice' in B Dahl et al (eds), *Festskrift til Jens Peter Christensen* (Copenhagen, Jurist- og Økonomforbundets Forlag, 2016) 709–29, 722f.

standing, an outcome contrary to an explicit provision in the relevant statute (H 2000:4394). Two years later (H 2003:2329), the majority found the application of a statutory provisions on taxation to be in violation of the Constitution's ban on retroactivity. In H 2002:3686, the Supreme Court refused to give a legislative ban on strikes effect on three labour unions for which the reasons underpinning the ban were not sufficient to outweigh the constitutionally guaranteed freedoms of association and of negotiating wages.

Finally, a case where the majority of the Supreme Court found the application of new tax legislation contrary to the ban on retroactive taxation according to Article 77(2) of the Constitution (H 2003:2329) deserves mention. In other cases (such as H No 274/2010 of 25 November 2010 and H No 600/2011 of 15 February 2012), the Court has confirmed that retroactive legislation interfering with property rights may under certain condition violate the right to property under Article 72.

In the Nordic context, the recent jurisprudence by the Supreme Court of Iceland has produced an exceptional number of cases concluding by the non-application of statutory law due to unconstitutionality. Besides, a number of cases where the Supreme Court found the opposite way clearly confirm the basic assumption about the Constitution as positive law. Most strikingly, this happened in as many as 11 judgments handed down in October 2011 regarding certain aspects of the legislation adopted in order to react to the collapse of the Icelandic banks and the extraordinary situation facing the financial market in the autumn of 2008. By acting in this way, the Supreme Court underpinned the need to give more extensive leeway to the political branches of government in situations of national crisis than would be the case under normal circumstances.

For a long time, quite a few Icelandic Supreme Court cases have been characterised by rather short reasoning on the constitutional issues at stake, while instead insisting on the factual aspects of the case. This tendency may be regarded as a reflection of the similar tradition cultivated by the 'mother' Supreme Court in Copenhagen. After 1995, however, the jurisprudence shows important signs of a shift in judicial attitudes.

The development might be understood as a somewhat discouraging sign of deficient quality in the preparation of legislation in a system with no independent abstract *ex ante* review similar to those found in Sweden and Finland. But at least in some cases, it is conceivable that the problem does not lie in bad legislation, but in deficient administrative action when applying the legislation to everyday life.

The Danish-Icelandic pattern of succinct reasons is far less apparent in Norway. Departing from the judges' obligation to vote individually and to outline the grounds for the outcome as imposed by statute in 1863, the Supreme Court has instead developed a tradition for lengthy opinions. Cases raising constitutional questions of some importance would normally count among those where the judges claim considerable space for their argument. When we add the fact that such cases are often heard in plenary (by a maximum of 19 judges) and that dissenting opinions are not infrequent, this tendency becomes even more apparent.

A case concerning the meaning of the constitutional requirement of 'full compensation' when property is taken (expropriation) is arguably the first case since the end of the Second World War where the Supreme Court refused to apply a statutory provision (Rt 1976, p 1, Kløfta). Seeking to reduce the level of compensation compared to the level developed by the judiciary acting directly by virtue of the constitutional clause, the relevant provision was at the political core of the statute itself and had been heatedly debated. Dispute followed the case all the way to the Supreme Court itself, where it was decided under strong dissent. Moreover, the outcome was presented as the result of constitutional-conform interpretation, not as a case where the statutory provision was openly unconstitutional.

Both the majority and the minority within the Court introduced a doctrine about setting aside Parliament's own interpretation of the Constitution, while adopting the statute only when this understanding goes beyond the scope of 'reasonable doubt'. Even if the majority chose an interpretation different from that retained by the majority in Parliament, it thus seems to have endorsed the prevailing opinion that judicial review of majority decisions by Parliament is problematic in a democratic system of government. In fact, leading scholars had recently predicted that judicial review was unlikely to ever being used again by the Norwegian courts for setting aside parliamentary legislation.

In a number of later plenary cases, this doctrine has been reiterated in the obiter part of the opinions. Gradually, however, it has become evident that this happens more as lip service to tradition than as a real fetter on the Court's attitude in matters of constitutional law. In any event, no similar self-restraint has been observed in the jurisprudence of the Supreme Court regarding the relationship between national legislation and international public law, in particular in the fields of human rights and EEA law, where it has developed a rather active review profile. Why then should the national judiciary be more reluctant when reviewing national legislation on behalf of the nation's own constitution?

After a number of precursors, including a 2007 case on property rights (Rt 2007, p 1308), the shift in judicial attitude towards constitutional adjudication strikingly appeared in three plenary cases in 2010. The two first (Rt 2010, p 143, Rt 2010, p 535) emerged from legislation adopted under sharp political dissent, while the third (Rt 2010, p 1445) arose from a provision adopted by a quasi-unanimous Parliament. In all three cases, the relevant provisions had been adopted after extensive debate over their constitutionality; as a consequence, they were all accompanied by thorough legal justification by Parliament. Moreover, all of them were handed down following more or less sharp dissent and invariably indicate that the contested provision were 'clearly' unconstitutional; the more cautious 're-interpretation' mode adopted back in 1976 seems far away.

The three judgments concern rather different fields of law. In Rt 2010, p 143, the key issue was the retroactive character of new legislation regarding a part of the taxation scheme for shipowners, with comparatively huge financial consequences for a limited group of shipowners or, alternatively, for the state. In Rt 2010, p 535, the Court was faced with legislation that sought to impose the idea that parts of the funds allotted to church affairs could be used in a way deviating from those admitted by a separate constitutional clause that had been left unaltered since 1814. Rt 2010, p 1445 dealt with the question of retroactivity of penal legislation on war crimes and crimes against humanity in a case against a person who had participated in war-like activities in Yugoslavia in the early 1990s. No argument concerning certain rights of freedoms enjoying better protection than others stood in the way of the Court's explicit striking down of the relevant pieces of legislation.

Later on, a more self-confident attitude seems to prevail, but not without sometimes apparent tendencies of tensions within the Supreme Court itself about which attitude to adopt. Such tensions also appear in some of the cases adjudicated after the insertion in 2014 of an extended bill of human rights in a new Chapter E of the Constitution of Norway. All agree that the new provisions should be used as positive law. But tensions seem to occur in relation to the question of whether the Court should take as its point of departure the applicable legislation and correct the outcome insofar as necessary for not violating the Constitution or whether it should take the new constitutional provisions as the legal position from which the concrete outcomes should be derived. For a telling example, see Rt 1015, p 93 (Maria) on the expulsion of a woman whose small daughter had obtained Norwegian citizenship.

It is well known, of course, that those who reason by way of 'principle' are likely to carve more room for their own appreciation of the proper outcome of the case than judges who base their reasoning on the applicable pieces of legislation, which is the approach that traditionally would have been chosen. For that reason alone, the two alternatives reflect different conceptions of the proper role of the judiciary in a democratic system of government.

The way in which one positions oneself on the scale between 'principle' and 'statute' may even be reflected in the weight that individual judges tend to allot to clarifying the law or to 'developing' it, a task that the Supreme Court of Norway has now adopted as its main 'purpose'. As interpretation by necessity commands a minimum level of creative activity, the distinction is not entirely clear. However, the more jurisprudential 'developing' of the law is stressed as an autonomous or even primary task for the judiciary, the more it takes upon itself a function that is eminently political *lato sensu*.

Along a number of parameters, we thus see that Norway confirms its particularity among the Nordic states in the field of judicial review of legislation. Parts of the recent development in and around the Supreme Court have actually sparked debate about individual cases or about the appropriateness of different attitudes towards the task of judicial review that may be discerned within the Court. Even the question of knowing if the strict 'apolitical' procedures nowadays applied for selecting new judges may be justified in a situation where the Supreme Court seems on its way to cultivate a more active political role needs to be asked.

V. The Constitution and International Law

In twenty-first-century Europe, national systems of judicial review can no longer be examined while ignoring the fact that the national judiciaries are increasingly called upon to review domestic legislation on behalf of international instruments by which the relevant state is bound.

When it comes to the position of international law in the domestic legal system, the Nordic countries adhere to a dualistic approach. But within the boundaries of this principle, the 'presumption' has grown strong that unless otherwise established, domestic legislation has not been drafted with the aim of violating the state's international obligations. More often than not, adherence to this 'presumption principle' is likely to avoid situations where the court would have to apply domestic provisions in conflict with a treaty obligation.

The dualistic approach has even formally been transgressed within the framework of EU membership of three of the five states (Denmark, Finland and Sweden), as well as in practice, although according to other techniques, by the two Nordic EEA states (Norway and Iceland). This clearly influences even judicial behaviour (see further Chapter 7). In fact, cases regarding the conformity of national law with EU/EEA and ECHR law tend to appear more frequently on the desk of the relevant Supreme Court than cases regarding the relationship between statutory law and the national constitution. As a consequence, the application of European law as a part of national law seems to have given an important impetus to the judiciary when facing cases of presumed conflict between statute and superior law at the national level. This effect should not be underestimated by those who want to understand the spread of judicial review not only in the states historically most resistant to the idea of judicial review (like Sweden and Finland), but even in those where judicial review is more deeply rooted.

On the position of international human rights in the Nordic domestic systems, see Chapter 6. In the following, we satisfy ourselves with a somewhat closer look at the role of ECHR law at points where it might work in tandem with the domestic constitution. It is important to recall that the subject matter in general includes much more than the position of ECHR law. However, practical reasons in combination with the existence of a strong international court at the European level command limiting the following remarks to this part of the matter only.

It is the domestic constitution that authorises the government to adhere to international obligations on behalf of the state. The legal point of departure must therefore be that the constitution is to be autonomously interpreted, that is, according to its own text and other relevant sources.

This approach has been used by the Supreme Court of Norway ever since ECHR law started to make its appearance in domestic jurisprudence; this had already been the case since the 1960s, but became increasingly so towards the end of the twentieth century. The reasoning in cases where both the constitution and ECHR law were invoked would typically address the constitutional point, followed by the ECHR argument insofar as necessary because the relevant party did not get satisfaction on constitutional grounds.

The Danish Supreme Court maintains a similar position on behalf of a constitution with few fundamental rights and no additions since 1953. The Norwegian judiciary is likely to do the same when dealing with rights inherited from 1814 (with a few later additions). But since 2014, Norway, like its other three neighbours, has had an updated constitutional rights catalogue. These four countries also have in common that their respective catalogues (or at least the recent additions to them, as in Norway) are heavily inspired by the ECHR (and some other instruments). To some extent, as in Norway, the new rights are generally framed as abbreviated versions of the relevant ECHR provisions.

As we have already seen, the striking developments in Icelandic jurisprudence regarding rights since the 1995 Constitution cannot be understood without taking the strong international influence or, rather, the Supreme Court's willingness to lean towards it into account.

Gradually developing from a much more reluctant past, Swedish and Finnish case law show a growing awareness about the question of knowing how to accommodate the ECHR and the jurisprudence of the ECtHR into the jurisprudence of the relevant judiciaries. In Finland, this has occurred in cases of doubt as to what might happen next in the jurisprudence of the European Court (as regards the *ne bis in idem* dilemmas in the field of administrative sanctions already mentioned above).

Almost immediately after the constitutional amendments in May 2014, the Norwegian Supreme Court started developing its own jurisprudence by adhering to a seemingly firm schema: the relevant constitutional provision is mentioned first. But the bulk of the argument that immediately follows almost invariably addresses the parallel ECHR provision and the way it has been handled by the ECtHR (or what might follow once a similar yet unsolved question is brought to Strasbourg).

This development may give rise to some intriguing paradoxes. The first one would recall the fact that in principle at least, the inter-European protection of human rights is meant to be a minimum level of protection that may be supplemented by more favourable protection at home (cf. Article 53 on the relationship with existing domestic rights). In practice, however, the standards seem effectively applied in domestic law in a way rarely going beyond the minimum level of protection required. Thus, in a sense, they tend to be used as if they indicate the maximum level the state is supposed to observe.

Another paradox is likely to appear over time, at points where the jurisprudence of the ECtHR develops further towards a more demanding level of protection. If the national judiciary follows, this would effectively end by giving the final word on the meaning of the national constitution to the ECtHR in what might be called a supranational way. This is a solution that none of the relevant states has actually authorised, at least explicitly, by constitutional amendment. But if the national judiciary does not follow this up, the Constitution might again gradually fade away as the apex instrument for human rights protection in the relevant state.

At a somewhat abstract level, the Supreme Court of Norway has addressed this dilemma in one of its first cases in the field after the adoption of the revised Bill of Rights in 2014 (Rt 2015, p 93, Maria). The unanimous chamber sets out by observing the clear resemblance between the relevant constitutional provision (on the right to family life) and Article 8 ECHR (and Article 17 of the UN Covenant on Civil and Political Rights). This observation is used as the basis for declaring that the constitutional provision should be interpreted 'in light of' its international models. On the other side, however, future ECtHR jurisprudence would not carry the same weight as case law preceding the adoption of the relevant constitutional provision. Then follows a self-confident statement about who has the last word in constitutional interpretation: 'According to the Constitution, the Supreme Court [of Norway], not the international institutions charged with supervising the respect for the international instruments, has the responsibility for interpreting, clarifying and developing the Constitution's provisions on human rights.'

It is reasonable to suppose that this basic approach might have been subscribed to by the neighbouring state courts as well. But it is unlikely to answer the abovementioned paradoxes. And should the statement about the Supreme Court's obligation to 'develop' the meaning of the Constitution's provisions on human rights come into life, it would be likely to revive the fundamental discussion about which courts, and what kinds of recruitment criteria, are best suited for taking charge of tasks that, in other countries, are invariably vested in genuine constitutional courts or in courts whose members are not appointed on legal-technical grounds only.

VI. Concluding Remarks

The comparison between the institutional and practical aspect of judicial review of legislation in the five Nordic countries has testified to a development that started two centuries ago, but even about important differences both in the way in which the relevant systems have developed and their present status. It is true that the impact of international instruments like the ECHR, and EU and EEA law in these last few decades is visible in all of them. But so far, the outcome does not show a striking degree of homogeneity across the borders. On the contrary, recent jurisprudence shows sometimes clear examples of how the national apex courts have made use of (or have exploited) such instruments in different ways.

To a large degree, it seems reasonable to assume that these differences reflect differences in the history of the relevant constitutional systems, not only interacting with but presumably also contributing to maintaining different patterns of thought in the respective legal-political communities. At the core of such differences, the different roles played by the national constitutions may be recalled.

In the East, Sweden maintains the name of its main institutional 'constitutional law', namely the 'Instrument of Government' (Regeringsformen), a text that contains many details and is frequently amended in a way that leaves little leeway for judicial creativity; even the 'evidence' requirement for setting aside legislation and governmental decrees was retained until quite recently. In Finland, a similar requirement was adopted as a part of a constitutional reform in principle opening up for judicial review; moreover, the quite particular system of abstract preview in the hands of a commission within Parliament (the Constitutional Law Committee) contributes to keeping the judiciary in a secondary role in the field of constitutional review and interpretation.

In the West, Denmark and Iceland (before the 1990s) maintained a relative standstill in terms of their constitutional text, thereby contributing to a certain marginalisation of the constitution as a political instrument in some of the fields most relevant for judicial action. Later on, Iceland has clearly departed from this line, namely in the field of human rights, and a series of crises has contributed to sparking a more active attitude from the Supreme Court. Even international (namely ECHR) influences have been increasingly visible in the development of domestic jurisprudence. The same goes for Norway, actually the only one of the five Nordic countries to have a constitution that seems to enjoy a high positive value as a symbol and where the present system of judicial review has comparatively very old roots.

In this way, many differences between East and West as well as between the individual Nordic countries may be observed. Across the different divides, however, the solidly embedded tradition that the political branches of government are at the head seems to survive. In this way, the inherited heavy emphasis on ordinary legislation, not jurisprudence, as the primary tool for political action or change is far from having perished. In terms of this pattern at least, a kind of Nordic political community remains strong.

6

Human Rights in Nordic Constitutions and the Impact of International Obligations

TUOMAS OJANEN

I. Introduction

The main aims of this chapter are twofold. First, the aim is to examine the Nordic constitutional systems for the protection of human rights (or constitutional rights or fundamental rights, whatever the terminology used in a given Nordic constitution). While the primary focus will be on the current state of evolution, several historical observations will also be made, especially for the purposes of illustrating the relatively rapid and profound constitutional transformations that have taken place in the field of constitutional protection of human rights in all five Nordic countries since the early 1990s onwards.

Aside from exploring human rights in light of the written provisions of the Nordic Constitutions, the focus will be on those constitutional doctrines and principles that underpin and condition the Nordic constitutional systems for the protection of human rights. However, it will follow from the inevitable incompleteness of all efforts of comparative constitutional law that several important issues pertaining to human rights will remain at least under-analysed, if not unexplored altogether. In particular, the content of individual human rights will fall outside the scope of this chapter, and one will also look in vain for a detailed account of the substantial human rights record, both in a positive and a negative sense, of the Nordic countries. Since other chapters in this book deal with such issues as judicial review and the division of powers in general, institutional arrangements and mechanisms of human rights protection and promotion will be dealt with in broad outline only.

Second, this chapter will deal with the relationship between the constitutional and international protection of human rights. It should be emphasised from the very outset that the European Convention on Human Rights (ECHR) and other international human rights treaties, including case law from the European Court of Human Rights (ECtHR) and other treaty bodies of international human rights treaties, have significantly shaped the Nordic domestic systems of human rights protection and promotion in recent decades. Hence, this chapter will deal with such issues as the domestic status and effects of international human rights norms in the Nordic legal orders. In addition, the impact of membership of the European Union (EU) and of the European Economic Area (EEA) will be covered, not least because most recent constitutional dynamics in the area of rights protection can be traced back to the ways in which EU or EEA law has affected domestic interpretations or doctrines pertaining to human rights. Ultimately, the most bewildering constitutional dynamics can be traced back to the ways in which interaction between international human rights treaties, EU law and EEA law, and domestic systems of rights protection have stimulated and reinforced the changes regarding human rights.

The reader is reminded that the protection and promotion of human rights depend on much more than simply human rights provisions of the Nordic constitutions or international human rights treaties. What eventually matters is how Nordic legislators, administrative organs and courts *de facto* respect, promote and enforce human rights in their decision-making. In this regard, today there is already an embarrassment of riches insofar as human rights case law by the Nordic courts is concerned. As it would be mission impossible to start discussing individual judgments by the Nordic courts even in broad outline in this chapter, the focus will instead be on those more encompassing patterns and trends that emerge from the case law of the Nordic courts.

This chapter is structured as follows: Section II will include general observations on the protection of human rights in the Nordic countries for the purpose of placing the topic within its broader historical and constitutional context. In particular, this section calls attention to certain idiosyncrasies and dualities that characterise the Nordic constitutional systems for the protection of human rights. Section III will deal with such issues as the sources of rights and major constitutional doctrines and principles shaping and directing the protection of human rights, including the domestic mechanisms of rights protection and promotion, in the Nordic countries. Section IV shifts the focus on to international human rights treaties and, accordingly, takes stock of the domestic validity, status and effects of international human rights treaties in the Nordic legal orders. This section will also outline the major effects of EU and EEA membership on the Nordic protection of human rights. Section V will provide a brief conclusion.

Finally, two important conceptual comments must be made. The first relates to the term 'human rights' in this chapter and the volume in general. The terms 'constitutional rights', 'fundamental rights' and 'basic rights' are often used interchangeably in European and Nordic constitutional discourse to refer to rights enshrined in the domestic constitutions. The term 'human rights', in turn, is typically used in international law to denote rights guaranteed by international human rights treaties such as the ECHR or the International Covenant on Civil and Political

Rights (ICCPR). However, in this chapter (and the volume in general), the concept of human rights denotes rights enshrined *both* in the domestic constitutions of the five Nordic countries *and* in international human rights treaties binding upon them. It thus follows that ordinary legislation providing in more detail rules on the guarantees of, exercise of or restrictions on human rights falls largely, if not exclusively, outside the scope of the following discussion. Again, therefore, the reader is reminded that ordinary legislation, as well as concrete decisions by courts and administrative authorities, really counts a great deal insofar as the actual protection and promotion of human rights is concerned.

The second terminological observation to be made relates to the term 'incorporation'. Below, this notion is only used for the purpose of referring to the specific method for the domestic implementation of international human rights treaties, according to which a treaty becomes part of domestic law in its original form through an act of parliament or some other form of domestic enactment. Hence, the notion of incorporation does not refer to all methods of implementing human rights treaties in the Nordic countries. As will be discussed in more detail below, Finland has adopted a systematic practice of incorporating the human rights treaties to which it is party into the domestic legal order. The other four Nordic countries, in turn, have traditionally taken advantage of the method of transformation. Accordingly, they have implemented these treaties by enacting domestic legislation for the purpose of achieving normative harmony with the human rights treaty in question.

II. General Observations on the Nordic Constitutional Systems of Rights Protection: Major Idiosyncrasies and Dualities

The Nordic constitutional approach to the protection of human rights can be characterised as ambivalent and even paradoxical. It involves a number of such idiosyncrasies and dualities that challenge certain widely held assumptions about human rights protection, such as the presumption that the effective protection of human rights inevitably requires strong mechanisms of judicial review.

On the one hand, the Nordic countries have a long constitutional history of acknowledging and safeguarding human rights. Human rights have traditionally assumed an important role in the written constitutions of the Nordic countries, in the legal enforcement of the constitution and within the framework of foundational constitutional aims and principles. Gender equality, freedom of expression, access to public documents and transparency in general, as well as such institutional arrangements as the institution of the Ombudsman, are examples of such areas where Nordic countries have carved out a worldwide reputation.

The Nordic constitutions have included provisions or even catalogues on rights from the very outset: the world's second-oldest still standing constitution, the Constitution of Norway adopted on 18 May 1814, already enumerated a range of such rights and freedoms that were regarded as being of particular importance at the time.[1] In Sweden, the constitutional recognition of rights can be traced as far back as the Freedom of the Press Act of 1766, prohibiting censorship and providing access to documents produced by public authorities. Similarly, the Swedish Constitution of 1809 afforded constitutional protection to such rights as the right to a fair trial, the right to property and freedom of religion.[2] The Constitutional Act of the Kingdom of Denmark of 1849 also contained some articles on rights and freedoms, and so did too the first Constitution of Iceland of 1874 and Chapter II of the Constitution Act of 1919 of Finland. As constitutional laws from the period of Swedish rule, enacted in 1772 and 1789, remained in force in Finland up to its independence in 1917 and the enactment of the Constitution Act of 1919, the origins of constitutional protection of human rights in Finland are actually as old as they are in Sweden.[3]

Aside from the constitutional protection of human rights, the Nordic countries have promoted the protection of human rights on European and international levels. Denmark, Norway and Sweden were among the 10 European states that founded the Council of Europe in 1949, and they signed and ratified the ECHR in the early 1950s. Moreover, human rights have traditionally played a prominent role in the foreign policy and European and international cooperation of the Nordic countries. The Finnish Constitution, for instance, provides explicitly in its very first provision that Finland 'participates in international co-operation for the protection of peace and human rights and for the development of society' (section 1, subsection 3).

The ratification record by all five Nordic countries of international human rights treaties stands out by comparative standards. The Nordic countries have signed and ratified almost without exception all human rights treaties adopted by the Council of Europe (CoE), the United Nations (UN) and the International Labour Organization (ILO).[4] By comparative standards, reservations to international human rights treaties by the Nordic countries have also remained relatively minor and small in number; Sweden, for instance, has made a reservation to Article 20 of the ICCPR prohibiting propaganda for war, but the explanation for

[1] M Andenæs and B Eirik, *Menneskerettighetene og oss* (Oslo, Universitetsforlaget, 2012).

[2] J Nergelius, *Constitutional Law in Sweden* (Alphen aan den Rijn, Kluwer Law International, 2015) 99–116.

[3] M Scheinin, 'Finland' in A Weber (ed), *Fundamental Rights in Europe and North America: Part A—Basic Work* (The Hague, Kluwer Law, 2001) 7–9.

[4] The exception is the *ILO Convention* No *169* concerning Indigenous and Tribal Peoples in Independent Countries. While Norway (1990) and Denmark (1996) have ratified this Convention, Finland and Sweden are still struggling to do so, since they have thus far failed to fully resolve the rights of the indigenous Sámi people, particularly insofar as their land rights are concerned. The Sámi live in Norway, Finland, Sweden and Russia, with the majority living in Norway.

this is the traditionally very strong protection of the freedom of the press by the Swedish Constitution.[5]

As Member States of the EU, Denmark, Finland and Sweden have also played an active role in endorsing and promoting such measures or institutional arrangements of fundamental rights protection within the framework of the EU as the creation of the Ombudsman of the European Union and transparency, access to information and good governance. These three Nordic EU Member States have also been active promoters of the accession of the EU to the ECHR; Finland, for instance, proposed a treaty amendment of the founding treaties of the EU in 1999 so as to enable the EU to become a party to the ECHR. Although the Finnish proposal was not adopted, it nonetheless contributed to the European discussion and debate on the issue of the EU's accession to the ECHR.[6] Until the entry into force of the Lisbon Treaty on 1 December 2009, the EU lacked the necessary competence to accede to the ECHR, but the Lisbon Treaty now provides such competence and also commits the EU to accede to the ECHR.

Last but not least, human rights performance by all five Nordic countries stands out compared to that of other countries internationally. Aside from promising a range of rights in their written constitutions and through their international human rights obligations, the Nordic countries tend to be more likely to *de facto* uphold and respect human rights compared to most other countries in Europe or elsewhere in the world. The fact that all five Nordic countries are strong democracies based on the rule of law, as well as being amongst the wealthiest countries in the world, significantly paves the way for their ability to meet their constitutional and international human rights obligations, particularly to the extent that these obligations, such as those pertaining to a right to education or health, entail public expenditure. Similarly, as the Nordic countries are still relatively homogeneous in ethnic, religious and linguistic terms, this fosters their ability to live up to their human rights commitments.

Of course, this is not to imply that the Nordic countries would be without human rights-related problems; judgments by the ECtHR confirming violations of the ECHR by the Nordic countries, alongside periodic reports by international treaty bodies on the compliance of the Nordic countries with their international human rights obligations, display a range of human rights concerns in the Nordic countries. Yet, such factors as the high level of democracy, the rule of law and economic wealth lay the groundwork for the ability of the Nordic countries to

[5] Aside from Article 20, Sweden has made reservations to Articles 10(3) and 14(7) of the ICCPR. The UN Human Rights Committee has on several occasions expressed its concern that Sweden should review its reservations with a view to withdrawing them. See Concluding observations by the UN Human Rights Committee on the seventh periodic report of Sweden, 28 April 2016, CCPR/C/SWE/CO/7, at para 7. See also G Melander, 'Setting the Stage: Wishful Thinking or Prospects for Development' in I Ziemele (ed), *Reservations to Human Rights Treaties and the Vienna Convention Regime: Conflict, Harmony or Reconciliation* (Dordrecht, Springer, 2004) xxiii.

[6] *ICG 2000: The Competence to Accede to the European Convention for the Protection of Human Rights and Fundamental Freedoms* (Brussels, 22 September 2000, doc Confer 4775/00).

effectively live up to (at least by and large) their constitutional and international human rights obligations.[7]

Up until the end of 2016, Denmark had received 15, Finland 139, Iceland 13, Norway 28 and Sweden 60 such judgments by the ECtHR finding at least one violation of the ECHR. The major problem area for the Nordic countries, notably Finland and Sweden, is the right to a fair trial, particularly insofar as the length of proceedings is concerned. In addition, violations of the ECHR by the Nordic countries have related to such rights as the right to respect for private and family life (Article 8) and freedom of expression (Article 10).[8]

In light of the recent concluding observations by the UN Human Rights Committee under Article 40 of the ICCPR, principal matters of concern and recommendations revolve around such human rights issues as detention conditions, domestic violence against women and children, and various deficiencies regarding the anti-discrimination framework, including human trafficking and the rights of migrants, refugees and asylum seekers.[9]

In addition, the absence of an independent national human rights institution in Iceland and Sweden, as well as the lack of incorporation of the ICCPR and several other core human rights instruments into the domestic legal orders in Denmark, Iceland and Sweden, are among the matters of concern. Finland and Sweden have also been criticised for failures to respect the rights of the indigenous Sami people. The Nordic approach regarding national human rights institutions and the domestic incorporation of human rights treaties are discussed in more detail below in section IV.

On the other hand, while the Nordic countries can be applauded as 'model countries' in relation to many human rights issues, it is somewhat paradoxical to note at the same time that the traditional Nordic constitutional position regarding human rights has been quite reserved and even reluctant, particularly to the

[7] See also DS Law and M Versteeg, 'Sham Constitutions' (2013) 101 *California Law Review* 863. This article empirically examines the global prevalence and severity of constitutional non-compliance over the last three decades and identifies the worst offenders, or 'sham constitutions', across several substantive categories. It lists (at 898–99) Finland, Iceland and Sweden among the 10 countries in the world that not only promise a wide range of human rights in their constitutions, but also make good upon those promises. Denmark and Norway, in turn, are mentioned as 'constitutional overperformers' because they uphold a much greater range of rights than their constitutions alone might suggest (at 900–01). The article deals with the situation in 2010 and, accordingly, does not take into account the reform of the Constitution of Norway in 2014 with the new Part E on human rights.

[8] Council of Europe, the European Court of Human Rights, Overview 1959–2016 ECHR, 8–9, available at: www.echr.coe.int/Documents/Overview_19592016_ENG.pdf.

[9] See Concluding observations by the Human Rights Committee on the latest periodic reports by the Nordic countries to the extent that principal matters of concern and recommendations are concerned; Concluding observations on the sixth periodic report of Denmark, 15 August 2016, CCPR/C/DNK/CO/6; Concluding observations on the sixth periodic report of Finland, 22 August 2013, CCPR/C/FIN/CO/6; Concluding observations on the fifth periodic report of Iceland, 31 August 2012, CCPR/C/ISL/CO/5; Concluding observations of the Human Rights Committee on the sixth periodic report of Norway, 18 November 2011, CCPR/C/NOR/CO/6; and Concluding observations of the Human Rights Committee on the seventh periodic report of Sweden, 28 April 2016, CCPR/C/SWE/CO/7.

extent that judicial safeguards for human rights are concerned.[10] The origins of this approach can partly be traced to the influence of Scandinavian legal realism, which is renowned for its almost nihilist approach to rights and courts.[11] However, the major explanation for the Nordic hesitance towards the judicial enforcement of human rights can be found in the traditional adherence to constitutionalist legislative supremacy, as well as to ideas about democracy as majority rule.[12] The exception to this has been Norway, where the Supreme Court has for a long time exercised the power of judicial review, with the outcome that it has struck down provisions of acts of parliament as unconstitutional (for more details on judicial review, see Chapter 5).

The rather marginal roles of rights and courts in Nordic countries except Norway have had a multi-faceted impact on the protection of human rights. For instance, it has been reflected in the Nordic welfare state model, which has lacked a strong tradition of defining welfare benefits and services as constitutionally entrenched human rights. Yet, the Nordic countries are globally regarded as renowned welfare states that emphasise positive duties and envision an active role for the state and the public authorities in pursuing social welfare.[13] Against this setting, the traditional Nordic constitutional reluctance vis-a-vis strong judicial safeguards for human rights may even be seen as challenging the presumption on the correlation between effective human rights protection and strong judicial review. To be sure, if the effective protection of human rights would inevitably require strong courts, then a failure to uphold these rights would be common to all the Nordic countries, since the Nordic constitutions adhere to various forms of weak judicial review. Hence, the experience of the Nordic countries suggests that the effective protection of human rights depends upon a variety of other factors than just judicial review.

[10] For an overview, see A Follesdal and M Wind, 'Judicial Review in the Nordic Countries' (2009) 27(2) *Nordic Journal of Human Rights* 131. See also JE Rytter and M Wind, 'In Need of Juristocracy? The Silence of Denmark in the Development of European Legal Norms' (2011) 9(2) *ICON* 470.

[11] See, eg, O Wiklund, 'The Reception Process in Sweden and Norway' in H Keller et al (eds), *A Europe of Rights* (Oxford, Oxford University Press, 2008) 172: 'The primacy of SLR ideas effectively prevented constitutional rights theories winning ground in the Scandinavian legal culture. The theory and ideology of SLR was detrimental to the legitimacy of constitutionally grounded rights arguments and principles in the legislative process as well as in the day to day adjudication of the Swedish judiciary.'

[12] See J Nergelius, 'The Nordic States and Continental Europe: A Two-Fold Story' in J Nergelius (ed), *Nordic and Other European Constitutional Traditions* (Leiden, Martinus Nijhoff, 2006) 3–4. See also E Smith, 'The Legitimacy of Judicial Review of legislation: A Comparative Approach' in E Smith (ed), *Constitutional Justice under Old Constitutions* (The Hague, Kluwer Law International, 1995); and J Lavapuro, T Ojanen and M Scheinin, 'Rights-Based Constitutionalism in Finland and the Development of Pluralist Constitutional Review' (2011) 9(2) *ICON* 511.

[13] M Scheinin, 'Introduction' in M Scheinin (ed), *The Welfare State and Constitutionalism in the Nordic Countries* (Copenhagen, Nordic Council of Ministers, 2001) 20. The argument is that the Nordic welfare state has by and large been built, developed and maintained through democratic decision-making by elected bodies and a large public sector, with the result that there has been no pressing need for anchoring these achievements in the form of constitutionally entrenched welfare rights. However, the argument is also that this traditional Nordic understanding of welfare is now increasingly challenged and, accordingly, more weight is attached to rights and courts.

However, these long-standing Nordic constitutional approaches towards rights and courts have been in a significant state of flux and transition since the early 1990s. As is discussed in more detail in other chapters of this book, Nordic constitutionalism has witnessed a remarkable shift from the legislative sovereignty paradigm to one in which domestic legislation and other legal measures are increasingly subordinated to rights-based judicial review, both by domestic courts and such European courts as the ECtHR and the Court of Justice of the European Union (CJEU).

The most significant impetus to this Nordic constitutional dynamic has probably been the incorporation of the ECHR into the domestic legal orders of all five Nordic countries in the course of the 1990s. In addition, the membership of Denmark, Finland and Sweden of the EU, as well as the accession of Iceland and Norway to the EEA in 1994, with a concomitant power granted to Nordic courts to review national law for its compatibility with EU/EEA law, have fostered constitutional tendency towards rights-based judicial review.[14]

However, it is premature to say that the traditional Nordic hesitance vis-a-vis human rights and strong courts has now been replaced by strong judicial safeguards for human rights. Instead, the current state of evolution assumes the nature of a transitional period: while constitutional hesitance towards strong judicial safeguards for human rights may no longer be the predominant dimension of Nordic constitutionalism, it is still tacitly and by implication shaping Nordic rights protection. In Denmark, for instance, the commission appointed by the Ministry of Justice recommended the incorporation of such core human rights treaties as the ICCPR, the UN International Convention on the Elimination of All Forms of Racial Discrimination (ICERD) and the UN Convention against Torture and Other Cruel, Inhuman or Degrading Treatment or Punishment. However, in 2014 the Danish government eventually decided *not* to incorporate these human rights treaties into Danish law, since their domestic incorporation, in the government's view, would entail a risk of a shift of competence from Parliament and the government to the Danish courts.[15] In other Nordic countries too, the traditional constitutional paradigm based on legislative supremacy is still strong enough to tempt the courts to exercise their powers of judicial review against a backdrop of judicial self-restraint.[16] Hence, the tendency towards stronger judicial protection of human rights is still far from such full-fledged forms of judicial review as are typical for continental constitutional courts in Europe.

[14] See Lavapuro et al (n 12) 507.

[15] Danish Institute for Human Rights, 'Human Rights in Denmark. Status 2014–15. A Summary'., 2015, 8, https://menneskeret.dk/files/media/dokumenter/udgivelser/status/2014-15/status_uk_2015.pdf.

[16] For the situation in Finland, see J Lavapuro, T Ojanen and M Scheinin, 'Intermediate Constitutional Review in Finland: Promising in Theory, Problematic in Practice' in J Bell and ML Paris (eds), *Rights-Based Constitutional Review: Constitutional Courts in a Changing Landscape* (Cheltenham, Edward Elgar, 2016) 218.

III. Nordic Constitutional Systems for the Protection of Human Rights

A. Sources of Human Rights

As already noted, human rights have traditionally been enshrined in the written constitutions of the Nordic countries. In recent decades, however, human rights have become even more central and visible in Nordic constitutions due to constitutional reforms or amendments in all Nordic countries except Denmark, where the most recent constitutional amendment dates as far back as 1953.

In Sweden, the domestic discussion and debate over the constitutional protection of civil rights and fundamental freedoms had already started before the Second World War, but it was not until 1974 that a compromise was reached and Chapter 2 of the Instrument of Government[17] was enacted. Subsequently, Chapter 2 has been modernised in 1976, 1979 and 1994. In addition, freedom of the press, the right of access to public documents and other dimensions of freedom of expression have always been accentuated in Swedish constitutional law: Sweden's first Freedom of the Press Act with a constitutional status was already adopted in 1766, and subsequent Freedom of the Press Acts followed in 1810, 1812 and 1949. In 2011, the Instrument of Government in Sweden underwent a further amendment, which inserted a new provision on the protection of personal privacy into the Constitution and extended the prohibition of discrimination to sexual orientation. In addition, this amendment enhanced the constitutional protection of the Sami people, as well as ethnic, linguistic and religious minorities to preserve and develop their own cultural and social life.[18]

In 1995, profound changes were made to the chapter of the Icelandic Constitution on human rights. The amendment[19] added a range of new rights to the Constitution, as well as rephrasing and modernising the existing human rights provisions. The bill accompanying the Act included references to the ECHR as well as to other CoE and UN human rights instruments binding upon Iceland. Until this amendment, the human rights provisions of the Icelandic Constitution had remained unaltered since the entry into force of Iceland's first Constitution in 1874.[20] In 2010, the Icelandic Parliament passed Act No 90 of 2010 establishing a

[17] By virtue of Article 3 of the Instrument of the Government, the following enactments enjoy constitutional status in Sweden: the Instrument of Government, the Act of Succession, the Freedom of the Press Act and the Fundamental Law on Freedom of Expression. Hereafter, the Instrument of Government and other enactments enjoying the status of the constitution will be referred to as the Swedish 'Constitution' unless otherwise explicitly mentioned.

[18] See M Isberg, *The Constitution of Sweden* (Stockholm, Sveriges Riksdag, 2016), especially 28–33 and 65–71; and Nergelius (n 2) 104–05.

[19] Constitutional Act No 97/1995.

[20] For the Icelandic constitutional reform, see H Torfason, 'Influential Constitutional Justice: Some Icelandic Perspectives', paper presented at the World Conference on Constitutional Justice, 23–24 January 2009, available at: www.venice.coe.int/WCCJ/Papers/ISL_Torfason_E.pdf.

consultative Constitutional Assembly, with the assignment of thoroughly revising the Constitution of Iceland. One of the fundamental aims of this reform was to involve the citizens in the making of a new Icelandic Constitution, partly through so-called 'crowd-sourcing'. Although the making of a new Constitution of Iceland eventually failed, the attempt fostered public awareness of the fundamentals of the Icelandic Constitution, including those relating to the rights and freedoms of individuals.[21]

Finland adopted a comprehensive reform of its constitutional catalogue of rights in 1995, with the outcome that the current Chapter 2 of the Constitution of Finland stands out as a broad and modern catalogue of rights compared to other European and international countries. It sets out a range of economic, social and cultural rights in addition to traditional civil and political rights. Moreover, there are specific provisions on everyone's responsibility for the environment and on environmental rights (section 20) as well as on the right to good administration (section 21:2).[22]

The most recent Nordic constitutional development aiming at bolstering the protection of human rights at the level of written constitution took place in 2014 in Norway, as part of its Constitution's bicentennial anniversary. Several rights already guaranteed by international human rights treaties binding upon Norway were then included in new Part E of the Constitution. Unlike the constitutional reforms in Finland, Iceland and Sweden, the 2014 Norwegian constitutional amendment did not aim at enumerating new rights. Instead, the major purpose was to clarify already-existing rights by bringing them together in a single chapter. The opening Article 92 of the new Part E of the Norwegian Constitution prescribes that the state authorities shall respect and ensure human rights as they are expressed in the Constitution and in the human rights treaties that are binding on Norway. This is followed by a number of provisions on such human rights that are also enshrined in the ECHR, the ICCPR[23] and the other international human rights treaties that are binding on Norway.[24]

[21] For the revision of the Icelandic Constitution and the constitutional reform process in more detail, see B Thorarensen, 'The Impact of the Crisis on Icelandic Constitutional Law: Legislative Reforms, Judicial Review and Revision of the Constitution', paper presented at the Workshop on Global Financial Crisis and the Constitutions, Athens, 4 May 2012, 13–24, available at: https://www.researchgate.net/profile/Bjoerg_Thorarensen/publication/289949295_The_impact_of_the_financial_crisis_on_Icelandic_constitutional_law_Legislative_reforms_judicial_review_and_revision_of_the_constitution/links/57865a2d08aec5c2e4e2e96c.pdf?origin=publication_list.

See also B Thorarensen, 'Why the Making of a Crowd-Sourced Constitution in Iceland Failed', *Constitution Making & Constitutional Change*, 26 February 2014, available at: http://constitutional-change.com/why-the-making-of-a-crowd-sourced-constitution-in-iceland-failed.

[22] See in more detail Scheinin (n 3) 1.

[23] In its periodic report to the UN Human Rights Committee, the Norwegian government noted that the constitutional provisions in Part E of the Constitution largely correspond to the following rights under Article 2, paragraph 1 of the ICCPR and to Articles 6, 7, 8, 9, 12, 14, 15, 17, 19, 21, 22, 26 and 27 of the Covenant. See Norway's seventh periodic report to the Human Rights Committee, para 10.

[24] A Kierulf, '*Norway: Human Rights and Judicial Review Constitutionalized*' *Blog of the International Journal of Constitutional* Law, 5 June 2015: www.iconnectblog.com/2015/06/norway-human-rights-and-judicial-review-constitutionalized.

However, separate chapters on human rights do not exhaust the spectrum of human rights in the Nordic constitutions. In addition, references to human rights can be found from those constitutional provisions that set out the fundamental principles and goals of these constitutions. For example, the opening provision of the Finnish Constitution provides that the Constitution 'shall guarantee the inviolability of human dignity and the freedom and rights of the individual and promote justice in society' (section 1:2). Similarly, the amendment of the Norwegian Constitution in 2012 inserted a new Article 2, which provides that the Constitution should ensure democracy, the rule of law and human rights. Article 2 of the first Chapter of the Instrument of Government of Sweden sets out in even more detail several such basic principles of the form of government that pertain to human rights. While such constitutional provisions setting out fundamental constitutional principles and aims with reference to human rights are not directly applicable and enforceable through the courts, they can assume interpretive effect, as well as providing guidelines and inspiration for policy-making.

Aside from written constitutional law, there is still room for the recognition of some human rights, or at least important dimensions of them, through unwritten constitutional principles or doctrines. This is especially so in Denmark, where the Constitution enshrines relatively few rights and is very difficult to amend. In the other four Nordic countries, the likelihood of regarding a certain right as protected through unwritten principles of constitutional law is limited due to the aforementioned constitutional amendments and reforms. In Iceland, for instance, the amendment of the Constitution's human rights provision in 1995 specifically aimed to redress the former inappropriate situation in which the Icelandic Constitution had lacked explicit provisions on various human rights, with the outcome that such rights were predominantly guaranteed by unwritten general principles of Icelandic law only. Similarly, one of the major reasons for the constitutional amendment of human rights provisions in Norway in 2014 was that the old Constitution failed to offer a sufficiently clear and comprehensive picture of the degree to which human rights are protected by the Norwegian constitutional law and legal order in general.

Finally, the significance of international human rights treaties with the ECHR at their apex as sources of human rights must be emphasised. The tendency in all Nordic countries has increasingly been towards the harmonisation of the constitutional and international protection of human rights, partly through the significant impact of international human rights treaties on the aforementioned domestic constitutional reforms and partly through the influence of international human rights norms, as seen in the light of the practice of international treaty bodies, on the interpretation of constitutional provisions on human rights and on the domestic constitutional principles and doctrines pertaining to human rights. The important role of international human rights norms in the operation of the Nordic constitutional system for the protection of human rights is discussed in more detail below in section IV.

The preceding discussion concerned sources of human rights at the level of the constitution and international human rights treaties. Beyond these, ordinary legislation often prescribes in more detail what the protection of human rights is all about. All Nordic constitutions proceed from the premise that the concretisation or regulation of human rights may take place only in the form of parliamentary legislation. Yet, it is also important not to assimilate constitutionally entrenched human rights, or international human rights treaty provisions, into ordinary legislation. Constitutional provisions on human rights, as well as international human rights treaty provisions, have their autonomous existence and meaning. They also condition and shape the enactment of ordinary legislation, as well as the interpretation and application of such legislation by the courts and authorities. Hence, there exists a qualitative difference between ordinary legislation providing more detail on the exercise of or restrictions on human rights, on the one hand, and human rights enshrined in the constitutions and human rights treaties, on the other hand. The reader must carefully keep this distinction in mind.

B. Major Principles and Doctrines Underlying the Constitutional Protection of Human Rights

As noted above, the purpose of this chapter is not to deal with the substance of human rights under the Nordic constitutions. Suffice to say that all the other Nordic constitutions except the Danish Constitution nowadays include fairly broad written catalogues of human rights due to the constitutional amendments or reforms discussed above. Hence, whereas the older Nordic constitutions primarily focused on traditional civil and political rights, the Constitutions of Finland and Sweden now include a broader set of rights, ranging from civil and political rights to various economic, social and cultural rights. In addition, some Nordic constitutions, such as the Finnish Constitution, offer explicit constitutional guarantees to environmental rights (section 20) and rights pertaining to good administration (section 21:2). As already mentioned, Sweden has traditionally emphasised the right of access to public documents and the right to information in general as important dimensions of freedom of expression and democratic discourse in its constitutional matrix. Nowadays, the Finnish (section 12) and the Norwegian (Article 100) Constitutions also enshrine these rights. Although the Danish Constitution is meagre and obsolete regarding its written provisions on human rights, it should be emphasised that the Danish Constitution considerably understates the country's actual commitment to and respect for human rights: Denmark *de facto* upholds a much greater range of human rights than its antiquated Constitution suggests.[25]

[25] Law and Versteeg (n 7) 900–01: 'As with the constitutional underperformance scores, each country receives a constitutional overperformance score between zero and one that is equal to the proportion of omitted rights that were nevertheless respected in practice. Thus, for example, Denmark's

The way in which human rights operate in the Nordic constitutional systems is shaped by the following conceptions, interpretations and doctrines.

i. The Personal Scope of Human Rights Protection under the Nordic Constitutions

The personal scope of the Nordic constitutional protections for human rights has widened due to constitutional revisions and doctrinal changes in recent decades. As a rule, the Nordic constitutions nowadays grant human rights to everyone, regardless of citizenship. Exceptions to the rule can be found in such constitutional provisions that regulate freedom of movement and certain electoral rights pertaining to national elections; such rights are given to the (adult) citizens of the five Nordic countries only. The Nordic constitutions also otherwise proceed from the principle of non-discrimination insofar as the enjoyment of human rights is concerned. Hence, the starting point is that the enjoyment of rights is not dependent upon such grounds as origin, nationality, language, religion, belief, opinion, political activity, trade union activity, family relationships, state of health, disability or sexual orientation. In addition, the Nordic constitutions include separate provisions on, for example, gender equality and the protection of the rights of the child. Aside from natural persons, the Nordic constitutions include provisions on the linguistic and cultural rights of various groups. The Finnish, Norwegian and Swedish Constitutions, for instance, include explicit constitutional provisions on the protection of the cultural and linguistic rights of the Sami people.

ii. Who is Bound by Human Rights?

The Nordic constitutions proceeded from the premise that human rights are binding on state authorities and public authorities in general. Hence, constitutional provisions on human rights are binding on municipalities or other public organs beyond the organisation of the state. Human rights are also understood as binding various semi-public or private organs or actors to the extent that they exercise public powers. As human rights are binding on state authorities and public authorities in general, it follows that Nordic legislatures and executive organs, as well as courts, are bound to observe human rights in their respective functions. However, the effects of human rights on the legislature, the executive and the judiciary can vary due to differences in the nature of the legislative, executive and judicial powers. Traditionally, the Nordic constitutions have proceeded from the premise that human rights are not directly binding on private subjects. Instead, the horizontal effect of human rights between private subjects is indirect and realised through the human rights-oriented interpretation of ordinary pieces of legislation applicable in legal relationships between private parties. In recent years,

perfect overperformance score of one (as of 2010) reflects the fact that its formal constitution understates its actual respect for rights: all seven of the rights absent from its constitution were nevertheless respected in practice.'

however, the trend has been towards recognising the more direct effects of human rights in horizontal relations between private actors.

iii. The Typologies of Rights and Obligations

The Nordic constitutions reflect the distinction between negative and positive state obligations and, accordingly, the typology of state obligations to respect, to protect and to fulfil. The application of human rights in private relationships is primarily realised through the positive obligations of the state to protect human rights and, accordingly, through the enactment of ordinary legislation and human rights-oriented interpretation of such legislation (indirect horizontal effect of human rights). Furthermore, the Nordic constitutional regimes reflect such well-established principles and doctrines of human rights law as the distinction between absolute (or non-derogable or inviolable) rights and rights that may be subject to limitations, provided that various conditions on these limitations are met.

iv. Limitations of Rights

The permissible limitation tests under the Nordic constitutions bear many similarities with those under Articles 8–11 of the ECHR or Article 52.1 of the Charter of Fundamental Rights of the European Union (EUCFR). Hence, these criteria revolve around the following cumulative conditions:

(i) The requirement that any limitation must be in accordance with the law; it follows from the rule of law principle endorsed by all Nordic constitutions that an act of parliament is always required for limitations on human rights. This requirement includes qualitative requirements such as that a legislative enactment entailing limitations must be sufficiently clear and precise.
(ii) The requirement of a legitimate aim, in that a limitation corresponds to the objectives of general interest such as security and/or the need to protect the rights and freedoms of others.
(iii) The requirements of necessity and proportionality.
(iv) The essence of rights cannot be subject to limitations.

These criteria for limiting human rights under the Nordic constitutions are not necessarily exhaustively expressed by written constitutional provisions. Instead, they may also be a matter of constitutional doctrine. For instance, Articles 20–25 of the Instrument of Government of Sweden set out in a quite detailed manner various conditions for limiting rights and freedoms guaranteed by the Constitution. By contrast, the Finnish Constitution lacks a general clause on the permissible limitations on human rights, although it includes several provisions defining in various ways the possibility of restrictions to these rights. Instead, the general permissible limitations test is set out in detail in the preparatory work of the reform of the constitutional catalogue of rights in 1995.[26] The Constitutions of Denmark,

[26] See Report 25/1994 of the Constitutional Law Committee of Parliament.

Iceland and Norway[27] lack a general clause defining the conditions for permissible limitations.

v. Derogations from Rights in Times of Public Emergency

The Nordic constitutional regimes reflect the possibility of derogations from human rights in times of public emergency which threaten the life of the nation. While the basics of the Nordic constitutional approach are similar in all five countries, there are notable differences between the Nordic approaches insofar as constitutional regulation is concerned.[28] Section 23 of the Finnish Constitution is most explicit and detailed in listing conditions for derogations from human rights in a manner that largely paraphrases provisions relating to human rights derogations under Article 4 of the ICCPR and Article 15 of the ECHR.[29] Article 7 of Chapter 15 of the Instrument of Government of Sweden also regulates limitations of rights and freedoms if the country is at war or is exposed to the immediate danger of war. It is noteworthy, particularly in light of the fact that the country has not been at war since 1814, that the text of the Swedish Constitution only focuses on war, thereby leaving such potential situations of public emergency as terrorism or natural disaster unregulated. In the other three Nordic countries, constitutional derogations in times of emergency are more a matter of unwritten constitutional principles and doctrines than something prescribed by the text of the Constitution.[30] In all Nordic countries, the constitutional doctrine is that derogations from human rights in times of public emergency must be in compliance with international human rights obligations. None of the Nordic states has declared a

[27] In Norway, the Report by the Human Rights Commission Concerning Human Rights in the Constitution, submitted 19 December 2011, recommended the adoption of Article 115, which would have included a general limitation clause. However, this recommendation was left out of the constitutional amendment; see https://www.stortinget.no/globalassets/pdf/diverse/report-from-the-human-rights-commission.pdf.

[28] For an overview of Nordic constitutional systems regarding derogations in times of public emergency, see R Helgadottir, 'Economic Crises and Emergency Powers in Europe' (2012) 2 *Harvard Business Law Review* 130. See also TO Johansen, 'Constitutional Necessity in Norway and Sweden', paper submitted to The Mutations and Transformation of Division of Powers: The Constitutional Organization Workshop, WCC 2014, Oslo.

[29] 'Section 23—Basic rights and liberties in situations of emergency' (1112/2011, entered into force 1 March 2012). Such provisional exceptions to basic rights and liberties that are compatible with Finland's international human rights obligations and that are deemed necessary in the event of an armed attack against Finland or in the event of other situations of emergency, as provided by an Act, which pose a serious threat to the nation may be provided by an Act or by a Government Decree to be issued on the basis of authorisation given in an Act for a special reason and subject to a precisely circumscribed scope of application. However, the grounds for provisional exceptions shall be laid down by an Act. Government Decrees concerning provisional exceptions shall without delay be submitted to the Parliament for consideration. The Parliament may decide on the validity of the Decrees.'

[30] In Norway, the Report by the Human Rights Commission Concerning Human Rights in the Constitution included a recommendation that a new Article 116 on derogations in times of war or other emergency situations, but the recommendation was eventually left out of the constitutional amendment of 2014. The report is available at: https://www.stortinget.no/globalassets/pdf/diverse/report-from-the-human-rights-commission.pdf.

state of emergency for the purpose of derogating from human rights. However, the financial crisis in the late 2000s in Iceland resulted in legislative reforms, including the enactment of the Emergency Act with implications on property rights and constitutional law in general. However, Iceland's financial crisis did not constitute a public emergency allowing derogations from human rights within the meaning of international human rights law, and the Icelandic government did not even try to declare a derogation from the ECHR or other human rights obligations.[31]

C. Nordic Mechanisms for the Protection and Promotion of Human Rights

Other chapters in this volume deal in detail with such issues as judicial review, separation of powers and supervision of legality. Suffice it here to recall that Nordic courts have started taking increasingly judicial notice of human rights in their decisions since the 1990s and that judicial safeguards for human rights are today much stronger than they were a couple of decades ago. As the Nordic courts tend to refer in tandem to constitutional, European and international sources of human rights, it is nowadays impossible to maintain a strong separation between the constitutional and international protection of human rights.

Aside from judicial safeguards, the effective protection of human rights inevitably requires contributions by all other branches of the government. After all, human rights cannot be fully implemented and realised without positive measures by the legislators and public authorities. For instance, the duty of state organs to respect and promote human rights entails the need to enact legislation forbidding violations of human rights by private parties. Human rights obligations can also give rise to wider programmes of legislation for the purpose of regulating in more detail what a certain human right is all about. Similarly, the administrative organs and public authorities in general contribute to the implementation of human rights through their decision-making in concrete cases and various other actions. The scope of this chapter does not permit a detailed account of the various ways in which constitutional and international human rights obligations may affect the works of the Nordic legislatures and administrative organs, but it is important to keep in mind that the effective protection of human rights is a matter for all branches of the government.

In the Nordic context, the role of the Ombudsman institution in the protection and promotion of human rights deserves particular attention. This derives from the Nordic model with particular focus on the handling of complaints relating to maladministration for the protection of individuals. All five Nordic countries

[31] On the constitutional implications of the financial crisis in Iceland, see B Thorarensen, 'The Impact of the Financial Crisis on Icelandic Constitutional Law: Legislative Reforms, Judicial Review and Revision of the Constitution' in X Contiades (ed), *Constitutions in the Global Financial Crisis: A Comparative Analysis* (Farnham, Ashgate, 2013) 263.

nowadays have Parliamentary Ombudsman institutions with the mandate[32] to monitor the observance of human rights by public authorities. These Ombudsmen have often been domestic trailblazers in the protection of human rights. For instance, the Parliamentary Ombudsman of Finland was at the forefront of change when Finnish courts and authorities started referring to human rights treaties in the late 1980s.[33] However, there are also significant differences between the East and West Nordic Ombudsman models and the scope of their control, as is discussed in more detail in Chapter 4.

The tendency in the Nordic countries has also been towards establishing specialised Ombudsman institutions with more exact and focused mandates to monitor the observance of human rights in such areas as equality, the principle of non-discrimination, the rights of the child and data protection.[34] A reference can be made here to such Ombudsman institutions in the field of equality and non-discrimination as the Non-discrimination Ombudsman of Finland and the Equality, Anti-discrimination Ombudsman of Norway, as well as the Ombudsmen for Children in all the Nordic countries. In Denmark, the National Human Rights Institute of Denmark is mandated with handling the promotion of equality and the protection of different grounds of discrimination. However, Sweden passed a legislative reform[35] in 2009 that merged the four pre-existing specialised Ombudsmen institutions into one new Ombudsman institution (the Equality Ombudsman) with a broad mandate to combat discrimination and promote equal rights and opportunities regardless of sex, transgender identity or expression, ethnicity, religion or other belief, disability, sexual orientation or age. Iceland still lacks comprehensive anti-discrimination legislation in the form that exists in other Nordic countries.[36]

It should be emphasised that the work of the various Nordic Ombudsmen institutions is not limited to such retroactive functions as the consideration of complaints in the light of human rights. In addition, their mandates often extend to cover a range of more preventive and proactive functions. For instance, the Norwegian Parliamentary Ombudsman has served since 2013 as the national preventive mechanism against torture and ill-treatment, which, among other things, entails that the Ombudsman regularly visits places where people are or

[32] The Constitution of Finland, for instance, explicitly obliges both the Chancellor of Justice (section 108) and the Parliamentary Ombudsman (section 109) to monitor 'the implementation of basic rights and liberties and human rights' when performing their duties.

[33] M Scheinin, 'Finland' in M Scheinin (ed), *International Human Rights Norms in the Nordic and Baltic Countries* (The Hague, Martinus Nijhoff Publishers, 1996) 257.

[34] In Finland, there are four specialised Ombudsmen in addition to the Parliamentary Ombudsman: one on equality between men and women; one on non-discrimination; one on children; and one on data protection.

[35] See the Equality Ombudsman Act No 568 of 2008.

[36] European network of legal experts in gender equality and non-discrimination, 'A Comparative Analysis of Non-discrimination Law in Europe', European Commission, Directorate-General for Justice and Consumers 2016, 134–40.

may be deprived of their liberty for the purpose of preventing these people from being subjected to torture and other cruel, inhuman or degrading treatment or punishment.[37] The Nordic Ombudsmen usually provide advice to parliaments and governments.

Aside from courts and Ombudsman institutions, there exist a range of other actors for the protection and promotion of human rights, such as advisory panels[38] or other specialised or even quasi-judicial bodies, such as the Board of Equal Treatment in Denmark, the National Non-discrimination and Equality Tribunal in Finland and the Equality and Anti-discrimination Tribunal in Norway.[39]

Actually, one problem of the Nordic mechanisms of human rights protection and promotion has not been so much the lack of human rights bodies, but, instead, the fragmented human rights architecture, with a variety of distinct institutions or other actors monitoring, promoting and protecting human rights in various ways. In order to provide a more coherent and comprehensive approach, some Nordic countries have established National Human Rights Institutions (NHRIs) for the promotion and protection of human rights institutions in accordance with the so-called Paris Principles of the UN, adopted by General Assembly Resolution 48/134 in 1993.[40]

The Danish Institute for Human Rights has since 1999 held 'A-status', which is given to national human rights institutions that fully comply with the UN Paris Principles.[41] In Finland, in which fragmented human rights structures for a long time hampered effective and coherent human rights protection and promotion, the Human Rights Centre was established in 2012; together with the Parliamentary Ombudsman, this Centre forms the NHRI of Finland. In Norway, the Norwegian NHRI has also been granted A-status.

In Sweden, the situation is nowadays different. While Sweden previously fulfilled the criteria for the NHRI in accordance with the Paris Principles, Sweden now lacks this status due to the reform that merged the four specialised Ombudsmen into one new institution.[42] Domestic discussions on the establishment of an NHRI

[37] Sivilombudsmannen/Norwegian Parliamentary Ombudsman, Annual Report 2015, 20–22.

[38] In Finland, for instance, there are such advisory panels as the Advisory Boards on Human Rights (within the Ministry of Foreign Affairs), the Advisory Board on Romani Affairs, and the Equality Board Council for Gender Equality.

[39] For equality and non-discrimination bodies in the Nordic countries, see in more detail European network of legal experts in gender equality and non-discrimination (n 36).

[40] The Paris Principles set out the six major criteria for NHRIs: mandate and competence; autonomy from government; independence; pluralism; adequate resources; and adequate powers of investigation. See in more detail European Union Agency for Fundamental Rights, *Handbook on the Establishment and Accreditation of National Human Rights Institutions in the European Union* (Luxembourg, Publications Office of the European Union, 2012).

[41] The Danish Institute for Human Rights previously had the competence to handle individual complaints, but this was transferred to the Board of Equal Treatment in 2009.

[42] In practice, Sweden did not submit the necessary supporting documents on time to the International Coordinating Committee of National Human Rights Institutions for the Promotion and Protection of Human Rights, See ICC, Sub-Committee on Accreditation (2008), point 3.10.

for Sweden are now taking place. In Iceland, the Draft Act on the Independent National Human Rights Institution of Iceland, designed to create a legal framework for the establishment of an independent NHRI for Iceland in compliance with the Paris Principles, is currently under consideration.

These Nordic mechanisms for the protection and promotion of human rights are complemented by European and international mechanisms of protection and promotion under the UN or the CoE's human rights treaty regimes, including the UN Charter-based monitoring mechanisms of human rights and the monitoring mechanisms by the ILO. As with human rights treaties in general, the Nordic countries have also systematically ratified various complaint procedures and other treaty-monitoring mechanisms of international human rights treaties. The relationship between the constitutional and international protection of human rights is dealt with in more detail below in section IV.

IV. The Relationship between Nordic and International Systems for the Protection of Human Rights[43]

A. The Domestic Validity of International Human Rights Norms: The Nordic Duality Regarding Incorporation

All five Nordic constitutions adhere to a dualist approach to international law, including international human rights treaties.[44] Hence, international human rights treaties do not enter into force in the Nordic legal orders only by means of their ratification. In addition, incorporation or some other domestic implementation measures are needed in order to make international human rights treaties formally parts of the Nordic legal orders.

In practice, various methods of implementation like incorporation fostering the direct application of international human rights norms by courts, and various rules of construction (see below, section IV.C) have mitigated the dualist approach of the Nordic constitutions. Similarly, the impact of international human rights treaties on domestic constitutional reforms and on the interpretation of

[43] For an overview of international human rights norms in the Nordic countries, see the chapters on Nordic countries in Scheinin (ed) (n 33). See also the country reports on Denmark, Finland and Sweden by J Christoffersen and M Madsen, 'Denmark', T Ojanen, 'Finland' and V Ndior, 'Sweden' in L Burgorgue-Larsen (ed), *La Chartre des droits fondamentaux de l'Union européenne saisie par les juges en Europe/The EU Charter of Fundamental Rights as Apprehended by National Judges* (Paris, Pedone, 2017).

[44] M Scheinin, 'Domestic Implementation of International Human Rights Treaties: Nordic and Baltic Experiences' in P Alston and J Crawford (eds), *The Future of UN Human Rights Treaty Monitoring* (Cambridge, Cambridge University Press, 2000) 229.

constitutional provisions on human rights has fostered the harmonisation of the constitutional and international protection of fundamental rights.

In addition, dualism has not prevented interpretive effects or other domestic effects of such international human rights instruments that have lacked formal domestic validity in the Nordic legal orders. In Norway, for instance, the Supreme Court already long ago showed its readiness to take judicial notice of non-incorporated international human rights treaties, including affording them priority over domestic law.[45] Similarly, the Finnish courts or authorities, such as the Parliamentary Ombudsman, were already citing non-binding international human rights instruments in their decisions in the late 1980s.[46]

With the exception of Finland, which has traditionally incorporated all international human rights treaties into domestic law, a notable characteristic of the other four Nordic countries was for decades a lack of incorporation. To be sure, while Denmark, Iceland, Norway and Sweden had ratified the ECHR in the 1950s, it was not until the 1990s that the ECHR was incorporated into their domestic law; the ECHR was incorporated into Danish law in 1992,[47] Icelandic law in 1994,[48] Swedish law in 1995[49] and Norwegian law in 1999.[50]

Monitoring bodies of international human rights treaties, such as the UN Human Rights Committee, have continuously criticised the lack of incorporation of human rights treaties by Denmark,[51] Iceland[52] and Sweden.[53] According to this criticism, certain areas of domestic law are not entirely aligned with international human rights norms. The lack of incorporation also induces domestic courts to give judicial effect to human rights treaties predominantly indirectly, through the interpretation of domestic law.

Together with critical observations by the international human rights treaty bodies on this lack of incorporation, the incorporation of the ECHR has stimulated the domestic debate on the incorporation of other international human rights treaties in Nordic countries, albeit with mixed outcomes. In 1999, Norway enacted an Act to strengthen the position of human rights in Norwegian law

[45] K Eggen, 'Norway' in Scheinin (ed) (n 33) 203.
[46] Scheinin (n 33) 257.
[47] Act No 285, 29 April 1992.
[48] Act No 62/1994.
[49] Act Concerning the European Convention for the Protection of Human Rights and Fundamental Freedoms (1994:1219).
[50] For the domestic status and effects of the ECHR in the Nordic countries, see I Cameron, 'Sweden', E More, 'Norway', P Germer, 'Denmark', G Gauksdóttir, 'Iceland' and A Rosas, 'Finland' in R Blackburn and J Polakiewicz (eds) *Fundamental Rights in Europe: The European Convention on Human Rights and its Member States, 1950–2000* (Oxford, Oxford University Press, 2001).
[51] See, eg, Human Rights Committee, Concluding observations on the sixth periodic report of Denmark, 15 August 2016, CCPR/C/DNK/CO/6, at paras 5–6.
[52] Human Rights Committee, Concluding observations on the fifth periodic report submitted by Iceland, 31 August 2012, CCPR/C/ISL/CO/5, para 4.
[53] See, eg, Human Rights Committee, Concluding observations on the seventh periodic report of Sweden, 28 April 2016, CCPR/C/SWE/CO/7, at paras 4–5.

(the Human Rights Act).[54] This Act includes six sections whereby the following international human rights treaties are given the force of national law to the extent that they are binding on Norway: the European Council's Convention for the Protection of Human Rights and Fundamental Freedoms, its Protocol of November 1950, its Protocol Nos 4 (securing certain other rights and freedoms), 6 (abolition of the death penalty) and 7 (furthering certain human rights and freedoms); the UN's International Covenants on Economic, Social and Cultural Rights, and on Civil and Political Rights, and the two optional Protocols to the ICCPR. In 2003, Norway incorporated the Convention on the Rights of the Child (CRC)[55] and took a further step of incorporation in 2009 by inserting the Convention on the Elimination of All Forms of Discrimination against Women (CEDAW) in the Human Rights Act of 1999, following the recommendations by the CEDAW Committee.

In contrast to Finland and Norway, Denmark, Iceland and Sweden have continued to follow a more cautious approach to incorporation: the ECHR is still the only human rights treaty incorporated into domestic law in Denmark, despite both international and domestic recommendations to incorporate human rights treaties.[56] Iceland, in turn, incorporated the CRC in 2013, but it is still to incorporate several other core UN human rights treaties. Sweden, too, has not incorporated other human rights treaties beyond the ECHR, but there is continuous debate on the issue of incorporation. The Swedish government recently submitted a proposal to the Council on Legislation to incorporate the CRC into Swedish law. Sweden has already ratified the CRC in 1990, but the government now considers that the Convention's domestic status must be strengthened and that a child rights-based approach must assume a stronger impact on the application of Swedish law. The incorporation enactment is scheduled to enter into force on 1 January 2020.

However, incorporation is not the only way of strengthening the position of international human rights norms in domestic legal orders, not to speak of giving effect to them. It should be emphasised that the Nordic countries have usually taken advantage of the method of transformation and, accordingly, have amended their domestic legislation so as to achieve harmony with the treaty in question. Similarly, the aforementioned constitutional amendments have enhanced the domestic status and applicability of international human rights treaties in the Nordic countries. In Iceland, for instance, the amendments made to the human rights provisions of the Icelandic Constitution in 1995 also enhanced the status of those international human rights conventions in Icelandic law that have not been

[54] Lov om styrking av menneskerettighetens stilling i norsk rett, Menneskerettsloven, No 30 of 1999.

[55] The CRC Committee had already earlier recommended the incorporation of the CRC. See the Norwegian NGO Coalition on the CRC, Supplementary report to the UN Committee on the Rights of the Child, 1999; UN Committee on the Rights of the Child, Concluding Observations: Norway, CRC/C/15/Add.126, 2000a.

[56] See Denmark, Third State Party report to the UN Committee on the Rights of the Child, CRC/C/129/Add.3, 2005, para 16.

incorporated into Icelandic law.[57] Accordingly, the influence of international treaties on human rights has increased due to the declared intention of the Icelandic legislature in the course of constitutional reform that these treaties should be taken into consideration in the interpretation of the human rights provisions of the Constitution.[58] In addition, some commentators have regarded constitutional provisions on the rights of the child as amounting to 'semi-constitutional incorporation' of the CRC, for example.[59]

B. The Domestic Status of International Human Rights Norms in the Nordic Legal Orders

Nordic constitutions lack explicit constitutional clauses on the domestic status of international law; one looks in vain for explicit constitutional provisions on the primacy or supremacy of international treaties in general, not to speak of international human rights treaties in particular. However, the Swedish Constitution adopts a kind of halfway house insofar as the ECHR is concerned by explicitly prohibiting the adoption of 'act of law or other provision', which contravenes Sweden's undertakings under the European Convention for the Protection of Human Rights and Fundamental Freedoms (Article 19 of the Instrument of Government). In Norway, the need to give human rights treaties the status of constitutional law was considered in the early 1990s, but the outcome was the adoption of section 3 of the Human Rights Act, which provided that: 'The provisions of the conventions and protocols mentioned in section 2 shall take precedence over any other legislative provisions that conflict with them.'

Yet, the relationship between Norwegian law and the ECHR, including the role of the Norwegian courts in the interpretation of the ECHR, has been subject to domestic debate after the Norwegian Supreme Court held in 2000[60] that it is primarily for the ECtHR to interpret the ECHR and that Norwegian courts should not be too active and dynamic in their interpretations of the ECHR. Especially, the Supreme Court emphasised the need to take account of traditional Norwegian

[57] See Fifth periodic report of States parties/Iceland; 27 November 2010, CCPR/C/ISL/5, at paras 7 and 8.

[58] See B Thorarensen, 'Judicial Control over the Legislature: Different Trends in Icelandic and Danish Practice' in B Dahl, MH Jensen and AH Mørup (eds), *Festskrift til Jens Peter Christensen* (Copenhagen, Jurist- og Økonomforbundets Forlag, 2016) 720.

[59] L Lundy, U Kilkelly and B Byrne, 'Incorporation of the United Nations Convention on the Rights of the Child in Law: A Comparative Review' (2013) 21(3) *International Journal of Children's Rights* 446.

[60] In 1994, ie, prior to the Human Rights Act of 1999, the Norwegian Supreme Court had required as a condition for giving priority to a treaty provision over conflicting Norwegian legislative provision that the treaty provision in question is sufficiently clear and ambiguous, but this requirement is no longer applied. See (1994) *Norsk Retstidende* 610. See in more detail M Andenas and E Bjorge, 'National Implementation of ECHR Rights' in A Follesdal, B Peters and G Ulfstein (eds), *Constituting Europe: The European Court of Human Rights in a National, European and Global Context* (Cambridge, Cambridge University Press, 2013) 198.

priorities in cases involving the balancing of various interests, and all the more so on occasions when the domestic legislator has considered the domestic enactment to be in harmony with the ECHR. The implications of the Supreme Court's judgment on the relationship between the ECHR and Norwegian law are still subject to domestic discussion.[61]

In addition, one can find in the Nordic constitutions special clauses that oblige State organs or public authorities in general to respect and ensure human rights. Such clauses can be found in the Finnish Constitution (Chapter 2, section 22), the Norwegian Constitution (Part E, Article 92) and the Swedish Constitution (Chapter 2, section 23). In Finland and Sweden, such constitutional provisions on human rights have been regarded as giving such semi-constitutional status to international human rights norms, thereby rendering them constitutionally special among international treaty obligations.[62] The Icelandic Constitution has also begun to reflect to a greater extent various international human rights instruments, both those adopted within the UN and the CoE, after the revision of the Constitution's human rights provisions in 1995, but no explicit provision on the issue can be found in the constitutional text.

As a rule, the incorporation of the ECHR and other international human rights treaties has taken place through ordinary acts of parliament in the Nordic countries.[63] As a result, such treaties have formally acquired the same hierarchical status as domestic ordinary laws, thereby giving rise to, at least in principle, the applicability of the rule of *lex posterior* for the purpose of solving a conflict between a human rights treaty norm and subsequent domestic legislation. In practice, however, the *lex posterior* rule has not significantly hampered the effective implementation of human rights in the Nordic countries. Aside from constitutional provisions giving rise to the semi-constitutional status of international human rights norms or making otherwise international human rights treaties something special among international treaty obligations, the inapplicability of the *lex posterior* rule to the detriment of human rights treaties follows from the principle of human rights-oriented interpretation of domestic law, which often gains more impetus from the rule of presumption (see in more detail below).

[61] (2000) *Norsk Retstidende* 996. See, eg, Andenas and Bjorge (n 60) 199–201; and G Ulfstein and A Follesdal, 'The European Court of Human Rights and the Norwegian Supreme Court: Independence and Democratic Control' in NA Engstad, AL Frøseth and B Tønder (eds), *The Independence of Judges* (The Hague, Eleven, 2014) 247–60. See also IJ Sand, 'Judicial Review in Norway under Recent Conditions of European Law and International Human Rights Law: A Comment' (2009) 27(2) *Nordisk tidskrift for menneskerettigheter* 160; and E Bjørge, 'The Status of the ECHR in Norway: Should Norwegian Courts Interpret the Convention Dynamically?' (2010) 16(1) *European Public Law* 45.

[62] Wiklund (n 11) 174; and Scheinin (n 33) 276.

[63] In Finland, a few older human rights treaties, such as the UN Covenant on Economic, Social and Cultural Rights and the Convention for the Elimination of Racial Discrimination, have been incorporated through government decrees only.

C. The Domestic Effects of International Human Rights Norms in the Nordic Countries

Today, there is an embarrassment of riches in terms of human rights case law from the Nordic courts. The growth in case law has been rapid particularly since the late 1990s onwards. The following judicial trends emerge from the maze of this case law:

(i) As with international treaties in general or EU law or EEA law for that matter, Nordic courts primarily tend to give judicial effect to international human rights treaties indirectly through the human rights treaty-oriented interpretation approach. Although the Nordic courts most frequently take judicial notice of the ECHR, they also cite other human rights treaties in their decisions. For instance, several judgments by the Danish,[64] Finnish,[65] Icelandic,[66] Norwegian[67] and Swedish[68] courts include references to the ICCPR.[69] As already noted, Nordic courts have occasionally given interpretive effect to those international human rights instruments that have lacked formal validity in the domestic legal order and therefore feature as soft law.

[64] According to the periodic report of the Danish government, Danish courts referred to various articles of the ICCPR in nine judgments between 1 January 2001 to 1 January 2014. Sixth periodic reports of States Parties due in 2013/Denmark, 10 November 2015, CCPR/C/DNK/6, para 23.

[65] As with Swedish courts, judgments of the Finnish courts most often cite Article 27 of the ICCPR in the context of cases involving the rights of the Sami people. See, eg, the judgments by the Supreme Administrative Court 2015:147, 2015:146 and 2013:179.

[66] For an overview, see Fifth periodic report of States Parties/Iceland; 22 November 2010; CCPR/C/ISL/5, paragraphs 8–11. See also Thorarensen (n 58), especially discussing the Icelandic court practice in the area of judicial control over the legislature, including the impact of international human rights conventions.

[67] The Supreme Court of Norway has frequently referred to and applied various rights enshrined in the ICCPR. Reference can be made to decisions cited in the Norwegian Supreme Court Reports 2014, 1105 (police storage of surplus material obtained through communications surveillance was deemed to be in violation of Article 17 of the Covenant); the Norwegian Supreme Court Reports 2015, 1142 (Article 9, paragraph 3 of the Covenant was deemed not to have been violated by a person not being brought before a judge until 52 hours after being detained); the Norwegian Supreme Court Reports 2015, 1467 (the prosecuting authority's denial of a request for access to recordings made by a surveillance camera was deemed to be in violation of Article 19 of the Covenant); and the Norwegian Supreme Court Reports 2015, 1085 (a convicted person's right to have his conviction and sentence reviewed under Article 14, paragraph 5 of the Covenant was deemed not to have been violated by the proceedings before the court of appeal being delayed by several years).

[68] Judgments by the Swedish courts have often dealt with issues pertaining to the Sami people and, accordingly, include references to Article 27 of the ICCPR. For an overview, see the seventh periodic reports of States Parties due in 2014/Sweden, 24 July 2015/CCPR/C/SWE/7, para 11.

[69] In Norway, judicial reference to the UN Convention on the Rights of the Child has also considerably increased after the domestic incorporation of the CRC. A Bårdsen, 'The Nordic Supreme Courts as Constitutional Courts: Main Features as Seen from the Norwegian Perspective', paper presented at the joint seminar between the Constitutional Court of Austria and the Supreme Court of Norway, Vienna, 29–30 October 2015.

(ii) The human-rights-oriented interpretation approach is often supported by the rule of presumption: when assessing the conformity of domestic law with international human rights norms, the Nordic courts tend to proceed from the presumption that the domestic legislator did not intend to derogate from international human rights treaty obligations unless such legislative intention is explicitly and clearly expressed. This presumption further fosters judicial efforts to resolve the ambiguity or uncertainty in domestic legislation in harmony with international human rights obligations. However, the rule of presumption has also been criticised to the extent that it prevents courts from conducting an independent assessment of whether this presumption is in harmony with international human rights obligations.

(iii) The direct application of international human rights treaty provisions by the Nordic courts has remained a secondary means of giving judicial effect to international human rights treaties. The exception to the rule is made by the ECHR because all Nordic countries have incorporated the ECHR into their domestic legal orders. As incorporation paves the way for (albeit that it does not fully guarantee)[70] the direct applicability of international human rights treaties by courts and authorities, the lack of systematic incorporation in the Nordic countries except Finland and, partially, Norway at least largely (if not exclusively) explains the limited significance of the direct applicability of other human rights treaties beyond the ECHR in the Nordic courts.

(iv) A significant dimension of the interpretive effect of international human rights treaties relates to the interpretation of constitutional provisions on human rights. Usually, the Nordic courts refer to international human rights treaties in tandem with the corresponding constitutional provisions. In Iceland, for instance, the provisions of the ECHR and other human rights treaties such as the ICCPR have often featured as a significant complementary material for the interpretation of the provisions of the Icelandic Constitution.[71] However, the impact of the case law of

[70] Although Finland has systematically incorporated international human rights treaties since the 1970s, it was not until the entry into force of the ECHR in 1990 that a rapid upswing of judicial references to international human rights treaties, including international human rights jurisprudence, took effect in Finland.

[71] Two judgments by the Supreme Court of Iceland are particularly worth mentioning. In these cases, the Supreme Court took judicial notice of Article 26 of the ICCPR when interpreting Article 65 of the Constitution for the purpose of applying the principle of equality before the law. In both cases, the conclusion by the Supreme Court was that the domestic legislation at issue was found to be at variance with the human rights provisions of the Constitution. In the first judgment, delivered on 3 December 1998 in Case No 145/1998, reference was made both to Article 26 of the Covenant and to Article 14 of the ECHR for the purpose of interpreting Article 65 of the Constitution. The Supreme Court concluded that the provisions of the Fisheries Management Act regarding the allocation of fishing permits violated the principle of equality set forth in the first paragraph of Article 65 of the Constitution, which had to be observed when applying a restriction on the right to employment under the first paragraph of Article 75 of the Constitution. In the second judgment, delivered

the ECtHR on the interpretation of Nordic constitutional provisions on human rights does not mean that the judgments of the ECtHR would be legally binding on the Nordic courts insofar as the interpretation of constitutional provisions are concerned. In Norway, for example, the Supreme Court has emphasised with reference to the constitutional amendment in 2014 that while the new human rights provisions in Part E of the Constitution must be interpreted in light of their international models, future practice by international human rights treaty bodies should not have the same judicial precedent in the interpretation of the Constitution as in the interpretation of the corresponding convention provisions.[72]

(v) In all the Nordic countries, the trend appears to be that the ECHR, as seen in the light of the case law of the ECtHR, is invoked by parties and adjudicated by the courts more frequently than constitutional provisions on similar human rights.[73] The judicial emphasis on the ECHR is presumably due, at least largely if not exclusively, to traditional constitutional restraints pertaining to judicial review insofar as the constitutionality of legislation is concerned in the Nordic countries except Norway. Another explanation is the richness of the case law of the ECtHR, often displaying in great detail what human rights norms are all about in a legal sense.

(vi) The significance of the ECHR and the case law of the ECtHR in the interpretation and application of human rights by the Nordic courts has been a source of domestic discussion and even criticism. As already noted, there has been domestic discussion and debate in Norway over the appropriate role of the Norwegian courts in the interpretation of the ECHR after the judgment by the Norwegian Supreme Court in 2000 to the effect that Norwegian courts should interpret the ECHR against the backdrop of a judicial restraint and by taking judicial notice of traditional Norwegian values, particularly in cases in which the domestic legislature has considered the enactment to be in harmony with the ECHR. According to the former President of the Supreme Court of Norway, this entails the adoption of the enforcement approach under which Norwegian courts assume a position of passive interpretation of the ECHR, as seen in the light of the case law by the ECtHR, instead of actively contributing to the evolution of the ECHR through more active interpretations.[74] In Finland too, it has been noted that Finnish courts are often content to analyse the existing case law

19 December 2000 in Case No 125/2000, the Supreme Court took judicial notice of Article 26 of the ICCPR, as well as Article 9 of the Covenant on Economic, Social and Cultural Rights, the European Social Charter and the Conventions of the ILO. The outcome was a new interpretation of the provisions of the Constitution regarding social rights.

[72] Norwegian Supreme Court Reports 2015, 93.

[73] See Wiklund (n 11) 168.

[74] See C Smith, 'Interaction between the European Convention and the Protection of Human Rights and Fundamental Freedoms within the Norwegian Legal System' in P Mahoney et al (eds), *Protecting Human Rights: The European Perspective* (Cologne, Carl Heymanns Verlag, 2000) 1307.

of the ECtHR without trying to adopt more independent and active interpretations of human rights, even in cases in which corresponding constitutional provisions on human rights exist. Such a judicial tendency has been regarded as creating the risk that the constitutional protection of human rights regresses to the minimum standard of protection under the ECHR. Yet, the domestic constitutional system of rights protection is supposed to offer a higher standard of protection than that under Finland's international human rights obligations.[75]

(vii) The fact that the Nordic courts so frequently and often in detail take judicial notice of the case law of the ECtHR effectively indicates their acceptance of the authority of the Strasbourg Court in the interpretation of the ECHR. Indeed, open judicial resistance from the Nordic courts towards the case law by the ECtHR has remained very rare. However, the Swedish courts have been noted to show some degree of judicial reluctance towards setting aside domestic legislation in favour of the ECHR, and the Supreme Court of Sweden even refused to uphold the ECHR against a demand from the Norwegian and Swedish authorities to execute a penal judgment from a Norwegian court. In addition, both Finnish and Swedish courts have been reluctant to take full judicial regard of the judgments by the ECtHR insofar as the *ne bis in idem principle* has been concerned.[76]

(viii) However, the willingness of the Nordic courts to take judicial notice of the ECHR, including referring to judgments by the ECtHR, has not been entirely unproblematic. First, the significance of the ECHR has come at the expense of other human rights treaties. Although it is possible to find judicial references by the Nordic courts to other international human rights treaties, these references remain few in number in comparison to the ECHR. The second problem is that there is more case law from the Nordic courts, except in Iceland, on the application of the ECHR than on their domestic constitutional provisions on human rights. Given that the Nordic courts often tend to assume a passive approach to the application of human rights by contenting themselves with the analysis of the case law of the ECtHR only, the outcome has been that the ECHR, as interpreted by the ECtHR, usually defines the standard of human rights protection in the Nordic countries. Yet, the ECHR does not exhaust the spectrum of human rights as it largely, if not exclusively, only protects classic civil and political rights. As with other international human rights treaties, the ECHR also only provides a minimum standard of rights protection below which Contracting States are not allowed to fall, but above which they are at least permitted, if not obliged, to go. In all the Nordic countries, the constitutional doctrine is that international human rights obligations 'only' feature as minimum

[75] Lavapuro et al (n 12) 523.
[76] See Nergelius (n 2) 100–01; and Lavapuro et al (n 16) 233–37.

> standards of rights protection and that the domestic system should offer a higher level of protection. In practice, however, the ECHR, as seen in the light of case law by the ECtHR, is often the highest yardstick of judicial enforcement of human rights. Such tendencies towards passive and minimalist interpretive approaches by the Nordic courts to human rights may, once again, stem from those traditional constitutional conceptions regarding rights, courts and majoritarian notions of democracy that still are strong enough to keep judicial protection of human rights at a minimum level unless authoritative reasons clearly require otherwise.

Aside from courts, international human rights treaties have had a significant impact on the work of the Nordic legislators, as well as the public authorities, thereby indicating that Nordic legislators and authorities regard international human rights treaties as binding on them. The various ways in which international human rights treaties have influenced the work of the Nordic legislatures have significantly increased from the 1990s onwards due to the entry into force of the ECHR in the Nordic legal countries and reforms of the Nordic constitutions as far as human rights provisions are concerned. As already noted, international human rights treaties have been a significant source of inspiration for the amendment of the human rights provisions of most Nordic constitutions in recent decades. The impact of international human rights treaties is most often visible in the concrete formulations of various material constitutional provisions on human rights, but it has also been extended to cover constitutional doctrines and principles, such as those relating to the permissible limitations tests under the constitutions, to the constitutional safeguards for human rights during times of emergency and necessity, or various domestic methods of giving legal protection to human rights.

A distinct dimension of legislative amendments influenced by the Nordic legislators is constituted by reactions to judgments of the ECtHR declaring a violation of the ECHR or other critical observations by an international treaty body, such as the UN Human Rights Committee. As Nordic countries have received dozens of such judgments from the ECtHR, and Finland even more than 100, examples abound to preclude a detailed illustration. However, reference can be made to such Nordic legislative reforms that have originated in those judgments of the ECtHR that have confirmed a violation of Article 6 ECHR on the right to a fair and public hearing within a reasonable time by an independent and impartial tribunal, established by law. As this right was extended to cover various decisions by administrative authorities due to a wide meaning given to 'civil rights and obligations' by the ECtHR, this resulted in legislative amendments in the 1990s in Finland[77] and Sweden.[78] However, the continued discussion in Denmark, Iceland

[77] For an overview of the impact of the observations by the UN Human Rights Committee on legislative reforms in Finland, see Scheinin (n 33) 272–74.

[78] For instance, Sweden adopted an Act on Judicial Examination of Certain Administrative Decisions which allowed a right to appeal to administrative courts against decisions of public authorities. Similar legislative reforms were made in Finland in the 1990s.

and Sweden on the domestic incorporation of human rights treaties beyond the ECHR also displays that repeated critical observations on the lack of incorporation by international treaty bodies, such as the UN Human Rights Committee monitoring the ICCPR, have not compelled domestic legislators of these three Nordic countries to enact the domestic incorporation enactments of the ICCPR. One of the explanations for this may be that while the ECtHR has the competence to hand down legally binding judgments on the compatibility of state actions or omissions with the ECHR, the critical observations by committees or other international treaty bodies are regarded as (legally) unbinding 'interpretations' or 'recommendations' of what a given treaty requires.

D. The Impact of Membership of the EU and EEA on the Nordic Systems of Human Rights Protection

The membership of Denmark (1973), Finland (1995) and Sweden (1995) of the EU, as well as the membership of Iceland and Norway[79] of the EEA since 1994, have strengthened the constitutional tendencies in the Nordic countries towards rights-based judicial review and the convergence between constitutional protection and European or international protection of human rights through Europeanisation and internationalisation.

In particular, the entry into force of the Lisbon Treaty in December 2009, rendering the EU Charter of Fundamental Rights a legal binding rights catalogue with the same legal value as the founding treaties of the EU, has brought about entirely new constitutional dynamics in the use of the EUCFR not only by the CJEU but also by domestic courts and other constitutional actors of the EU Member States, including the Nordic ones. Courts and other constitutional actors, such as the Nordic Ombudsmen or the Constitutional Law Committee of Parliament of Finland,[80] attach growing attention to the EUCFR, as interpreted by the CJEU, in Denmark, Finland and Sweden.[81] Usually, the Danish, Finnish and Swedish

[79] For human rights in EEA law from the perspective of a national court, see A Bårdsen, 'Fundamental Rights in EEA Law: The Perspective of a National Supreme Court Justice', paper presented at the EFTA court spring seminar, Luxembourg, 12 June 2015, available at: https://www.domstol.no/globalassets/upload/hret/artikler-og-foredrag/fundamental-rights-in-eea-law---bardsen-03062015.pdf.

[80] *Ex ante* constitutional review by the Constitutional Law Committee of Parliament provides the constitutional framework for the Committee to address questions pertaining to the Charter. It is worth noting from a European perspective that the Committee has systematically taken constitutional notice of the Charter rights when reviewing *either* proposals for EU measures *or* domestic implementing enactments of EU legislative instruments for their compatibility with the Constitution and international human rights treaties since the parliamentary session of 2001, ie, at the time when the Charter was still non-binding. The very first reference by the Committee can be found in Opinion 1/2001 of the Constitutional Law Committee.

[81] For the application of the EU Charter of Fundamental Rights in the Danish, Finnish and Swedish constitutional settings, see J Christoffersen and MR Madsen, 'Denmark', T Ojanen, 'Finland', and V Ndior, 'Sweden' in Burgorgue-Larsen (n 43).

courts or other actors refer to the EUCFR in parallel with the ECHR and the corresponding constitutional provisions on human rights. For instance, it is typical for the Finnish Constitutional Law Committee of Parliament to make reference to Articles 7 and 8 of the Charter on respect for private life and protection of personal data alongside the corresponding rights under Article 8 of the ECHR and section 10 of the Constitution of Finland when reviewing EU legislative proposals or their domestic implementing enactments for their compatibility with privacy and data protection rights.

Up to now, the *real* impact of the Charter on deliberations by the Nordic courts or other constitutional actors has often remained quite slight in comparison to the ECHR. However, during the 2010s, the EUCFR has truly started affecting constitutional interpretations or doctrines. Reference can be made to a series of decisions by both Swedish and Finnish courts regarding the *ne bis in idem* principle. In that context, the case law of both the ECtHR and the CJEU has resulted in the revision of the Swedish and the Finnish approach and, accordingly, replacing it with the new interpretation, according to which a final decision in one set of proceedings would prohibit both the initiation and continuation of proceedings in the other set of proceedings if the matter was the same.[82]

Another example of the impact of the EUCFR on the Nordic constitutional doctrines can be found in the area of privacy and data protection rights—the judgments by the CJEU in such cases as *Digital Rights Ireland*[83] and *Tele2.*[84] The former ruling made it necessary for the Constitutional Law Committee of the Finnish Parliament to reconsider the constitutional protection of the so-called metadata of electronic communications (ie, information about the parties and about a message being sent and delivered between them). Earlier, the processing of metadata was understood by the Committee as falling within such 'peripheral areas' of privacy and data protection, where the legislator was understood to enjoy a wide margin of discretion to enact limitations.[85] However, the Constitutional Law Committee took the view in light of the CJEU's judgment in *Digital Rights Ireland* that a combination of various forms of metadata can reveal a lot of confidential and sensitive personal information on the individual and sensitive personal relationships, particularly when combined with information obtained from other sources. Hence, it is important to analyse which types of metadata are at issue and what their combined effect is upon the right to privacy and data protection.

The judgment by the CJEU in *Tele2*, in turn, has brought about constitutional and legal ramifications in Sweden and Finland to the extent that EU law precludes

[82] See in more detail Nergelius (n 2) 100–04; and Lavapuro et al (n 16) 233–37.

[83] Case C-293/12 and C-594/12, *Digital Rights Ireland and Others*, judgment of 8 April 2014.

[84] Joined Cases C-203/15 and C-698/15, *Tele2 Sverige AB et al*, judgment of 21 December 2016.

[85] See, eg, Opinions 6/2012, 67/2010, 66/2010, 62/2010, 29/2008 and 23/2006 by the Constitutional Law Committee on the position that such metadata as location data and traffic data of electronic communications fall within the 'peripheral areas' of privacy and data protection, with the result that the legislator enjoys a wide margin of discretion to enact legislation constituting an interference with privacy and data protection.

a general and indiscriminate retention of traffic and location data. In Finland and Sweden, providers of electronic communications services are currently obliged to retain data on a rather generalised basis.

Some references for a preliminary ruling by the Nordic courts have also been significant from the point of view of the evolution of the EU system of human rights protection. Reference can be made here to the case of *Satakunnan Markkinapörssi*, in which a reference by the Supreme Administrative Court of Finland had an impact on the evolution of EU law in the field of privacy and data protection rights to the extent that the reference necessitated the CJEU to strike a balance between the right to privacy and the protection of personal data, on the one hand, and freedom of expression and the right to information, on the other hand, as well as to define the notion of journalism in the age of electronic communications.[86] Similarly, the request by a Swedish district court in *Åkerberg Fransson* for a preliminary ruling by the CJEU clarified the interpretation of the *ne bis in idem* principle in EU law, as well as the question of the scope of application of the EUCFR to Member States. In addition, the preliminary ruling by the CJEU in *Åkerberg Fransson*[87] clarified the obligations of the national courts in situations involving a conflict between provisions of domestic law and rights guaranteed by the Charter, as the CJEU ruled that EU law precludes judicial practice which makes the obligation for a national court to disapply domestic provisions that conflict with a fundamental right guaranteed by the EUCFR conditional upon that infringement being clear from the text of the Charter or the case law relating to it.[88]

Finally, the Nordic constitutional resistance towards EU law warrants attention to the extent that it involves human rights. In Finland, the supreme authority of constitutional review and constitutional interpretation—the Constitutional Law Committee of Parliament—took the view in the early 2000s that the domestic implementation of EU legislation is not permitted to weaken the domestic constitutional standard of rights protection. This view originated in the domestic concern that the more general domestic concern that Finland's membership of the EU might dilute the domestic standard of rights protection, particularly insofar as social rights, access to documents and good administration are concerned. Due to such concerns, some constitutional provisions on human rights were actually designed to counter such problematic tendencies that might arise from membership of the EU. On the basis of these constitutional premises, the Constitutional Law Committee has on a few occasions effectively demanded such changes to domestic implementing enactments of EU legislation that have compromised the 'maximal' implementation of such EU measures as Council Framework Decision 2002/584/JHA of 13 June 2002 on the European Arrest Warrant and the surrender

[86] Case C-73/07 *Satakunnan Markkinapörssi and Satamedia*, judgment of 16 December 2008.
[87] Case C-617/10 *Åkerberg Fransson*, judgment of 26 February 2013.
[88] See Nergelius (n 2) 103–04.

procedures between Member States and Council Framework Decision 2002/475/JHA of 13 June 2002 on Combating Terrorism.[89]

Similarly, it is possible to see a constitutional challenge to EU law in the background of the aforementioned *Åkerberg Fransson* case to the extent that the Swedish Supreme Court had decided not request a preliminary ruling by the CJEU on the applicability of the EUCFR in a case concerning the *ne bis in idem* principle. As the Haparanda District Court later decided to make such a reference, and the CJEU emphasised in its ruling that national courts may, or sometimes must, refer questions to the Court for a preliminary ruling in case of doubt, the *Åkerberg Fransson* case amounted to a challenge against the Swedish Supreme Court itself rather than EU law.[90]

The most recent Nordic constitutional challenge towards the CJEU in the area of rights protection has come by the Danish Supreme Court[91] challenging the preliminary ruling by the CJEU in *Ajos* on the general principle of non-discrimination on the grounds of age, adding to the case law by the ECJ on this principle in *Mangold* and *Kücükdeveci*.[92] The judgment by the Supreme Court of Denmark in *Ajos* is discussed in more detail elsewhere in this book.[93]

Iceland and Norway's membership of the EEA has shaped the protection of human rights in these countries. In Iceland, EEA law has for its part paved the way for a new way of legal thinking that puts the protection of individuals and their rights more at the forefront than before. Icelandic courts now proceed from the presumption that the text of the constitutional provisions on human rights no longer exclusively determines the content and effect of rights. Instead, judicial notice is also taken of the wider context and intent, and, in particular, requirements arising out of international obligations in the area in question.[94] In particular, Iceland's membership of the EEA has had an impact on human rights in the areas of social policy, employment and gender equality.[95]

[89] For the Finnish constitutional challenge towards EU law, see T Ojanen, 'The European Arrest Warrant in the Midnight Sun: The Implementation and Application of the EAW in Finland' in E Guild and L Marin (eds), *Still Not Resolved? Constitutional Issues of the European Arrest Warrant* (Nijmegen, Wolf Legal Publishers, 2009) 143.

[90] See Nergelius (n 2) 103.

[91] Supreme Court of Denmark, Case No 15/2014 *Dansk Industri (DI) Acting for Ajos A/S v The estate Left by A*, judgment of 6 December 2016.

[92] Case C-441/14 *Danske Industri (DI) Acting on Behalf of Ajos A/S*, judgment of 19 April 2016.

[93] See also MR Madsen, HP Olsen and U Sadl, 'Legal Disintegration? The Ruling of the Danish Supreme Court in AJOS', *Verfassungsblog*, 30 January 2017, http://verfassungsblog.de/legal-disintegration-the-ruling-of-the-danish-supreme-court-in-ajos.

[94] Thorarensen (n 58) 721. See also ÓI Hannesson, 'The Status of Non-implemented EEA Law in Iceland: Lessons from the Judicial Reactions of the Supreme Court to International Law' (2011) 80(4) *Nordic Journal of International Law* 425, 441.

[95] B Thorhalslsson and B Thorarensen, 'Iceland's Democratic Challenges and Human Rights Implications' in HF Carey (ed) *European Institutions, Democratization, and Human Rights Protection in the European Periphery* (London, Lexington Books, 2014) 232–40. For the approach of the Icelandic courts to EEA law, see P Hreinsson, 'The Interaction between Icelandic Courts and the EFTA Court' in EFTA Court (ed), *Judicial Protection in the European Economic Area* (Stuttgart, German Law Publishers, 2012) 90.

The somewhat troublesome approach taken by the Norwegian courts, notably the Supreme Court, to EEA law is discussed elsewhere in this book (see Chapter 7).[96] While case law from Norwegian courts is usually most significant from the perspective of competition and trade law, cases such as *Holship* have also involved questions pertaining to human rights. *Holship* is also in interesting contrast to the judgment of the Danish Supreme Court in *Ajos* to the extent that the Norwegian Supreme Court decided to follow the EFTA Court's judgment by a margin of 10 votes to 7 votes.[97]

V. Concluding Observations

The contemporary protection of human rights in the Nordic countries is essentially composed of layers of protection where constitutional, European and international layers of protection complement each other and contribute to the overall protection and promotion of human rights. Hence, it is no longer possible or even meaningful to strongly distinguish between constitutional, European and international systems for the protection of human rights.

One major dimension of constitutional dynamics in the Nordic courts has been the tendency towards stronger judicial safeguards for human rights, with the result that this has had implications on the traditional Nordic constitutional relationships between legislatures and courts.

The other significant tendency has related to the influence of international human rights treaties, notably the ECHR, as seen in the light of the case law of the ECtHR, on the domestic constitutional systems for the protection of human rights. Aside from offering a major source of inspiration for constitutional reforms of human rights provisions of the Nordic constitutions since the 1990s, international human rights treaties with the ECHR at their apex have assumed a significant role in the interpretation of domestic constitutional provisions and doctrines on human rights. This strand of constitutional development has not been entirely unproblematic to the extent that it has resulted in minimalist and uninventive approaches to human rights by Nordic courts and other constitutional actors; it often suffices for Nordic courts and other actors to take notice of the existing case law of the ECtHR only, with the result that they end up enforcing the minimum standard of protection under the ECHR at the expense of the (potentially) higher standard of protection under their own constitutions. After all, all other Nordic

[96] For the approach of the Norwegian courts, particularly the Supreme Court, to EEA law, see HH Haukeland, 'One Market, Two Courts: Legal Pluralism vs. Homogeneity in the European Economic Area', (2010) 79(4) *Nordic Journal of International Law* 481. For a recent overview, see C Baudenbacher, 'Reciprocity' in C Baudenbacher (ed), *The Fundamental Principles of EEA Law* (Cham, Springer, 2017) 35.

[97] Norwegian Supreme Court, judgment of 16 December 2016, HR-2016-2554-P.

countries except Denmark nowadays have a fairly broad and progressive constitutional catalogue of human rights, and they are at least permitted, if not even obliged, to offer a higher standard of rights protection as a matter of both domestic constitutional law and international law.

By and large, it is possible to observe patterns of constitutional similarity and convergence between the Nordic constitutional systems insofar as the protection of human rights is concerned. Yet, there are also patterns of constitutional difference, some of them breaking through the traditional divide between the Eastern (Finland and Sweden) and Western (Denmark, Iceland and Norway) Nordic countries. One such divide is currently made by the approach to the incorporation of international human rights treaties into domestic legal orders: while Finland has systematically incorporated international human rights treaties into its domestic law since the 1970s and Norway is also increasingly doing the same, Denmark, Iceland and Sweden are still following a much more cautious approach to the domestic incorporation. Despite repeated recommendations by international treaty bodies such as the UN Human Rights Committee to incorporate the core human rights treaties of the UN, the ECHR is still the only human rights treaty incorporated by Denmark and Sweden. Iceland incorporated the CRC in 2013 after having incorporated the ECHR in 1994.

Another noteworthy divide between the five Nordic countries has been introduced by the EU Charter of Fundamental Rights particularly after the entry into force of the Lisbon Treaty, which rendered the Charter legally binding in 2009. The Charter's role, including the case law of the CJEU on the Charter, is rapidly growing, with the result that many of the transformations at work in the area of rights protection and constitutional law in general in the EU Member States, including the three Nordic Member States, can increasingly be traced back to the ways in which the ECHR, the Charter and constitutional systems of rights protection interact and reinforce the changes in the other two.

7

Impact of the EU/EEA on the Nordic Constitutional Systems

HELLE KRUNKE

I. Introduction

As discussed in previous chapters there is a historical divide between the Nordic countries into an East and a West. The West consists of Denmark, Norway and Iceland, and the East consists of Sweden and Finland. However, cooperation with the European Union (EU) and the European Economic Area (EEA) has introduced a new divide into the Nordic region. Whereas Denmark, Sweden and Finland are full Member States of the EU, Norway and Iceland are only members of the EEA. Until 1995, only Denmark was a full Member State of the EU, having joined the EC (as it was then called) in 1973 at the same time as the UK and Ireland. This might even be said to constitute yet another divide linking Denmark more strongly to the rest of Europe than the rest of the Nordic countries are. In this chapter the impact of the EU/EEA on the Nordic countries will be analysed. Through this analysis, it will be possible to determine the importance of the described divisions and maybe even to discover new hidden divisions.

II. The Nordic Countries and EU/EEA Membership

Denmark was the first Nordic country to join the European Community (EC) back in 1973. Prior to the Danish accession, a referendum had taken place in accordance with Article 20 of the Danish Constitution on the transfer of sovereignty to international organisations. The referendum took place on 2 October 1972 and the outcome was 63.4 per cent in favour and 36.6 per cent against membership of the EC. A total of 90.1 per cent of the voters voted in the referendum. On 28 November 1972, a referendum on EC membership was also held in Norway. However, with 53.5 per cent against EC membership, Norway stayed outside the EC.

The EEA Agreement was signed in Porto on 2 May 1992, entering into force on 1 January 1994. More than 20 years would pass before Sweden and Finland joined the EU in 1995. In the Finnish referendum on EU membership on 16 October 1994, 56.89 per cent voted in favour of membership. Only 70.8 per cent of the electorate participated in the referendum. On 13 November 1994, 52.3 per cent of Swedes voted in favour of EU membership, while 46.8 per cent voted against; 83.3 per cent of those eligible to vote participated in the referendum. At around the same time, the Norwegians once more chose to stay outside the EU. In a referendum on 28 November 1994, 52.2 per cent voted against EU membership. This meant that a divide was created between the Nordic countries, with Denmark, Sweden and Finland as EU Member States, and Norway and Iceland as EEA members.

Iceland entered into negotiations with the EU on membership of the EU in 2009. However, following the 2013 election, Iceland chose to withdraw from the negotiations. As a result, the Nordic EU divide was sustained.

III. How is the EU/EEA Cooperation Embedded in the Nordic Constitutions/Constitutional Systems?

A. The Danish Constitution

The constitutional embedding of participation in the EU/EEA differs among the Nordic countries. One might presume that the EU is reflected the most in the Constitution of the oldest Nordic Member State, Denmark; however, that is not the case. The Danish Constitution has not been revised since 1953. Although Denmark did not enter the EC until 1973, the drafters of the Constitution foresaw that Denmark might one day enter a supranational organisation, since the European Coal and Steel Community had already been established in 1951 and hence Article 20 prescribes how sovereignty can be transferred to an international organisation. Article 20 is a general provision which does not mention specific organisations, including the EU. In this way, Denmark's membership of the EU is not visible in the Constitution. Article 20 reads:

(1) Powers vested in the authorities of the Realm under this Constitutional Act may, to such extent as shall be provided by statute, be delegated to international authorities set up by mutual agreement with other states for the promotion of international rules of law and cooperation.

(2) For the enactment of a Bill dealing with the above, a majority of five-sixths of the members of the Folketing shall be required. If this majority is not obtained, whereas the majority required for the passing of ordinary Bills is obtained, and if the Government maintains it, the Bill shall be submitted to the electorate for approval or rejection in accordance with the rules for referendums laid down in section 42.

Danish membership of the EU is regulated by the Act of Accession.[1]

According to case law[2] and legal literature,[3] the following limits for transferal exist as regards Article 20:[4]

- Only specific powers vested in Danish authorities under the Constitution can be transferred and the extent of transferred powers must be provided by statute. There must be a positive delimitation of which competences are transferred as regards topics and the character of the competences.[5]
- Not all legislative, executive or judicial power can be transferred.[6]
- Powers which no Danish authority has cannot be transferred.[7]
- The power to change the Constitution cannot be transferred.[8]
- The power to decide upon the age of voting cannot be transferred.[9]
- Provisions on national elections cannot be transferred.[10]
- The competence of the Court of Impeachment is excluded from transfer.[11]
- Denmark must remain an independent state.[12]
- Denmark must have a democratic form of government.[13]
- The Supreme Court reserves the final right to decide whether an EU act or judgment exceeds the powers transferred in the Danish Act of Succession.[14]
- The national separation of powers model must to some extent be respected as regards the relationship between legislators and courts.[15]
- The rule of law and legal certainty are important legal principles.[16]

[1] Law no 447 of 11 October 1972, Act on Denmark's Accession to the European Communities.

[2] U 1998.800H (*Maastricht* judgment), U 2013.1451H (*Lisbon* judgment) and U 2017.824H (*Ajos* judgment).

[3] See, eg, H Zahle, *Dansk forfatningsret* (Copenhagen, Jurist- og Økonomforbundets Forlag, 2001) 401ff.

[4] The following list is almost identical to the list in H Krunke, 'Constitutional Identity in Denmark: Extracting Constitutional Identity in the Context of a Restrained Supreme Court and a Strong Legislator' in C Calliess and G van der Schyff (eds), *Constitutional Identity in a Europe of Multilevel Constitutionalism* (Cambridge, Cambridge University Press, forthcoming).

[5] U 1998.800H; and see, eg, H Zahle, *Dansk forfatningsret* (Copenhagen, Jurist- og Økonomforbundets Forlag, 2001) 401ff.

[6] ibid.

[7] See, eg, ibid 401ff.

[8] ibid.

[9] ibid.

[10] ibid.

[11] ibid.

[12] U 1998.800H.

[13] ibid.

[14] U 1998.800H and U 2013.1451H.

[15] U 2017.824H.

[16] The Supreme Court does not express this directly in U 2017.824H. However, these principles seem to be inherent in the judgment when the Court states that the Supreme Court 'would be acting outside its limits of powers as a judicial authority if it was to dis-apply the national provision in this situation'.

If a transfer of sovereignty falls outside the above-mentioned limits, it would be possible to amend the Constitution. The Constitution has no eternity clauses. However, constitutional amendment (Article 88) is regarded as de facto difficult to carry out because of the arduous process, which requires the following to occur:

> Should the Folketing pass a Bill for the purposes of a new constitutional provision, and the Government wish to proceed with the matter, writs shall be issued for the election of members of a new Folketing. If the Bill is passed un-amended by the Folketing assembling after the election, the Bill shall, within six months after its final passage, be submitted to the electors for approval or rejection by direct voting. Rules for this voting shall be laid down by statute. If a majority of the persons taking part in the voting, and at least 40 per cent of the electorate, have voted in favour of the Bill as passed by the Folketing, and if the Bill receives the Royal Assent, it shall form an integral part of the Constitutional Act.

It should also be mentioned that EU treaties which do not require transfer of sovereignty can be adopted according to the normal procedure for entering into international cooperation in Article 19, which only requires the consent of a majority in Parliament.

It is necessary to study the Danish Act on Accession to the EC/EU in order to get an impression of Danish EU membership. Since some competences mentioned in the Constitution have been transferred to the EU, which is an important actor in daily political life, one might say that the Constitution does not reflect the reality of contemporary governance in Denmark. This is further reflected in the fact that the 'King' is mentioned as having several competences which have today been transferred to ministers. Some constitutional provisions date back to 1849. Many reasons can be given as to why the Danish Constitution has not been amended during the more than 40 years that Denmark has been a member of the EC/EU. Some of these have a legal nature. First, the constitutional design with Article 20 as the main provision has been able to handle EC/EU membership. None of the treaties has gone beyond Article 20 so far and required an amendment of the Constitution. Second, the amendment procedure in the Constitution is very arduous and this prevents constitutional change. However, a number of other reasons of both a legal and political nature can also be given as to why the Danish Constitution has not been amended in order to mention the EU cooperation. Political actors have found Article 20 flexible enough to embrace new EU treaties until now. The Supreme Court has supported this view in the *Maastricht* judgment and the *Lisbon* judgment. An amendment as regards the EU would most likely be part of a complete revision of the Constitution. There is not a political majority in favour of that. A revision would entail discussions not only on the EU but also on controversial topics, such as whether the European Convention on Human Rights (ECHR) should be mentioned in the Constitution and whether the human rights catalogue should be updated, whether Denmark should have a state church in the future and the role that the monarch should play in the Constitution in the future.

As regards Denmark and EU membership, major discussions in Danish legal theory have been as follows:[17]

— How to draw the line between Article 19 and Article 20 when accessing a new EU treaty—the lower limit of Article 20. This is primarily a procedural question, since Article 19 requires a majority in Parliament and Article 20 requires either a five-sixths majority in Parliament and, if that cannot be reached, a referendum. The major question is whether sovereignty is ceded, since this will require an Article 20 procedure. Important case law in this field is the judgment on the Lisbon Treaty (U 2013.1451H).[18]
— How to draw the line between Article 20 and Article 88 when accessing a new EU treaty—the upper limit of Article 20. This is primarily a procedural question since Article 88 requires that a majority of the persons taking part in the voting, and at least 40 per cent of the electorate, have voted in favour of the Bill as passed by Parliament. The limits of Article 20 were listed above. An example is as follows: if no positive delimitation of which competences would be transferred as regards topics and the character of the competences exists, an Article 88 procedure must be followed. Important case law in this field is the judgment on the Maastricht Treaty (U 1998.800H).[19]
— How to handle the dynamic nature of judgments from the Court of Justice of the European Union (CJEU) in relation to transfer of sovereignty in the Danish Constitution. This is the question of creeping competence transference of powers to the EU through its case law. Important case law in this field is the judgment on the Maastricht Treaty (U 1998.800H), the judgment on the Lisbon Treaty (U 2013.1451H) and the *Ajos* judgment (U2017.824H).[20]
— Whether the mandates given by Parliament's Committee on European Policy are politically or legally binding on the government.[21]

[17] This is not an exhaustive list.

[18] See, eg, H Krunke, 'The Danish Lisbon Judgment: Danish Supreme Court, Case 199/2012, Judgment of 20 February 2013' (2014) 10(3) *European Constitutional Law Review* 542; and HP Olsen, 'The Danish Supreme Court's Decision on the Constitutionality of Denmark's Ratification of the Lisbon Treaty' (2013) 50 *CMLR* 1489.

[19] See, eg, H Zahle, *Dansk forfatningsret* (Copenhagen, Jurist- og Økonomforbundets Forlag, 2001) 401ff; and O Spiermann, 'Hvad kommer efter tyve? En analyse af Højesterets dom i "grundlovssagen"' (1998) *Ugeskrift for Retsvæsen*, section B, 325.

[20] See, eg, MR Madsen, HP Olsen and U Sadl, 'Competing Supremacies and Clashing Institutional Rationalities: The Danish Supreme Court's Decision in the Ajos Case and the National Limits of Judicial Cooperation' (2017) 23(1–2) *European Law Journal* 140; R Nielsen and CD Tvarnø, 'Præjudikat eller ikke præjudikat—Chartrets retsvirkning i dansk ret efter EU-domstolens og Højesterets afgørelser i Ajos-sagen' (2017) 02–03 *Tidsskrift for Rettsvitenskap* 218; J Kristiansen, 'Grænser for EU-rettens umiddelbare anvendelighed i dansk ret—Om Højesterets dom i Ajos-sagen' (2017) *Ugeskrift for Retsvæsen*, section B, 75; and O Spiermann 'En højesteretsdom om EU-tiltrædelsesloven' (2017) *Ugeskrift for Retsvæsen*, Section B, 297.

[21] See, eg, H Krunke, *Den Udenrigspolitiske Kompetence* (Copenhagen, Jurist- og Økonomforbundets Forlag, 2003) 200–19; H Krunke, 'Folketingets kontrol med den europæiske udenrigs- og sikkerhedspolitik' (2001) *Ugeskrift for Retsvæsen*, section B, 401; H Krunke, 'Developments in National

— Whether referendums on EU treaties can be held in situations where at least a five-sixths majority in Parliament support transfer of sovereignty.[22] Such referendums have been held in practice.

The Danish Ministry of Justice considers whether all new draft legislation is compatible with the Constitution, EU law and other international obligations, including the ECHR.

In the Danish *Ajos* judgment from 2016 (U 2017.824H), the Danish Supreme Court found it impossible to follow an interpretation by the CJEU in a preliminary ruling. The reasons for this were that: (1) it was not possible within the Danish Accession Act to give precedence to the unwritten principle on age discrimination in a horizontal relationship; and (2) the Supreme Court would be acting outside the limits of its powers as a judicial authority if it were to disapply the national provision in this situation. Hence, the Supreme Court—for the first time in history—did not follow an interpretation suggested by the CJEU in a preliminary ruling and applied national legislation instead of EU law to the case.

B. The Swedish Constitution

Though they have been members of the EU for a shorter period than Denmark, Sweden and Finland have chosen to let their membership be clearly reflected in their constitutions through the constitutional amendments in 2011 and 2012 respectively. Already in Chapter 1, Article 10 of the Instrument of Government, it is mentioned that Sweden is a member of the EU. Furthermore, the Constitution has a specific provision on the transfer of decision-making authority within the framework of the EU cooperation in Chapter 10, Article 6:

> Transfer of decision-making authority within the framework of European Union cooperation
>
> Art. 6. Within the framework of European Union cooperation, the Riksdag may transfer decision-making authority which does not affect the basic principles by which Sweden is governed. Such transfer presupposes that protection for rights and freedoms in the field of cooperation to which the transfer relates corresponds to that afforded under this Instrument of Government and the European Convention for the Protection of Human

Parliaments' Involvement in Ordinary Foreign Policy and European Policy—Denmark' (2007) 13(2) *European Public Law* 335; JA Jensen, *Parlamentarismens statsretlige betydning* (Copenhagen, Jurist- og Økonomforbundets Forlag, 1997) 136; and H Zahle, *Dansk forfatningsret* (Copenhagen, Jurist- og Økonomforbundets Forlag, 2001) 437ff.

[22] H Rasmussen, '§ 20' in H Zahle (ed), *Danmarks Riges Grundlov med kommentarer*, 2nd edn (Copenhagen, Jurist- og Økonomforbundets Forlag, 2006) 217f. Against this, see H Koch, 'Grundlovsstridige folkeafstemninger' in H Koch (ed), *Politik og Jura—Festskrift til Ole Espersen* (Copenhagen, Thomson/GadJura, 2004) 497–523.

> Rights and Fundamental Freedoms. The Riksdag may approve a transfer of authority, provided at least three fourths of those voting and more than half the members of the Riksdag vote in favour of the decision. The Riksdag's decision may also be taken in accordance with the procedure prescribed for the enactment of fundamental law. Such a transfer cannot be decided until the Riksdag has approved the agreement under Article 3.

This provision has existed since the 1970s, but it was amended in 1994 when Sweden joined the EU and once again in 2002.[23] An important difference compared to the Danish Constitution is that only the Parliament is involved in the decision to transfer powers to the EU in the Swedish context. This requires a majority of three-quarters of Parliament. Joakim Nergelius has referred to the Swedish model as 'probably one of the most flexible solutions among the EU Member States'.[24] According to him, an official investigative committee suggested an even more radical solution in 1993, namely inserting a new provision into the Constitution declaring total supremacy of EU law also in relation to the Constitution.[25] However, this solution did not gain enough political support.

The transfer of powers after Article 6 is limited in the following ways:

— The basic principles by which Sweden are governed must not be affected.
— Transfer presupposes that the protection of rights and freedoms in the field of cooperation to which the transfer relates corresponds to that afforded under the Instrument of Government and the ECHR.

Otherwise, a constitutional amendment is necessary. According to Chapter 8, Article 14 of the Instrument of Government, this requires two identically worded decisions separated by a general election. If at least one-third of the Riksdag members support a referendum on a proposal to amend a fundamental law, a referendum must be held. In the referendum, all those entitled to vote in the election are entitled to state whether or not they accept the proposal on fundamental law which is being held in abeyance. The proposal is rejected if a majority of those taking part in the referendum vote against it and if the number of those voting against exceeds half the number of those who registered a valid vote in the election. In other cases, the proposal goes forward to the Riksdag for final consideration (see Chapter 8, Article 16 of the Instrument of Government). However, until now this has not been necessary.

Until the constitutional reform of 2011, the common view was that Article 6 was aimed at the Parliament (and not the courts). However, in the preparatory works to the constitutional reform, this view was challenged and it was stated that the courts can use Article 6 as a last resort.[26] In NJA 2014, p 79, the Swedish

[23] See, eg, J Nergelius, 'Constitutional Reform in Sweden: Some Important Remarks' (2013) *Tijdschrift voor Constitutioneel Recht* 372, 378.

[24] ibid.

[25] ibid.

[26] See SOU 2008:125, 500.

Supreme Court confirmed that the courts can apply Article 6 as a limit on the effect of EU law in Sweden. The scope of the second limitation was interpreted by the Swedish Supreme Court in the judgment. The plaintiff questioned whether an interpretation by the CJEU in a preliminary reference violated the ECHR. The Supreme Court stated that a Swedish court may overrule an interpretation by the CJEU only in cases which would otherwise lead to a serious and clear violation of the ECHR. Furthermore, it is stated that this exemption is very limited. Following this, it found that there was no foundation for setting aside the interpretation by the CJEU in the concrete case. The judgment must be viewed as progressive because it is the first case in which the Supreme Court has applied Article 6, which has commonly been viewed as an article aimed at the Parliament. In NJA 2014, p 79, the Swedish Supreme Court might be said to show willingness to set limits on the effect of EU law, but unwillingness to state where the limit lies.

It has been stated in the legal literature that in the years immediately after the Swedish accession to the EU, preliminary CJEU rulings were in some cases misinterpreted by the Supreme Court and the Supreme Administrative Court.[27]

In the Swedish context, it is important to mention that prior review of legislation in relation to the Constitution, the ECHR and EU law is performed by the Law Council, which consists of jurists and former judges from the two Supreme Courts.[28] The reviews of the Council are provided in opinions. Opinions can be requested from the government or by a parliamentary committee according to Article 21 of the Instrument of Government. However, it does not constitute an obstacle to the application of law if the Law Council is not consulted.[29] Apparently, the main reason why the Law Council has criticised much draft legislation since 2000 is the fact that the Law Council must review compatibility with EU law and the ECHR.[30]

Sweden has a long and strong tradition of openness and transparency. In 2016, it celebrated the 250th anniversary of the Swedish Freedom of the Press Act. Naturally, Sweden has much focus on openness and transparency in the EU. Compared to Sweden, the EU has a weaker tradition in this field, though progress is being made. Therefore, Swedish legal literature has focused heavily on how membership of the EU might cause a weaker level of protection of openness and transparency for Swedish citizens.[31]

[27] Nergelius, 'Judicial Review in Relation to European Law' (2009) *Nordisk Tidsskrift for Menneskerettigheter* 142, 149.

[28] See, eg, Nergelius (n 23) 374.

[29] ibid 375.

[30] ibid 378, with reference to an analysis by Council judge Danelius in (2009) 1 *Svensk Juristtidning* 25–33.

[31] See, eg, AS Lind, J Reichel and I Österdahl, *Transparency in the Future: Swedish Openness 250 Years* (Tallinn, Ragulga Forläg, 2017).

The Swedish membership of the EU is regulated by the Act of Accession.[32] Sweden has a 'de facto exception' from the euro, as it has deliberately avoided satisfying the mandatory criteria to enter into the EMU.[33]

C. The Finnish Constitution

Whereas the Danish Constitution does not refer to the EU at all, the Finnish Constitution—like the Swedish Constitution—already mentions that Finland is a Member State of the EU in its first section:

> Finland is a sovereign republic. The constitution of Finland is established in this constitutional act. The constitution shall guarantee the inviolability of human dignity and the freedom and rights of the individual and promote justice in society. Finland participates in international cooperation for the protection of peace and human rights and for the development of society. Finland is a Member State of the European Union (1112/2011, entry into force 1.3.2012).

Even though the Finnish Constitution refers to Finland's membership of the EU in section 1, it also emphasises in the very first sentence of that section that Finland is a sovereign republic. It might be recalled that the Danish Supreme Court in its *Maastricht* judgment stated that Denmark must remain an independent state. In this way, both section 1 of the Finnish Constitution and the Danish Maastricht judgment provide a maximum limit for how far the EU can develop without constitutional amendments in the two countries.

The main provision on the transfer of sovereignty to the EU is section 94, according to which:

> [I]f the proposal concerns the Constitution or an alteration of the national border, or such transfer of authority to the European Union, an international organisation or an international body that is of significance with regard to Finland's sovereignty, the decision shall be made by at least two thirds of the votes cast [in Parliament].

Otherwise, acceptance of an international obligation only requires a simple majority vote in Parliament.

As is the case in Sweden—and unlike Denmark—only the Finnish Parliament is included in the procedure for ceding sovereignty. However, compared to Sweden, the Finnish Parliament is more restricted in the sense that there are more limitations to decision-making by a simple majority than is the case in

[32] Law no 1500 of 29 December 1994, Act Concerning the Accession of Sweden to the European Union.

[33] R Adler-Nissen, *Opting out of the European Union* (Cambridge, Cambridge University Press, 2014) 10.

Sweden. In the following situations, the Finnish Parliament will need a two-thirds majority:

— if the proposal concerns the Constitution;
— if the proposal concerns an alteration of the national border;
— if such transfer of authority to the EU, an international organisation or an international body is of significance with regard to Finland's sovereignty.

The two-thirds requirement in section 94 matches the procedure for amendment of the Constitution in section 73, though that procedure is altogether more arduous than the one in section 94.

It should also be mentioned that the Constitution makes a distinction between 'acceptance' of international obligations (Article 94) and 'bringing into force' international obligations (Article 95). According to Article 95:

> The provisions of treaties and other international obligations, in so far as they are of a legislative nature, are brought into force by an Act. Otherwise, international obligations are brought into force by a Decree (1112/2011, entry into force 1.3.2012). A Government bill for the bringing into force of an international obligation is considered in accordance with the ordinary legislative procedure pertaining to an Act. However, if the proposal concerns the Constitution or a change to the national territory, or such transfer of authority to the European Union, an international organisation or an international body that is of significance with regard to Finland's sovereignty, the Parliament shall adopt it, without leaving it in abeyance, by a decision supported by at least two thirds of the votes cast.

Finnish membership of the EU is incorporated into Finnish law by the Incorporation Act of the Accession Treaty.[34]

Contrary to the other Nordic constitutions, the Finnish Constitution contains detailed regulation on the participation of Parliament in the national preparation of EU matters in section 96 and on Parliament's right to receive information on EU affairs in section 97:

> Section 96—Participation of the Parliament in the national preparation of European Union matters
>
> The Parliament considers those proposals for acts, agreements and other measures which are to be decided in the European Union and which otherwise, according to the Constitution, would fall within the competence of the Parliament. The Government shall, for the determination of the position of the Parliament, communicate a proposal referred to in paragraph (1) to the Parliament by a communication of the Government, without delay, after receiving notice of the proposal. The proposal is considered in the Grand Committee and ordinarily in one or more of the other Committees that issue statements to the Grand Committee. However, the Foreign Affairs Committee considers a proposal pertaining to foreign and security policy. Where necessary, the Grand Committee or the Foreign Affairs Committee may issue to the Government a statement on the proposal. In addition, the Speaker's Council may decide that the matter be taken up for debate in

[34] Act no 1540 of 1994.

> plenary session, during which, however, no decision is made by the Parliament. The Government shall provide the appropriate Committees with information on the consideration of the matter in the European Union. The Grand Committee or the Foreign Affairs Committee shall also be informed of the position of the Government on the matter.
>
> Section 97—Parliamentary right to receive information on international affairs
>
> The Foreign Affairs Committee of the Parliament shall receive from the Government, upon request and when otherwise necessary, reports of matters pertaining to foreign and security policy. Correspondingly, the Grand Committee of the Parliament shall receive reports on the preparation of other matters in the European Union. The Speaker's Council may decide on a report being taken up for debate in plenary session, during which, however, no decision is made by the Parliament. The Prime Minister shall provide the Parliament or a Committee with information on matters to be dealt with in a European Council beforehand and without delay after a meeting of the Council. The same applies when amendments are being prepared to the treaties establishing the European Union. The appropriate Committee of the Parliament may issue a statement to the Government on the basis of the reports or information referred to above.

Later on in this chapter, there is a specific section on EU/EEA cooperation and the Nordic Parliaments, especially in light of the Early Warning System and the Barroso initiative.

Importantly, in the Finnish context, the Constitutional Law Committee of Parliament is regarded as the primary authority of constitutional interpretation. This is different from the situation in Denmark, Norway and Iceland, in which the Supreme Courts must be viewed as the primary interpreter of the constitutions. On the other hand, Sweden is closer to Finland with its Law Council (discussed above). The members of the Finnish Constitutional Law Committee are members of Parliament; however, they hear experts in constitutional law. The Committee traditionally has high level of integrity and authority. Its reviews are treated as binding by the Parliament.[35] In this way, the Finnish Constitutional Law Committee is stronger than the Swedish Law Council. The power of the Constitutional Law Committee was, among other examples, clear when it stated that 'domestic implementation of EU law may not lower the level of national protection of constitutional rights and the implementation of EU measures should conform to the requirements originating in the domestic system for the protection of constitutional and human rights'.[36] In this way, constitutional and human rights define the limits of primacy of EU law over Finnish law and this has had an impact, for example, in relation to the implementation of the European Arrest Warrant and the Council Framework Decision of 13 June 2002 on combating terrorism, since the 'maximal' implementation of EU law was limited.[37]

[35] See, eg, T Ojanen, 'From Constitutional Periphery toward the Center: Transformations of Judicial Review in Finland' (2009) 27(2) *Nordisk Tidsskrift for Menneskerettigheter* 194, especially 196.

[36] ibid 202.

[37] See, eg, T Ojanen, 'The European Arrest Warrant in Finland' in E Guild (ed), *Constitutional Challenge to the European Arrest Warrant* (Oisterwijk, Wolf Legal Publishers, 2006); and Ojanen (n 35).

The Finnish courts are traditionally rather weak in the sense that until 2000, they did not have the competence to review the constitutionality of Acts of Parliament. As a result, one might say that membership of the EU has had a significant impact on the competence and role of the Finnish courts. The Finnish Supreme Court has not (yet) challenged the primacy of EU law—it has dealt with a few cases concerning this topic, but not 'hard' cases.[38] Later on in this chapter, we shall see that the Finnish courts are the most active among the Nordic courts as regards preliminary references. This shows an interest from the side of the Finnish Supreme Court in learning how the CJEU interprets EU law. Another impact of Finland's EU membership is that the Finnish courts have been inspired by the legal reasoning and interpretation methods in EU law. This has meant a 'shift in legal reasoning from formal, rule-focused reasoning toward relying more heavily on reasoning from principle' and EU law has 'affected the methods of interpretation, attaching more significance to what can be described as the teleological or purposive interpretation approach'.[39] Furthermore, as a source of law, case law is now considered to be of greater significance.[40]

Finland is the only Nordic country which participates in the Economic Monetary Union (EMU) zone. Both Denmark and Sweden have exceptions in this field. This might be said to make a distinction between the Nordic EU Member States. Especially during the eurozone crisis, this distinction became clear, since Finland was more directly affected by the crisis than Denmark and Sweden. Furthermore, the EMU cooperation has created some constitutional concerns in Finland. Through its efficient *ex ante* review process in the Constitutional Law Committee, Finland was actually the first EU Member State to express constitutional concern regarding the draft European Stability Mechanism (ESM) Treaty.[41] Concern was expressed by the German Federal Constitutional Court more than a year later.[42] The Finnish Constitutional Law Committee has especially scrutinised various instruments related to the eurozone crisis in relation to their impact on the budgetary powers of Parliament.[43] Furthermore, the Committee has emphasised the need to observe the strong constitutional prerogatives of Parliament as regards the rights of information and participation in domestic decision-making pertaining to EU affairs in accordance with sections 96–97 of the Constitution (quoted above).[44] These constitutional obligations set out constitutional limits to EMU-related measures and crisis management measures.[45]

[38] ibid 200.
[39] ibid 202.
[40] ibid.
[41] See, eg, Opinion 27/2011, Opinion 1/2012 and Opinion 13/2012 of the Constitutional Law Committee.
[42] See Judgment of 12 September 2012, 2 Bv 1390/12.
[43] See Opinion 13/2012 of the Constitutional Committee.
[44] ibid.
[45] ibid.

D. The Approach of the Norwegian and the Icelandic Constitutions towards EEA

As could be expected, the Constitutions of Norway and Iceland do not mention the EEA cooperation. In these countries it is viewed as ordinary international cooperation; however, it is the most extensive and influential treaty to which these countries have acceded, imposing wide obligations on them, including the transfer of powers in more areas. The main difference between the nature of the cooperation in the EU system and the EEA system is that the latter does not create supranational powers for its institutions. Accordingly, the EEA Agreement is based on the main foundation that legislative powers are not delegated to international institutions, EEA decisions need to be implemented into national law by the legislature and EEA legislation does not have priority over other national legislation. However, in some limited areas such as competition law, the EEA Agreement presupposed from the outset that executive powers were transferred to the main control body of the EEA, the European Free Trade Association (EFTA) Surveillance Authority. Furthermore, the EEA Agreement establishing new supervisory bodies in the financial market (the European Banking Authority, the European Insurance and Occupational Pensions Authority and the European Securities and Markets Authority) is challenging the Norwegian and Icelandic Constitutions.[46] The powers given to the new supervisory authorities include making directly and legally binding decisions in relation to companies and individuals which go far beyond the criteria established when Iceland and Norway joined the EEA.[47]

In Norway, the Parliament consented to the ratification of the EEA Treaty under Article 115 (formerly Article 93), but the ongoing cooperation follows the dualistic principle. The dualistic principle follows from Article 1 of the Constitution.[48] Even though the Norwegian Constitution was amended in 2007, 2012, 2014 and 2016, the EEA was not written into the Constitution. The Constitution has a number of general provisions on international cooperation in Articles 25–26 and 115.

Even though Norway is not a member of the EU, transfer of sovereignty to international organisations with supra-national powers is possible either by amending the Constitution (Article 121, but within the 'sovereignty' clause in Article 1) or by parliamentary consent under Article 115 (within the limits in Article 115

[46] See Regulations (EU) Nos 1093, 1094 and 1095/2010 and Regulation (EU) No 1092/2010.

[47] See B Thorarensen, 'The Nordic Constitutions in a Multilevel Constitutional Order' in H Krunke et al (eds), *Festskrift til Henning Koch. Rettens Magt. Magtens Ret* (Copenhagen, Jurist- og Økonomforbundets Forlag, 2014) 415–16.

[48] See, eg, E Smith, *Konstitutionelt demokrati. Statsforfatningsretten i prinsipielt og komparativt lys* (Bergen, Fagbokforlaget, 2015) 151–52 and 163ff. For a critique of the classic distinction between traditional international law and international law with direct effect, see T Bekkedal, 'Suverenitet og samarbeid. Grunnlovens skranker for delegasjon av statsmakt (2016) 42(1) *Kritisk Juss* 3, especially 5.

and Article 1). Some provisions set limits on the powers which Norway could transfer to such an organisation:

— Norway must be a free, independent, indivisible and inalienable realm (Article 1).
— The armed forces may not be transferred to the service of foreign powers (Article 25).
— The power to alter the Constitution cannot be transferred (Article 115).
— Amendment of the Constitution must never contradict the principles embodied in the Constitution, but must solely relate to modifications of particular provisions which do not alter the spirit of the Constitution (Article 121).[49]

The main provision for transfer of sovereignty is Article 115, which reads:

> In order to safeguard international peace and security or to promote the international rule of law and cooperation, the Storting may, by a three-fourths majority, consent that an international organisation to which Norway belongs or will belong shall have the right, within specified fields, to exercise powers which in accordance with this Constitution are normally vested in the authorities of the state, although not the power to alter this Constitution. For the Storting to grant such consent, at least two thirds of its Members shall be present, as required for proceedings for amending the Constitution. The provisions of this Article do not apply in cases of membership in an international organisation whose decisions only have application for Norway exclusively under international law.

Discussions in relation to Article 115 have been:[50]

— how to delimit 'within specific fields';
— the dynamic character of EU law;
— the divide between Article 115 on the transfer of sovereignty and Article 26 on traditional international cooperation.

According to Article 115, it requires the support of three-quarters of Parliament to transfer sovereignty. Interestingly, this is a larger majority than is required in order to amend the Constitution and it is meant to compensate for the absence of elections between the proposal and the vote under Article 121. Constitutional amendment requires the support of a two-thirds majority of three Parliaments following each other after elections support the amendments (Article 121). The voters are not directly involved through the medium of elections when sovereignty is ceded and when the Constitution is amended, unlike in Denmark, where the voters are involved in transfer of sovereignty if a five-sixths majority in Parliament is not possible and in constitutional amendment through an election and a referendum. As a result, the Norwegian Constitution seems easier to amend—as practice also

[49] This exception has now lost some of its importance. See E Smith, 'Old and Protected? On the "Supra-constitutional" Clause of the Constitution of Norway' (2012) 44(3) *Israel Law Review* 369.
[50] Smith (n 48) 164, 168–69.

shows—though it might take some time. On the other hand, whereas Denmark has no eternity clauses, Norway has the provision on the principles of the Constitution which must be upheld. Transfer of sovereignty is also easier in Norway than in Denmark. This is even further underlined by the following practice discussed below.

A major discussion in constitutional theory in relation to the transfer of sovereignty has been the application of Article 26(2) and Article 115. How far can Article 26(2) be stretched in relation to EEA cooperation? Some legal theorists have criticised the fact that a practice has developed according to which this provision has been used as a legal basis for ceding sovereignty when transfer can be characterised as a 'minor intrusion', even though a new provision on the transfer of sovereignty was introduced in Article 93 in 1962 precisely on the basis that it was unclear whether Article 26 could be the legal basis for transfer of sovereignty.[51] No clear criteria exist for how to distinguish 'minorly intrusive' transfer of sovereignty from more intrusive transfer.[52] Article 26(2) reads:

> Treaties on matters of special importance, and, in all cases, treaties whose implementation, according to the Constitution, necessitates a new law or a decision by the Storting, are not binding until the Storting has given its consent thereto.

The impact of applying Article 26(2) is that Parliament has made decisions by a simple majority, whereas Article 115 demands a three-quarters majority. Some legal theorists have put forward that Article 93 has not been violated since governments and parliaments over a long period have developed a practice and interpreted the Constitution through a dynamic interpretation.[53] Article 115 has only been applied twice, namely in 1992 for the entire EEA accession, but motivated in particular by supra-national elements, such as when competence to impose fines was ceded to the EEA in the field of competition law[54] and in 2016 when Norway joined EU's Finance Supervisory Authority.[55]

The Norwegian Supreme Court has in the *Finanger I* case from 16 November 2000, HR-2000-49-B, Rt-2000-1811, stated that EEA law must be given considerable weight when interpreting Norwegian legislation, although not so much weight that it can set aside a clear Norwegian provision, and this applies even when Parliament is under the impression that a directive has been correctly incorporated into national law.[56] Like the Danish *Ajos* case, the *Finanger I* case concerned direct

[51] See, eg, E Holmøyvik, 'Grunnlova og avtalerne med EU: Pragmatismens siger, det konstitusjonelle demokratiske tap' in EO Eriksen and JE Fossum (eds), *Det Norske Paradoks. Om Norges forhold til Den Europæiske Union* (Oslo, Universitetsforlaget, 2014) 42–59.

[52] See, eg, Smith (n 48) 164.

[53] See, eg, F Sejersted, 'Suverenitet og samarbeid i 2014' (2014) 72(3) *International Politik* 418.

[54] See, eg, T Bekkedal, 'Suverenitet og samarbeid. Grunnlovens skranker for delegasjon av statsmakt' (2016) 42 *Kritisk Juss* 3, especially 4; and Case E-15/10 *Posten Norge AS* from the EFTA Court.

[55] Smith (n 48) 165.

[56] F Veggeland, 'EØS, folkerett og maktfordeling: Høyesteretts dom i Finanger-saken' (2002) 18 *Norsk Statsvidenskapelig Tidsskrift* 328.

horizontal effect in the relationship between two private parties. The majority in the Norwegian Supreme Court applied national legislation to the case. A clear inconsistency between EEA law and Norwegian law existed. The Norwegian Parliament was under the impression that Norwegian law was consistent with EEA law. The Supreme Court found that it is the role of the legislator to make Norwegian legislation comply with EEA law.[57] Though, differences exist between the *Finanger I* judgment and the *Ajos* judgment, the two judgments seem to share the same approach to the role of courts and legislators, and thereby to the separation of powers. It is for the legislator—and not the courts—to make national legislation comply with EU/EEA law. The Danish Supreme Court's respect of the Danish legislator is also reflected in the Danish *Maastricht* case.[58] However, as mentioned below, the Norwegian Supreme Court did not follow this line of thinking in the more recent *Holship* judgment from 2016.

Norway also has an Act of Accession to the EEA, which entered into force on 1 January 1994 and was last amended on 12 April 2014.

Like Norway, Iceland is a member of the EEA. The EEA is not mentioned in the Icelandic Constitution, which was adopted in 1944. The general provision on international cooperation is Article 21, which reads:

> The President of the Republic concludes treaties with other states. Unless approved by Althingi, he may not make such treaties if they entail renouncement of, or servitude on, territory or territorial waters, or if they require changes in the state system.

This provision dates back to the 1920 Constitution of Iceland, which was enacted after Iceland became a sovereign state in union with Denmark on the basis of an Act of Union between the states of 1918. It was almost identical to Article 18 of the Danish Constitution of 1915 (article 19(1) of the 1953 Constitution).[59]

Article 21 is still the only provision of the Icelandic Constitution which deals with international cooperation. It has a very narrow scope and its main objective is to stipulate that treaty-making powers are in the hands of the executive branch; however, the ratification of some treaties needs to be approved by the Alþingi. Icelandic theory and practice regarding Article 21 has not been interpreted as authorising the transfer of powers to international institutions. The Icelandic Constitution is the only Nordic constitution which is completely silent with respect to cooperation through international institutions.[60]

This has raised the question of and heated debates as to whether and to what extent sovereignty can be transferred or whether it would require a constitutional amendment after the procedure in Article 79, which like the Danish Constitution

[57] However, in the more recent *Holship* case (HR 2016-2554-P), the Norwegian Supreme Court decided the opposite way in a comparable question.

[58] See, eg, Krunke (n 18).

[59] B Thorarensen (n 47) 414–15.

[60] ibid.

requires both an election and a referendum, but without the percentage requirement. When Iceland became a party to the EEA Agreement, the conclusion was that the Alþingi had a certain 'political margin' to decide 'a minor transfer of executive power' as required by the agreement in certain areas, without any constitutional amendment. This conclusion was challenged before the Icelandic courts as being in violation of the Constitution, mainly Article 2, which describes the highest holders of state powers and separation of powers. In a judgment in Hrd 1994, 1451, the Supreme Court of Iceland dismissed the claims on the grounds that the plaintiff—a private individual—lacked a specific individual and legal interest in the case and that the procedural requirements were thus not fulfilled.

Like the other Nordic countries, Iceland has a dualistic approach to international law.[61] This means that EEA law must be incorporated into national law in order to have effect, as described previously.

The EFTA Court has established a 'quasi-direct effect' principle in Case E-1/94 *Restmark* and a 'quasi-primacy' principle in Case E-1/01 *Einarsson* based on Protocol 35 of the EEA.[62] The 'quasi-direct effect' principle states that 'a national rule implementing EEA obligations must create invocable rights for individuals', while the 'quasi-primacy' principle states that 'other national Acts cannot prevail against such obligations', meaning that 'preference should be given to transformed EEA law when a conflict between the two sets of rules occurs'.[63] The *Einarsson* case concerned Iceland and it is therefore interesting how the Icelandic Supreme Court reacted to the decision of the EFTA Court. The argument made by the Supreme Court in the Icelandic *Einarsson* judgment (Hrd 2003, 2045) has been debated.[64] However, it seems that the Supreme Court, by applying the *lex specialis* principle even though it could have applied the *lex posterior* principle, shows its willingness to give the EEA provision priority over other national legislation.[65] In later case law, the *Tobacco* judgment[66] and the Icelandic *Alcohol Legislation* judgment,[67] both from 2006, the Supreme Court has applied a more restrictive approach.[68] In the *Tobacco* judgment, the Supreme Court held that it 'would not disregard national legislation that was incompatible with the EEA Agreement'.[69] Following that line, it

[61] See, eg, B Thorarensen, *Stjórnskipunarréttur. Undirstöður og handhafar ríkisvalds* (Reykjavík, Codex Publications, 2015) 679–85 (English summary).

[62] ME Méndez-Pinedo and OI Hannesson, *The Authority of European Law: Exploring Primacy of EU Law and Effect of EEA Law from European and Icelandic Perspectives* (Reykjavik, Ritröd Lagastofnunar Háskóla Íslands, Bókaútgáfan Codex, 2012) 196ff.

[63] ibid 205–06.

[64] D Björgvinsson, *EES-réttur og landsréttur* (Reykjavik, Bókaútgáfan Codex, 2006); and DS Tynes, 'Ys og þys út af engu?: hugleidingar um bókum 35 vid samninginn um Evrópska efnahagssvædid' (2002) 3 *Úlfljótur* 473.

[65] Méndez-Pinedo and Hannesson (n 62) 201–03.

[66] Supreme Court case No 220/2005.

[67] Supreme Court case No 274/2006.

[68] Méndez-Pinedo and Hannesson (n 62) 203.

[69] ibid 204.

stated in the *Alcohol Legislation* judgment that 'since Icelandic legislation could only be set aside on grounds of the Constitution, it could be applied without any thought as to whether it was a violation of the EEA Agreement'.[70] The approach taken by the Supreme Court contradicts the quasi-primacy principle established by the EFTA Court.

E. Sub-Conclusion

If we look across the five Nordic countries, we see that whereas the Eastern countries, Finland and Sweden, explicitly mention the EU in their constitutions, there is no trace of the EU in the constitutions of the Western countries, Denmark, Norway and Iceland. At least formally, it might seem natural that Norway and Iceland do not mention the EU, since they are only part of the EEA cooperation. However, in reality, the EU plays a major role in their legal systems in any case. Interestingly, while Denmark has not amended its Constitution since 1953, Norway has amended its Constitution many times since 1992, thus having the chance to introduce the EEA into its Constitution. As regards Denmark, it has been shown that it is not an argument in itself that it is difficult to amend the Constitution when trying to explain why the Danish Constitution does not mention the EU. Denmark has been a Member State for more than 40 years and the argument ought to be turned around into the following question: why has the Danish Constitution not been amended in such a way that it reflects EU membership and hence the contemporary constitutional reality? So surprisingly, maybe there does exist an East/West divide here in the sense that the countries of the Nordic East shows an honest and visible approach to the EU in their constitutions, while those of the Nordic West 'deny' its existence in the Constitutions, even though the EU in reality plays an important role in the lives of their citizens and in the national separation of powers. Perhaps this division reflects an important feature of the Nordic West. Although Denmark has been a Member State for longer than Sweden and Finland, it also has a number of exceptions from the treaties and a number of referendums relating to the EU have had a 'negative' outcome. In Norway, the voters have twice turned down the possibility of membership of the EU instead of EEA membership. While Iceland was in negotiations with the EU in 2009 on possibly joining the EU, it withdrew from the negotiations after the election in 2013.

As regards the procedure for ceding sovereignty to the EU, a look across the Nordic countries shows that the voters only have an influence on this in: (1) Denmark and formally only if five-sixths of Parliament do not vote in favour of the treaty; and in (2) Iceland, given that Article 21 of the Icelandic Constitution cannot be used to cede sovereignty and that a constitutional amendment is necessary, including the participation of the voters in an election. In Finland, Sweden

[70] ibid 205.

and Norway, the Parliament can decide to cede sovereignty by itself with respectively two-thirds, three-quarters (from at least half of the members) and formally three-quarters (in practice one-half). This means that the Swedish Parliament is in reality probably the most powerful as regards the sovereignty procedures.

In the Nordic West, the constitutions seem to have been 'stretched' a little in practice or interpreted in a pragmatic or perhaps legal realistic way as regards the transfer of sovereignty. In Denmark, Article 20 has so far been able to embrace great developments in terms of EU cooperation (at least until the recent *Ajos* judgment). In Norway, the government has interpreted Article 26(2) in a way that arguably contradicts Article 93 (both on 'transfer of sovereignty' and on the requirement that transfers may only be made to international associations of which Norway is a member). Iceland, which is still lacking any explicit authority under the Constitution, is experiencing growing pains in stretching the 'political margin' to decide to transfer powers while the EEA Agreement is increasingly developing in directions where new powers are transferred to new institutions and agencies.[71] Most recently, this was reflected in the implementation of the EU regulations under the EEA Agreement establishing new supervisory bodies in the financial market.

Even though the Nordic countries are in general loyal to their EU/EEA obligations when applying EU/EEA law, we also find a few interesting judgments in Denmark and Iceland which seem to underline the dualistic principle and to reflect a specific 'Nordic' approach to the separation of powers between courts and legislators (see the Danish *Ajos* judgment, the Icelandic Tobacco judgment and the *Alcohol Legislation* judgment). Whereas the Norwegian *Finanger I* judgment might be said to reflect the same line of thinking, newer cases such as the *Finanger II* judgment and the *Holship* judgment depart from it.

IV. EU Cooperation and the National Nordic Parliaments

Parliamentary scrutiny and control of the government in the Nordic countries is discussed in general in Chapter 4 of this volume. Hence, this section's focus will be strictly on the national parliaments and EU cooperation, with emphasis on the new scrutiny instruments for national parliaments introduced by the EU—the Early Warning System and the Barroso initiative—analysed in a Nordic context.

Parliaments in the EU have been provided with two new instruments for influence on EU legislation. The first instrument is the Early Warning System (EWS), which has its legal basis in Protocol No 2 to the Lisbon Treaty on the application of the principles of subsidiarity and proportionality. In short, the

[71] Thorarensen (n 59) 415.

EWS provides national parliaments with the possibility to scrutinise draft EU legislation in relation to subsidiarity and to send a reasoned opinion to the EU institutions in the event that they find that the draft legislation violates the principle of subsidiarity. If a certain threshold is reached among all the national parliaments, they can collectively influence the EU legislation process.[72] The other instrument is of a more political and informal nature and is normally referred to as the 'Barroso initiative'.[73]

How have these initiatives affected the parliaments in the Nordic EU Member States? First, the discussion will focus on how active Denmark, Finland and Sweden are as regards reasoned opinions under the EWS and the reasons for this. Second, the discussion will move on to examining whether the Nordic EU Member States focus on specific policy areas as regards the substance of the opinions.

Sweden is the Member State in the EU that has submitted the most reasoned opinions under the EWS, Denmark has submitted an average number of opinions and Finland is among the Member States with the fewest submitted opinions.[74] Why do we see these differences? Through a comparative analysis of Sweden, Denmark and Finland, Anna Cornell has identified a number of possible factors.[75] First, the scrutiny undertaken by the Swedish and Finnish Parliaments is decentralised, with considerable emphasis on the scrutiny of EU affairs through the ordinary select committees. In Denmark, parliamentary scrutiny of EU affairs is highly centralised around the European Affairs Committee. It should be added to Cornell's analysis that the ordinary select committees are actually more involved in the scrutiny work than was previously the case, based on the fact that EU legislation now covers so many areas and is sometimes quite detailed and technical. However, it is true that the mandate procedure lies with the European Affairs Committee. Second, Denmark has a strong mandate procedure which is binding on the government. If the government wants to change its position within the Council, it must contact the European Affairs Committee. Mandates are provided by the European Affairs Committee. In Finland, mandates are provided by the Grand Committee; however, they have a less binding character on the government than is the case in Denmark. In Sweden, mandates are provided by the select committees and are less binding compared to those in Denmark. Third, unlike what we find in Denmark and Sweden, Finland has a clear strategy for speaking with one voice in Brussels through the government. Fourth, Denmark and Sweden have for long periods had minority governments which strengthen the Danish and Swedish Parliaments. Taken together, these factors seem to explain the differences

[72] For the detailed procedures, see Protocol No 2 to the Lisbon Treaty.

[73] See, eg, Commission of the European Communities, COM (2006) 211, 'A Citizen's Agenda—Delivering Results for Europe' (10 May 2006).

[74] AJ Cornell, 'Similar But Different: Comparing the Scrutiny of the Principle of Subsidiarity within the EWM in Denmark, Finland and Sweden' in AJ Cornell and M Goldini (eds), *National and Regional Parliaments in the EU-Legislative Procedure Post-Lisbon* (Oxford, Hart Publishing, 2017) 201.

[75] ibid 201–23.

in the level of parliamentary activity as regards reasoned opinions. Compared to Denmark, the Swedish Parliament has a weaker position in European affairs and therefore the reasoned opinions stand out as a new valuable instrument for Parliament. In Denmark, the European Affairs Committee has a long and strong tradition of influence on EU affairs and therefore the reasoned opinion instrument is not as tempting for the Danish Parliament as it is in Sweden. The Finnish scrutiny system is strongly influenced by the Finnish one-voice strategy, which we do not find in Sweden and Denmark, and this at least partly explains why Finland has a very low number of reasoned opinions. One might add one more factor to Cornell's analysis as regards Finland. The Constitutional Law Committee of Parliament, which is regarded as the primary authority of constitutional interpretation, is also important in the Finnish context. Such interpretations also regard the EU, and the existence of the Constitutional Law Committee strengthens the powers of the Finnish Parliament. Interestingly, even though the Danish Parliament is a strong player in EU affairs, the mandate and scrutiny procedures are only described in political agreements between the Parliament and the government, while in Finland parliamentary scrutiny is mentioned in the Constitution. In Sweden, scrutiny is regulated in legislation. One might—like Cornell—be surprised that the Danish mandate and scrutiny system can be so strong despite only being regulated in details in political agreements. However, it should be emphasised that the Danish European Affairs Committee—but not the procedures on mandate and scrutiny—is mentioned in the Danish Act of Accession to the EU and that the political practice on the mandate procedure has been carried out for more than 40 years. It can therefore be—and has been—discussed whether the mandate procedure has already hardened or whether in the future it will harden into a legally binding convention.[76] Cornell's analysis is very valuable not only as regards the EWS, but also as a comparison of Nordic EU scrutiny systems as such.

This leads us to the second question regarding which policy areas the Nordic EU Member States focus on in their reasoned opinions. Are the Nordic EU Member States interested in some specific areas which might also tell us something about Nordic identity? In our data, both opinions under the EWS and the Barroso initiative, including opinions on White and Green Papers, are included. If we study the opinions issued by the Danish Parliament, we see that special attention is paid to the following areas: environmental issues, social policy and labour policy, democratic initiatives, rule of law, gender balance and criminal matters.[77] In the Swedish context, we find a high rate of opinions within a very broad spectrum of areas, but special focus seems to

[76] H Krunke, 'Developments in National Parliaments' Involvement in Ordinary Foreign Policy and European Policy—Denmark' (2007) 13(3) *European Public Law* 335.

[77] H Krunke, 'Constitutional Identity in Denmark: Extracting Constitutional Identity in the Context of a Restrained Supreme Court and a Strong Legislator' in C Calliess and G van der Schyff (eds), *Constitutional Identity in a Europe of Multilevel Constitutionalism* (Cambridge, Cambridge University Press, 2017).

be on tax law,[78] criminal law,[79] environment,[80] democratic initiatives,[81] market and consumer protection,[82] data protection,[83] health,[84] social policy and labour policy,[85] and traffic and development policy.[86] We see several overlaps in focus areas in the Danish Parliament. Finally, as mentioned earlier, Finland has a quite low number of opinions. The Finnish Parliament has among other things focused on the environment,[87] criminal law[88] and social and labour policy.[89] If we look across the three Nordic countries, the aforementioned focus areas seem to reflect Nordic values, such as democracy, openness, strong welfare states with many social rights financed by the public taxation system and protection of the environment.

V. EU/EEA Cooperation and the National Nordic Courts

Above in section III, a number of important judgments from the Nordic Supreme Courts which contribute to the interpretation of the constitutional provisions that regulate the EU cooperation were included in the analysis, including:

— the *Maastricht* judgment (Denmark).
— the *Lisbon* judgment (Denmark).

[78] COM/2016/0025, COM/2016/0026, COM/2016/0198, COM/2016/0683, COM/2016/0685, COM/2016/0686, COM/2016/0687, COM/2015/0135, COM/2013/0071, COM/2013/0814, COM/2011/0121, COM/2011/0594, COM/2010/0695.

[79] COM/2016/0050, JOIN/2016/0018, COM/2014/0144, COM/2012/0010, COM/2012/0363, COM/2011/0327, COM/2011/0429, COM/2011/0573, COM/2010/0311, COM/2010/0776, COM/2009/0624.

[80] COM/2015/0614, COM/2014/0015, COM/2013/0027_28_29_30_31, COM/2013/0133, COM/2013/0169, COM/2012/0473, COM/2012/0576, COM/2011/0370, COM/2011/0424, COM/2011/0889, COM/2010/0066, COM/2010/0212, COM/2010/0799, COM/2009/0147, COM/2009/0163, COM/2009/0279, COM/2008/0811.

[81] COM/2014/0506_507, COM/2013/0506_566, COM/2012/0375, COM/2011/0345, COM/2010/0291, COM/2009/0622.

[82] COM/2016/0283, COM/2015/0550, COM/2015/0600, COM/2015/0630, COM/2014/0464, COM/2014/0469, COM/2013/0036_37, COM/2013/0122, COM/2013/0627, COM/2012/0048_49, COM/2012/0049, COM/2012/0372, COM/2012/0511, COM/2012/0698, COM/2012/0788, COM/2011/0015, COM/2011/0128, COM/2011/0144, COM/2011/0393, COM/2011/0427, COM/2011/0436, COM/2011/0747, COM/2011/0834, COM/2011/0895, COM/2011/0941, COM/2010/0183, COM/2010/0245, COM/2010/0348, COM/2010/0368, COM/2010/0370, COM/2010/0371, COM/2010/0561, COM/2010/0579, COM/2010/0608, COM/2010/0799, COM/2009/0279, COM/2009/0324, COM/2009/0614, COM/2008/0794.

[83] COM/2012/0010, COM/2012/0011, COM/2011/0225, COM/2010/0492.

[84] COM/2014/0219, COM/2012/0048_49, COM/2012/0049.

[85] COM/2012/0130, COM/2012/0614, COM/2012/0617, COM/2011/0060, COM/2011/0367, COM/2011/0455, COM/2011/0608, COM/2011/0609, COM/2011/0634, COM/2010/0486, COM/2010/0636, COM/2009/0329, COM/2008/0725.

[86] COM/2015/0598, JOIN/2015/0033, COM/2013/0027_28_29_30_31, COM/2013/0092, COM/2013/0296, COM/2012/0380, COM/2011/0144, COM/2010/0586, COM/2010/0629, COM/2009/0044, COM/2009/0279.

[87] COM/2013/0133, COM/2011/0370.

[88] COM/2015/0750, COM/2013/0534.

[89] COM/2012/0130.

— the *Ajos* judgment (Denmark).
— NJA 2014, p 79 (Sweden).
— the *Finanger I* judgment (Norway).
— the *Finanger II* judgment (Norway).
— the *Holship* judgment (Norway).
— the *Einarsson* judgment (Iceland).
— the *Tobacco* judgment (Iceland).
— the alcohol legislation judgment (Iceland).

These judgments will also to some extent be included in the following analysis of EU/EEA cooperation and the Nordic courts.

Like all the other national courts in the Member States of the EU, the Danish, Swedish and Finnish courts have an obligation to apply EU law in their judgments. They have to respect EU principles such as primacy and direct effect. However, the Danish Supreme Court has in the *Maastricht* case and the *Lisbon* case expressed that the Supreme Court has the competence to conduct ultra vires review. The Supreme Court has the final competence to review whether an EU act or an EU judgment falls outside the competences which Denmark has ceded to the EU through the Act of Accession.[90]

The aforementioned case law from the Nordic Supreme Courts expresses how the Supreme Courts view the limits of the impact of EU law. In Danish case law, we see a line from the *Maastricht* judgment, over the *Lisbon* judgment to the *Ajos* judgment. In the *Lisbon* judgment, the Supreme Court emphasised that the CJEU may not expand the powers of the EU by means of its interpretations and the Supreme Court underlined its jurisdiction to carry out judicial review if 'an Act or a judicial decision that has a specific and real impact on Danish citizens etc raises doubts as to whether it is based on an application of the Treaties which lies beyond the surrender of sovereignty according to the Accession Act'. In the *Ajos* judgment, the Supreme Court found that it was not possible to apply EU law as interpreted by the CJEU to the case within the powers transferred to the EU through the Act of Accession and within the role of courts in the Danish separation of powers. Interestingly, a parallel can be drawn with the Norwegian *Finanger I* judgment. Both courts emphasised that EU/EEA law would have direct effect in a horizontal relationship between two private parties. Legal certainty as an important legal principle has clearly played a role in this, as has an approach to the separation of powers with strong parliaments and reluctant courts. However, whereas case law from the Danish Supreme Court could be interpreted as moving towards a more critical approach to EU law, the Norwegian Supreme Court has moved towards a more integration-friendly approach in its recent *Holship* judgment, which interestingly is from 2016, like the Danish *Ajos* judgment. In the Swedish judgment NJA 2014, p 79, the Swedish Supreme Court shows a willingness to set limits for EU law. However, at the same time, the Court also shows an unwillingness to define this limit.

[90] On the Danish *Lisbon* judgment, see, eg, Krunke (n 18).

The courts in Norway and Iceland are formally in a different situation from the courts in Denmark, Sweden and Finland, since Norway and Iceland are only members of the EEA. Beginning with Norway, the starting point is that the Supreme Court has the final right to interpret EEA law in Norway. Interpretations from the EFTA Court are not legally binding. The Norwegian Supreme Court has in a number of judgments stated that it has the competence and a duty to perform an independent review of the extent to which interpretations by the EFTA Court should be applied in Supreme Court judgments.[91] The Supreme Court will give interpretations from the EFTA Court considerable weight; however, it feels free to depart from them if necessary and has done so in a few cases.[92] As regards case law from the CJEU, the following distinction must be made. Relevant judgments from before the EEA Agreement was signed 2 May 1992 must be applied to interpretations of the EEA Agreement. This follows from Article 1 of the Act on the EEA. Such a formal obligation on the Norwegian courts does not exist for judgments after this date, even though they are normally applied by the courts.[93]

This is the formal starting point. However, in some specific fields Norway has actually ceded sovereignty to the EFTA Court and the CJEU. When executive power is transferred to the Commission, judicial power is at the same time transferred since cases against the Commission must be submitted to the CJEU.[94] Furthermore, seen from the point of EU and EEA law, it is of course unacceptable that all the Member States have their own interpretation of, for instance, free movement.[95] Hence, in reality, courts in Norway are not as free to have the last word on the interpretation of the EEA Agreement as one might think, given the fact that Norway is not a member of the EU. Despite the formal state of the law, the CJEU in reality decides how the EEA Agreement should be interpreted.[96] This contradiction between formality and reality has been pointed out by several legal scholars.[97]

We now turn to the Icelandic context. As mentioned earlier, case law from the Icelandic Supreme Court shows a move from the willingness in the *Einarsson* judgment from 2002 to give EEA law priority over national legislation to the *Tobacco* judgment and the *Alcohol Legislation* judgment from 2006, which both show a more restrictive approach. The approach taken by the Supreme Court in the latter case law contradicts the quasi-primacy principle established by the EFTA Court. The Court stated that Icelandic legislation can only be set aside on the grounds of the Constitution. It follows from case law from the Icelandic Supreme Court that

[91] HH Fredriksen, 'Dømmer Høyesterett, EFTA-domstolen eller EU-domstolen i siste instans på EØS-rettens område?' in Eriksen and Fossum (n 51) 75–88; and the *Finanger I* judgment (Rt-2000-1811).
[92] Fredriksen (n 91); and the *STX* judgment (Rt-2013-258).
[93] Fredriksen (n 91) 79.
[94] See, eg, Fredriksen (n 91).
[95] ibid.
[96] ibid.
[97] See, eg, ibid; and Sejersted (n 53).

the Supreme Court has the competence and a duty to perform an independent review of the extent to which interpretations by the EFTA Court should be applied in Supreme Court judgments. The case law also shows that the Supreme Court feels free to depart from case law from the EFTA Court and from EEA law.

As a sub-conclusion, the Nordic courts have in reality become 'European' courts which apply EU/EEA law as interpreted by the CJEU and the EFTA Court.[98] The divide between Nordic EU Member States and EEA Member States is not as deep as it might seem at first sight. In a few cases where the limits of the impact of EU law in the national jurisdictions is tested, we see some resistance. This has been especially clear in the *Ajos* judgment, the *Finanger I* judgment, the *Tobacco* judgment and the *Alcohol Legislation* judgment.[99] The resistance from the Supreme Courts of Denmark and Iceland in particular transgresses the divide between EU Member States and EEA Member States, and it could perhaps imply that an East/West divide still exists to a certain extent.

As regards the resistance reflected in the recent *Ajos* judgment (as opposed to the Norwegian *Holship* case), this resistance of the court does not seem to be an isolated Danish or Nordic phenomenon. We see the same concerns in judgments from the Italian Constitutional Court,[100] the British Supreme Court[101] and the German Constitutional Court.[102] This resistance appears across different legal systems and families linking Denmark to a Europe outside the North.

The general picture of the Nordic courts as European courts will now be analysed in light of the Nordic countries' use of requests for preliminary rulings from the CJEU. These requests reflect a national interest in applying EU law in accordance with the interpretations by the CJEU. The list below shows a simple calculation based on the number of preliminary references and the average per annum up to 2016:[103]

— *Denmark*: 181 (member since 1973). Average p.a.: 4.11. Average per million citizens: 0.72 (population: 5,707,251).
— *Finland*: 100 (member since 1995). Average p.a.: 4.55. Average per million citizens: 0.83 (population: 5,487,308).

[98] See also H Krunke, 'Towards a Complex Matrix of New Formal and Informal Ways of Compensation of Lost National Powers to the EU' in JP Christensen, J Christoffersen, JH Danielsen and S Ebdrup (eds), *Max Sørensen 100 år* (Copenhagen, Jurist- og Økonomforbundets Forlag, 2013) 438.

[99] As mentioned above, the Norwegian Supreme Court has followed a different line in its recent case law.

[100] The Italian Constitutional Court Order No 24/2017 and Case C-105/14 *Ivo Taricco and Others* [2015] EU:C:2015:555.

[101] *R (HS2 Action Alliance Ltd) v Secretary of State for Transport* [2014] UKSC 3, judgment given on 22 January 2014.

[102] BVerfG, Judgment of the Second Senate of 21 June 2016— 2 BvR 2728/13— paras 1–220; and Case C-62/14 *Gauweiler and Others v Deutscher Bundestag* [2015] EU:C:2015:400.

[103] http://ec.europa.eu/eurostat/tgm/table.do?tab=table&init=1&language=en&pcode=tps00001&plugin=1.

- *Sweden*: 120 (member since 1995). Average p.a.: 5.45. Average per million citizens: 0.55 (population: 9,851,017).
- *Italy*: 1,094 (member since 1958, counted from 1961). Average p.a.: 19.54. Average per million citizens: 0.32 (population: 60,589,445).
- *The Netherlands*: 853 (member since 1958, counted from 1961). Average p.a.: 15.23. Average per million citizens: 0.9 (population: 17,081,507).
- *The UK*: 583 (member since 1973). Average p.a.: 13.25. Average per million citizens: 0.20 (population: 65,808,573).
- *Germany*: 2134 (member since 1958, counted from 1961). Average p.a.: 38.1. Average per million citizens: 0.46 (population: 82,800,000).

It is the subject of debate whether EFTA countries must ask the EFTA Court for advisory opinions. Therefore, it can be difficult to make a direct comparison between Nordic EU Member States and Nordic EFTA countries as regards preliminary references and advisory opinions. However, the average advisory opinions per annum per million citizens can be calculated as follows:[104]

- *Iceland*: 36 (member since 1994). Average p.a.: 1.57. Average per million citizens: 4.69 (population: 335,000).
- *Norway*: 52 (member since 1994). Average p.a.: 2.26. Average per million citizens: 0.43 (population: 5.305,000).

The Icelandic population of 335,000 citizens is very small compared to the countries in the sample and this might explain why the Icelandic average per million citizens is very high compared to Norway, Nordic EU Member States and the other EU Member States. Even though the average per million citizens in Norway is lower than in Finland and Denmark, it is close to Sweden and Germany and higher than in Italy and the UK. This is quite interesting since it might also reflect that EEA Member States through requests for advisory opinions from the CJEU show a strong national interest in applying EEA law in accordance with the interpretations by the EFTA Court.

If we return to the EU Member States, the first list shows that the Nordic EU Member States have a quite high frequency of preliminary requests compared to their size measured in number of inhabitants if we view preliminary rulings per million citizens over a long time period. As mentioned above, this could be interpreted as an interest in interpreting EU law in accordance with the CJEU's interpretations. This seems to indicate that EU law has had a quite significant impact on the behaviour of the courts. This is interesting because it is often emphasised that the Nordic Member States (including Denmark) are traditionally quite reluctant and show great respect for the national political institutions

[104] www.eftacourt.int/cases; and UN Population Division, www.un.org/en/development/desa/population/publications/index.shtml.

compared to other European national courts, which is sometimes said to affect their behaviour towards EU law.[105] It has also been stated that Danish courts have fewer preliminary requests than other European courts because of the aforementioned characteristics.[106] However, simply counting the number of preliminary references in all EU Member States and comparing them to each other does not provide a satisfactory impression of the differences between the national courts. Many factors play a role in this complex picture, for instance, differences in population size, litigation patterns and the level of compliance with EU law.[107] Broberg and Fenger have compared Member State activity as regards predicted average annual preliminary references based on the structural country differences. This has produced to the following figures:[108]

— Denmark: 15 per cent above average.
— Finland: 5 per cent above average.
— Sweden: 9 per cent below average.

In conclusion and with respect of the complexity of comparing the different national European court systems, the picture that seems to emerge is that the Nordic EU Member States are in general active in posing preliminary references. This especially applies to Denmark and Finland, but so less so to Sweden. Though Sweden seems to be below average in this respect, the numbers still seem to reflect a real interest on the part of the national Nordic courts to learning how the CJEU interprets EU law. This supports our sub-conclusion that the Nordic courts have to a large extent also become 'European' courts, which seems to be especially the case in Denmark and Finland.

VI. EU/EEA and the Nordic Separation of Powers

The dynamic interpretation style adopted by the CJEU is different from the more traditional careful positivist interpretation style evident in the Nordic countries. Nordic courts view a very dynamic interpretation style as stepping into the role of the legislator and entering the political arena. This follows from the Danish case law (especially the *Maastricht* judgment and the *Ajos* judgment), earlier Norwegian case law (the *Finanger I* judgment) and Icelandic case law (the *Tobacco* judgment and *Alcohol Legislation* judgment). For instance, in the *Ajos* judgment

[105] See, eg, JE Rytter and M Wind, 'In Need of Juristocracy?: The Silence of Denmark in the Development of European Legal Norms' (2011) 9(2) *International Journal of Constitutional Law* 470.

[106] See, eg, M Wind, 'The Nordics, the EU and the Reluctance towards Supranational Judicial Review' (2010) 48(4) *Common Market Studies* 1039.

[107] M Broberg and N Fenger, *Preliminary References to the European Court of Justice* (Oxford, Oxford University Press, 2014) Chapter 2.

[108] ibid 48.

and the *Finanger I* judgment, which set limits for the impact of EU/EEA law on national law, the Supreme Courts based their judgments on separation of powers arguments. As mentioned above, the Norwegian Supreme Court has in the recent *Holship* judgment chosen a more EEA integration-friendly approach. Another difference between the traditional Nordic constitutional and legal systems and the EU legal system is the role of unwritten legal principles. Even though unwritten legal principles exist in the Nordic legal systems, this is not to the same extent as in EU law. For instance, in the *Ajos* judgment, there seems to be a clash between the Danish legal system and culture and the EU legal system and culture. The case concerned the unwritten EU principle on age discrimination which, according to the CJEU, is an EU constitutional principle with the same rank as the Treaties. However, seen from a traditional Danish legal reasoning perspective, such an unwritten principle is problematic. If we turn to Finland, there seems to be a different pattern. Here the EU and the ECHR seem to have had an impact on judicial review and the role of courts. This shift has strengthened the courts in the constitutional and political system.[109] Interestingly, it seems that the Danish and Icelandic courts hang on to the traditional Nordic approach to legal reasoning and view on the role of courts, despite the influence of the CJEU/EFTA Court and the ECHR/ECtHR. As mentioned above, Finnish courts on the other hand have to a greater extent adapted to the interpretation style of the CJEU and the ECtHR, and thereby have also strengthened their own role. Furthermore, before Finland joined the EU, its courts did not have the competence to review the constitutionality of legislation.[110] In this way, EU membership has had a significant impact on the powers of the courts in Finland. An interesting development in the Swedish separation of powers is that the courts can now apply Article 6 of the Instrument of Government and as a result set limits for the impact of EU law, a competence which was commonly viewed as reserved for the Swedish Parliament until the last constitutional revision in 2011.

The strong prior review of draft legislation in Finland (the Constitutional Law Committee) and Sweden (the Law Committee) as regards EU law and the ECHR should also be mentioned in relation to the separation of powers. If a strong review is carried out by the political institutions, one might say that less power is left for the courts in this field.

In the relationship between legislator and government, EU and EEA cooperation moves power away from the legislator and towards the executive. The reason for this is that discussions on new legislation which would formerly have taken place in the national parliaments are now taking place in the EU institutions. Since the

[109] Ojanen (n 35) 207.

[110] This was introduced in the Finnish Constitution in 2000. See Article 106 and J Lavapuro, T Ojanen and M Scheinin, 'Rights-Based Constitutionalism in Finland and the Development of Pluralist Constitutional Review' (2011) 9(2) *International Journal of Constitutional Law* 505.

government represents the Member State in Council meetings on new legislation, the governments in Denmark, Sweden and Finland have been strengthened. How much power the governments gain depends on the strength of the parliaments' scrutiny of EU affairs and not least the mandate procedure. As mentioned earlier, the Danish mandate procedure seems to be the most binding on the government. As regards EEA cooperation, the Norwegian and Icelandic governments are also strengthened in relation to the parliaments, as is the case with all international cooperation, since the government represents the country in international fora. Another challenge for Norway and Iceland is that the two countries do not have as much influence on EU legislation as the EU Member States, even though EU legislation in reality has a significant impact on them.

Legislators in Denmark, Sweden and Finland—but also Norway and Iceland—now have a new role as implementers of EU law and as 'watchdogs' as regards EU legislation. In relation to the implementation of EU law in the national Nordic legal systems in Denmark, Sweden and Finland, we refer to the following statistics on infringement:[111]

Formal notice, Article 258 of the Treaty on the Functioning of the European Union (TFEU) (past 10 years):
Denmark: 234 (27 active), Sweden: 228 (41 active), Finland: 370 (48 active)

Reasoned opinion, Article 258 TFEU (past 10 years):
Denmark: 53 (six active), Sweden: 88 (16 active), Finland: 108 (18 active)

Referral to the CJEU, Article 258 TFEU (past 10 years):
Denmark: 10 (one active), Sweden: 20 (four active), Finland: 16 (none active)

An example that combines the two functions as implementers of EU law and as watchdogs as regards EU legislation is an initiative from 2016, when the Danish legislator reacted to what it saw as a Danish practice of 'over-implementation' of EU law, meaning that Denmark followed EU legislation further than was necessary when implementing it. This has resulted in new procedures in the ministries with the purpose of making sure that Denmark only meets the precise requirements of EU law when implementing it. The purpose of this initiative is twofold for the legislator: first, it keeps as much room for manoeuvre vis-a-vis political decision-making as possible with the Danish legislator in relation to the EU legislator; and, second, the intention is to make it clearer in the relationship between the Danish legislator and executive how far Denmark's EU obligations go and what room for manoeuvre vis-a-vis legislative competence is left. This is a good example of how the EU cooperation impacts the relationship between the legislator and the executive at the national level, and how the legislator fights to gain back as much competence as possible.

[111] http://ec.europa.eu/atwork/applying-eu-law/infringements-proceedings/infringement_decisions.

VII. EU/EEA Cooperation and the Nordic Voters

As mentioned in section II above, referendums have been held regarding EU membership in Denmark (1972), Sweden (1994), Finland (1994) and Norway (1972 and 1994). Furthermore, Denmark has had a number of referendums on new EU treaties in 1992 (Maastricht), 1993 (Maastricht, including the Edinburgh Agreement) and 1998 (Amsterdam). The second Danish referendum on the Maastricht Treaty included the four Danish exceptions on the euro (EMU), the Common Security and Defence Policy (CSDP), Justice and Home Affairs (JHA) and the Citizenship of the European Union.[112] Finally, both Denmark and Sweden have had referendums on whether to abandon exceptions in the EU treaties. As regards Denmark, a referendum on whether to abandon the euro exception took place in 2000 (the outcome was a 'no') and a referendum on whether to abandon the exception on judicial cooperation took place in 2015 (again, the outcome was a 'no'). Sweden held a referendum on whether to abandon the euro exception in 2003 (the outcome was a 'no').

In general, the referendums show support for the EU cooperation in Denmark, Sweden and Finland. However, in Denmark and Sweden in particular, the outcomes of some of the referendums also reflect some scepticism regarding specific parts of this cooperation. In Norway, the two referendums show general scepticism towards entering the EU. In Iceland, no referendum has taken place; however, in the general election in 2013, voters clearly rejected the political parties which supported continuing the application process for membership of the EU.

With the Lisbon Treaty, the EU Citizens' Initiative was introduced. It has its legal basis in Article 11, Part 4 of the Treaty on European Union:

> Not less than one million citizens who are nationals of a significant number of Member States may take the initiative of inviting the Commission, within the framework of its powers, to submit any appropriate proposal on matters where citizens consider that a legal act of the Union is required for the purpose of implementing the Treaties. The procedures and conditions required for such a citizens' initiative shall be determined in accordance with Article 24 of the Treaty on the Functioning of the Union.

How have the citizens in the Nordic EU Member States reacted to this new opportunity to gain more influence on EU legislation? If we study data on (1) taking the initiative to start a new Citizen Initiative and (2) supporting an

[112] The Danish opt-out of EU citizenship was only against giving up Danish citizenship in exchange for EU citizenship. Thus, when the Treaty of Amsterdam clarified that EU citizenship is only supplementary to national citizenship, this opt-out became redundant. See, eg, H Krunke, 'From Maastricht to Edinburgh: The Danish Solution' (2005) 1(3) *European Constitutional Law Review* 339. See also Adler-Nissen (n 33).

initiated Citizen Initiative, we see some interesting aspects as regards the Nordic Member States.[113] In relation to taking the initiative on a new EU Citizens' Initiative, only Sweden has been active, and compared to other Member States in which citizens have been involved in new EU Citizens' Initiatives, Swedish citizens are placed in the middle of this group as regards activity. If we turn to activity in terms of already supporting new EU Citizens' Initiatives, Finland is the most active Nordic country and compared to the other Member States in which citizens have shown support to EU Citizens' Initiatives, it is placed in the middle. Denmark and Sweden appear on the list of Member States in which there was some support but not sufficiently to pass the threshold.[114] In one case, Denmark actually reached the threshold, but a week too late. Interestingly, Sweden and Denmark have no political culture as regards Citizens' Initiatives at the national level, while Finland does. This might explain why more Finnish citizens have supported already initiated Citizens' Initiatives. Denmark introduced a national Citizens' Initiative on 1 January 2018 and it will be interesting to see whether this will have an impact on how Danish citizens act in relation to the EU Citizens' Initiative. When studying the activity of all the Member States, this seems to be a general trend: if a Member State has a political tradition for national Citizens' Initiatives, the citizens are normally more active in terms of supporting EU Citizens' Initiatives than is the case as regards citizens in Member States with no such tradition at the national level.[115]

Finally, we turn to elections for the European Parliament. Here we see the following level of activity in the Nordic Member States.

Table 7.1: Voter turnout in elections for the European Parliament[116]

Voter turnout (%)	1999	2004	2009	2014
Denmark	50.46	47.89	59.54	56.32
Sweden	38.84	37.85	45.53	51.07
Finland	30.14	39.43	38.60	39.10
EU average	49.51	45.47	42.97	42.61

[113] The study is based on the analysis in H Krunke and JC Dalsgaard, 'Towards Increased Citizen Participation in Europe: Impact of Current Developments on Political Decision Making and Democracy' (2016) 2 *Revue Internationale des Gouvernements Ouverts* 135.

[114] According to Article 7 in Regulation 211/2011 of 16 February 2011, the proposed EU Citizens' Initiative must be signed by citizens from a minimum of one-quarter of all the Member States and in each of these Member States it must be supported by a least the number of members of the European Parliament from the Member State times 750.

[115] ibid 155.

[116] See TNS/Scytl in cooperation with the European Parliament: www.europarl.europa.eu/elections2014-results/en/turnout.html.

This table shows that the voters in the Nordic EU Member States have in general shown an increasing level of interest in participating in the elections for the European Parliament. Interestingly, Denmark has always had a higher participation percentage than the average percentage in the EU, and since 2009, we can see the same tendency in Sweden. Finland, on the other hand, has the lowest participation percentage of the Nordic Member States, with the exception of the 2004 election. This is quite interesting since Finland is the Nordic EU Member State in which citizens are the most active in supporting EU Citizens' Initiatives. Finally, if we compare the participation in elections for the European Parliament to the participation in national elections, we see that Nordic voters are much more active in national elections:

- Denmark (2015): 85.9%[117]
- Sweden (2014): 85.8%[118]
- Finland (2015): 70.1%[119]
- Norway (2017): 78.2%[120]
- Iceland (2017): 81.2%[121]

An interesting observation is that Finland has a lower level of participation in national elections than Denmark and Sweden. This seems to reflect the differences as regards elections for the European Parliament as well.

VIII. Conclusion: How Deep is the EU Divide?

In the first section of this chapter, we emphasised the traditional divide between the Nordic East and the Nordic West, and we asked whether membership of the EU might have created new divides among the Nordic countries. The Nordic countries have made different choices and at different times as regards European integration. As mentioned above, Denmark is the oldest participant in the European cooperation project, having joined the European Community in 1973. Sweden and Finland joined the EU in 1995. Norway and Iceland are only EEA members. Norway has twice held referendums on accession to the EU which have resulted in a negative outcome. Iceland has been in negotiation with the EU on membership, but withdrew from the negotiations after the 2013 election.

In this chapter we have analysed the individual Nordic countries' systemic relationship to the EU, including possible differences in legal reactions to the EU legal

[117] See Danmarks Statistik: https://www.dst.dk/pukora/epub/upload/22259/headword/dk/44.pdf.

[118] See Statistika Centralbyrån: www.scb.se/hitta-statistik/sverige-i-siffror/val-och-partier/valdeltagande.

[119] See Statistics Finland: www.stat.fi/til/evaa/2015/evaa_2015_2015-04-30_tie_001_en.html.

[120] See Statistics Norway: https://www.ssb.no/valg/statistikker/valgdeltakelse.

[121] See Statistics Iceland: www.statice.is/publications/publication-detail?id=59055.

system. Such national reactions can be initiated by courts, national parliaments, governments and electorates. Many findings and comparisons appear through the chapter and we will only be able to draw on some of them in this section.

If we start with the *constitutional embedding* of the EU/EEA cooperation, we can see an interesting pattern. Whereas Sweden and Finland have chosen to clearly mention the EU cooperation in their constitutions, the EU does not appear in the Danish Constitution, even though Denmark is the oldest Member State among the Nordic countries. Nor does the EEA cooperation appear in the Norwegian and Icelandic Constitutions. As a result, we apparently see an East/West divide as regards the visibility of EU/EEA cooperation. Other findings support the idea that such an East/West divide still exists to some extent, even though Denmark, like Sweden and Finland, is a member of the EU.

If we turn to *case law from the courts*, we find the judgments that signal the most resistance towards primacy and direct effect of EU law and quasi-primacy and quasi-direct effect of EEA law coming from the Danish Supreme Court and the Icelandic Supreme Court. In Norway we seem to find a development in case law from the Supreme Court towards a more EU-friendly approach with the *Holship* judgment from 2016. The Danish *Ajos* judgment can also be linked to a broader reaction in several European Supreme Courts and constitutional courts (in Italy, Germany and the UK) towards interpretations by the CJEU which have an impact on fundamental legal principles, such as the rule of law and legal certainty. If we turn to the Nordic East, we do not find the same resistance in case law from the courts. In Finland and Sweden, the prior review of legislation, including whether it is compatible with EU law, is carried out in the Constitutional Law Committee and the Law Committee, respectively. In particular, the Finnish Constitutional Law Committee has considerable authority in this respect. Interestingly, we find some resistance towards the primacy of EU law in its opinions regarding human rights and constitutional rights. This might reflect that the West/East divide in this field is closely linked to the traditional differences in terms of review of legislation and differences in separation of power. However, one more interesting finding appears in relation to the case law from the courts. The Finnish courts seem have been heavily inspired by the legal reasoning and interpretation of the CJEU. This reflects that the impact of EU membership is broader than that EU legislation has supremacy over national legislation and in many cases direct effect. EU membership not only brings substantial EU law which becomes part of national law to the Member States, it also represents a specific legal tradition as regards interpretation, legal sources, the role of courts etc. The EU legal tradition differs from those in the Nordic legal systems. However, some of the Nordic legal systems—primarily the Finnish system—seem to have been inspired by the EU legal tradition, resulting in a move towards a more positivistic approach to legal reasoning and from reluctant courts to more dynamic interpretations with more focus on rights. Such a development naturally has an impact on the traditional national separation of powers. Finally, we focus on preliminary references. Here Finland seems to be the most active Nordic Member State—followed by Denmark—and also compared to other European Member States. Sweden, on the other hand, is less active and in Broberg and Fenger's analysis, which attempts to erase structural differences, Sweden was even a little below the EU average. Activity as regards preliminary references can be interpreted as a sign of a court's willingness to comply with EU law. The East/West divide was not underlined in this field.

Yet another example of national reactions towards EU integration is *exceptions from EU treaties*, which we find in Denmark and Sweden—Denmark being the Nordic Member State with the most exceptions. Does this mean that we do not see an East/West divide in this field? This might be the conclusion if we only look at the Nordic EU Member States. However, if we include the fact that Norway and Iceland are not even members of the EU, but only of the EEA, the picture looks somehow different and might be said to reflect a more EU-sceptic Nordic West. Exceptions are normally initiated by the national parliaments, in some cases being brought to a referendum and finally negotiated with the EU by the governments. In Denmark, the public voted on the four exceptions when voting for the second time on accession to the Maastricht Treaty. In both Denmark and Sweden, the electorate have been asked if they want to abandon the exceptions, but so far the majority have voted against removing such exceptions. This naturally leads us to the next expression of national reactions to EU integration.

National reactions to EU integration can find expression in the *outcome of referendums* on further EU integration through new treaties. A clear difference between the Nordic EU Member States exists in the field of the involvement of the electorate in further EU integration through referendums. Denmark stands out as having the most involvement of the voters when entering into new EU treaties. Interestingly, voters have even been involved to a greater extent than is required by the Constitution.

Nordic citizens can also react to EU integration by proposing new EU legislative initiatives to the EU Commission through the EU Citizens' Initiative. In this field, our analysis showed that whereas Sweden was the only Nordic Member State in which the citizens had started a new *EU Citizens' Initiative*, Finnish citizens were the most active in supporting already initiated EU Citizens' Initiatives. Here we see a dominance of the Nordic East, which at least in the Finnish context might be explained by the fact that Finland has a political culture in this field at the national level with a national Citizens' Initiative.

So far, as regards Sweden, the results of our comparative analysis have not shown that much reaction on EU integration. However, interestingly the picture changes when we turn towards the *EWS*. Here the Swedish Parliament stands out as extremely active compared to the other Nordic Member States. We find Denmark in the middle and Finland with the lowest number of reasoned opinions. These differences were, among other factors and with reference to Cornell, explained by a weak Swedish European Affairs Committee, a strong Danish European Affairs Committee and a Finnish 'one-voice' in the tradition in relation to EU affairs. However, if we in very general terms compare the areas of interest among the Nordic Member States as regards the EWS and the Barroso initiative, we see some common policy areas which at the same time fit well with the identity of the Nordic welfare states. The East/West divide is not underlined as regards the level of activity, but the Nordic similarity and unity can be seen as regards the topics.

If we combine our analyses into a broad overview of institutional reactions to EU integration and possible changes to the separation of powers in the Nordic Member States, we see the following patterns. In general we see an attempt—at least on the side of the courts—in the West (Denmark, Norway and Iceland) to hold on to the traditional role of courts on the one hand and political institutions on the other hand. This is of course a challenge when EU integration reflects another perspective on legal reasoning, dynamic interpretation and the role of courts from the traditional Nordic more positivistic legal reasoning, interpretation and courts which are careful not to enter what they consider the 'political rule-making zone'. The important judgments from the Supreme Courts of Denmark, Iceland and Norway show how the courts refer to the role of courts and legislators in their legal argumentation, respectively. In Finland we see the opposite development, namely a Supreme Court which has been empowered by the EU cooperation. Until Finland's accession to the EU, the Finnish courts did not even have the competence to review legislation; furthermore, the courts have been heavily inspired by the more active and dynamic CJEU in their legal reasoning and style. In Sweden since 2011, the courts have had the competence to apply Article 6 of the Instrument of Government and thereby set limits on the effect of EU law, a competence which before 2011 was only viewed as a competence of Parliament. In Finland and Sweden, we have a stronger system of prior review than in Denmark, Norway and Iceland. This strengthens the political institutions, primarily the parliaments, also in relation to the courts as regards EU integration. The fact that the Swedish Parliament is so active in relation to the EWS also strengthens the Parliament. Interestingly, important case law from the Finnish Constitutional Law Committee which attempts to set limits on the primacy and direct effect of EU law also has a strong focus on human rights in relation to the ECHR. This is not the case in the judgments from the Western Nordic courts which we have analysed. In conclusion, if we look at how the national institutions have reacted to EU integration and how the national separation of powers in the Nordic countries has been impacted by EU/EEA integration, there does seem to be an East/West divide.

In other words, though the picture is quite complex as regards the impact of EU/EEA integration on the Nordic constitutional systems, to some extent there still seems to exist an East/West divide. This is remarkable since membership of the EU has broken up the traditional divide with Denmark, Sweden and Finland being members of the EU, while Norway and Iceland are only members of the EEA. Several reasons might lie behind this. First of all, it seems that at the national legal, historical and cultural traditions in EU Member States still play a big role, even though EU integration is extensive. These traditions are reflected by political institutions, courts and the electorate. The Finnish case, where the courts have benefited from EU integration, and the Swedish case, where the Parliament uses the EWS to gain influence, of course show that—especially in the East—we also see institutional moves made possible by EU integration. Second, it seems that the formal difference between EEA membership and EU membership may not be as important and deep in reality. It should also be emphasised that, as shown above, we also see reactions from institutions and voters which transgress the East/West divide. Third, though a traditional East/West divide might have existed in the Nordic countries, it has never been a rigid division. Finally, it should be emphasised that in some fields, we see reflections of a common Nordic heritage across the East/West divide, for instance, as regards topics/values which the Nordic Member States raise and protect through the EWS and the Barroso initiative. In the concluding chapter of the book, there will be a more general discussion, which includes coverage on the impact of both the EU/EEA and the ECHR, on where the Nordic countries are heading: towards greater unity or towards more differences. In the concluding chapter we shall also return to the micro-level and macro-level of comparison.

8

Concluding Thoughts

HELLE KRUNKE AND BJÖRG THORARENSEN

I. Introduction

We now return to the main thesis of the book, which was laid out in the first chapter, and hold it up against the analyses conducted in Chapters 2–7. The main thesis of the book was that viewed from the outside, from a European or global perspective, the Nordic constitutional systems share some common features at both a more functional level and at the deeper level of values. However, viewed from a closer Nordic perspective, differences appear in the aforementioned general pattern.

Through the comparative analyses undertaken in this book, we have tried to identify both the broader common features and the more detailed differences, thereby applying both a macro- and a micro-perspective to the comparison of the Nordic constitutional systems. This was conducted through a comparison of some key features of constitutional systems and an analysis of the common historical roots of the Nordic constitutional systems. Furthermore, we have especially focused on how the EU/EEA and international human rights conventions (especially the ECHR) impact the Nordic constitutional systems, and whether this impact creates new differences and similarities in the Nordic context.

II. Nordic Values in Constitutions, Legislation and Policy Outcomes

The Nordic constitutions are interesting in the sense that they do not have a tradition of preambles or unamendable constitutional provisions, which express core constitutional values.[1] Nevertheless, viewed from the outside in a European/global

[1] As shown in Chapter 6, this might be changing, since some of the Nordic constitutions have recently adopted provisions that state general constitutional principles. This is a development that seems to be inspired by international human rights.

context, the Nordic countries share a number of common values, which seem to be especially strong in these constitutional systems, including strong welfare states, transparency, public trust in state institutions, consensus-based politics, human rights, democracy, the rule of law, good governance, clean environment/sustainability, gender equality etc. These are values that the Nordic countries defend together in European and international institutions, as pointed out in the chapters by Krunke and Ojanen. Interestingly, not all of these values are directly expressed in (all) the Nordic constitutions, or are only expressed to some extent, but instead may be regulated by ordinary legislation (or not at all). This observation might surprise the foreign reader. One might say that such values are an inherent part of the modern Nordic culture and hence part of the deeper layers of the Nordic identity.

However, if we take a closer look, we will see that some of the above-mentioned values actually play an important role in the *overall* constitutional design in the Nordic countries. For instance, the Nordic countries share strong parliaments, whereas the courts, compared to many other countries, are rather reluctant to intervene in 'political' matters. There are of course differences within the Nordic countries, with Norway at the more activist end of the scale and Denmark at the more reluctant end of the scale. Furthermore, none of the Nordic countries has a constitutional court. However, there are clear signs (as discussed in Chapters 5 and 6) that judicial control over the legislator has been growing in all the Nordic countries with respect to international human rights obligations, particularly in Norway and Iceland. The general constitutional design with strong parliaments and relatively cautious courts reflects the Nordic perception of democracy very well. Public trust in state institutions and de facto quite well-functioning state institutions with a very low level of bad governance and corruption also seems to be a core feature in this separation of powers design. A fairly strong system for parliamentary control of the executive, including the Nordic 'Ombudsman design', combined with a tradition for minority governments in Denmark, Norway and Sweden supports values such as transparency, well-functioning democracy, state institutions and high levels of public trust, as pointed out in Thorarensen's chapter. Not only politicians and judges but also civil servants contribute to upholding this strong public trust.

Respect for human rights could also be mentioned as a core feature in the Nordic constitutional systems. Human rights are of course part of all the Nordic constitutions, but are more extensively regulated in some of the recently revised constitutions in Finland, Norway, Sweden and Iceland, and are supplemented in all the states by international treaties. As mentioned above, values like welfare rights, gender equality and a sustainable environment are often associated with the Nordic constitutional systems. Such values are reflected in the Nordic constitutional texts. Social rights are an important feature of a strong welfare state and even though such rights are mainly regulated through extensive legislation in the Nordic countries, we also find general provisions in the constitutions often with a long history, like the provision in the Danish Constitution (Article 75, part 2) on the right to social security if one has no other income or financial support, which dates back to 1849. Equivalent provisions can be found in all the other Nordic constitutions (Article 19 of the Finnish Constitution, Article 110 of the Norwegian Constitution, Article 76 of the Icelandic Constitution and Article 2 of Chapter 2 of the Swedish Instrument of Government). In the more recently revised Nordic constitutions, we find provisions of a more modern character, for instance, a provision on everyone's responsibility for the environment and environmental rights in Article 20 of the Finnish Constitution. Equivalent provisions on the environment are found in Article 112 of the Norwegian Constitution and Article 2 of Chapter 2 of the Swedish Instrument of Government. Finally, gender equality is explicitly mentioned in Article 65 of the Icelandic Constitution, Article 13 of Chapter 2 of the Swedish Instrument of Government and Article 6 of the Finnish Constitution.

As a result, following a closer look, Nordic values and constitutional design might be said to go hand in hand. This underlines our main thesis well: from the outside perspective, we see some general patterns both at the deeper level of values/identity and at the functional level. Viewed at the micro-level—the Nordic perspective—individual nuances appear. We will go into more detail on the functional level below.

III. The Legal Historical Context

Chapter 2 showed that the historical context might provide less support for explaining similarities and differences in the Nordic constitutional systems than might at first be expected. The chapter also showed that the East/West divide between the constitutional systems in Sweden and Finland on the one hand, and Denmark, Norway and Iceland on the other hand cannot be explained entirely based on the historical context, among other things, because the East/West borders have not been upheld throughout history. However, this does not mean that there is no such divide at a functional or value-based level and in terms of policy outcomes; it only means that the explanations for such a divide and for possible general Nordic similarities are mainly based on a modern context and not a historical one. The analyses of the present constitutional settings will answer whether this or not is the case.

Nevertheless, Chapter 2 emphasises some features that have a historical background: first, the position of the Evangelic-Lutheran Church or at least its faith, which according to Suksi 'has been (and to some extent still is) a common denominator between the countries', has common historical roots in the Reformation; and, second, the tradition of quite strong local decision-making power. Here Suksi makes an interesting parallel between the Nordic tradition for collective cooperatives and associations outside the cities pooling together, for instance, the resources of agricultural society, local self-government in municipalities and even a sympathetic approach towards special forms of self-government that breaks up the unitary state. Suksi refers to the Åland Islands, Greenland, the Faroe Islands and the Sami population in his analysis. The historical background behind the quite strong tradition of local self-government might be explained by the fact that two Nordic states, Denmark and Sweden, eventually became five Nordic countries. Finally, the fact that Denmark, Norway and Iceland are members of NATO, while Sweden and Finland are not, might be a consequence of the historical fact that the Western Nordic countries were all placed under occupation during the Second World War II, while the Eastern countries were not.

These general observations bring us to the functional comparison of the present constitutional settings.

IV. Comparing the Nordic Constitutional Systems at the Functional Level

A. Analysis and Comparison of Some Key Features

Moving on to the more functional analyses of specific key features of constitutional systems, we bear in mind an observation from Suksi's chapter, namely that not only elements present in the Nordic constitutional systems but also common elements in other constitutional systems which are missing in the Nordic context are interesting from a comparative point of view. First, we focus on some general common characteristics, then we focus on the East/West divide and finally we focus on diversity.

As shown in this volume, the Nordic constitutional systems share several characteristics. One of the features that stands out when viewed from the outside is the fact that the Nordic countries are very well-functioning democracies with a high level of respect of human rights. At the same time, none of the Nordic countries has a constitutional court. Judicial review of the constitutionality of legislation is carried out by the Supreme Courts (with Finland as a latecomer in this respect) and is only carried out as a concrete *ex post* review. The courts do not apply legislation which turns out to be unconstitutional; however, they do not have the authority to annul legislation. Accordingly, such laws would not be enforced and the legislatures would react to such conclusions from the court by amending the law. *Ex ante* review is only carried out in the political institutions, with a distinction between the East (Denmark, Norway and Iceland), in which the ministries are the primary controllers of constitutionality, and the West (Finland and Sweden), where special strong parliamentary committees are the main controllers of constitutionality. The Nordic countries in general have strong parliamentary control over the executive through a system of parliamentary committees and the Ombudsman. As discussed by Thorarensen, there is a growing demand in the

Nordic countries to strengthen means to control their governments' activities. This can in part be seen as a reaction to the growing Europeanisation of politics. Nordic parliaments have sought to compensate for their alleged decline in legislative activity by developing their oversight and control mechanisms with respect to EU affairs. Furthermore, new patterns of parliamentary practices have emerged in order to ensure the ability of Nordic parliaments to control national governments, for instance, more emphasis on the appointment of independent special investigation commissions to investigate events that have seriously impacted the public and to assign responsibility for the situation or identify a possible abuse of power.

The legislative process in the Nordic countries is characterised by hearing processes with interest groups, NGOs, scholars and other parties who might have some relevant comments to make on draft legislation. According to Bull, this also reflects a Nordic preference for consensus in politics. In general, the Nordic constitutional systems are based on openness, transparency and public trust in state institutions. The fact that the Nordic countries score highly in relation to democracy and human rights, even though the courts do not play as important a role as they do in many other countries shows that a strong tradition for upholding principles of the rule of law and good governance in the legislative and administrative processes is just as important. If quality and high standards in the legislative and administrative processes are present, the courts will play a less important role.

Ojanen also refers to the fact that the Nordic countries are wealthy welfare states as an important context surrounding the Nordic constitutional systems. Hence, the structure of the Nordic constitutional systems reflects a common Nordic approach to democracy that emphasises the importance of majority-democracy and with less emphasis on the courts than we see in many other countries. However, as mentioned above, this must be seen in the special Nordic context.

The table below provides an overview of some main common features.

Table 8.1: Main common features of the Nordic constitutional systems

Democratic form of government	Parliamentary democracies (with a long history)
Number of chambers in parliament	Single-chamber parliaments
Election period	Members of parliament are elected for four years (if an election is not called before)
Voters	Voting age 18, non-citizens cannot vote in national elections
Election system	Proportional representation
Parliamentary control of the executive	Strong tradition including, among other things, parliamentary committees and an Ombudsman

(continued)

Table 8.1: (*Continued*)

Decision to prosecute ministers on unlawful conduct in office (legal responsibility)	Lies with the parliament
Motions of no confidence against a government (political responsibility)	Can be passed in the parliament
Legislative initiative:	New draft legislation can be proposed by the government and by individual members of parliament, and committees in some cases.
Independent courts	Personal and functional protection
Constitutional court tradition	No such tradition
Human rights catalogue as part of the Constitution	Yes
Judicial control with the executive	Strong tradition, performed by administrative courts in the East
Federalism	No such tradition
Preambles in the constitution	No such tradition
Eternity clauses	No such tradition
Dualism/monism	Dualism

Having pointed out some major common features reflected in the functional comparative analysis of the Nordic constitutional systems, we move on to take a closer look at the traditional East/West division in the Nordic constitutional systems. As emphasised by Smith, the traditional East/West division is primarily reflected in the institutional design of the Nordic constitutional systems. The table below provides a comparative overview of some of the traditional institutional characteristics of the West and the East.

Table 8.2: Comparative overview of traditional institutional characteristics of the West and the East

	West (Denmark, Norway and Iceland)	**East (Sweden and Finland)**
Judicial system for supreme instances	Single-tier judicial system with a single supreme instance (civil, criminal and administrative cases)	Two supreme instances (one for civil and criminal cases and one for administrative cases)
Court review (concrete *ex post*) of constitutionality of legislation	Long tradition (especially in Norway)	New tradition (especially in Finland)

(*continued*)

Table 8.2: (*Continued*)

	West (Denmark, Norway and Iceland)	East (Sweden and Finland)
Prior review (*ex ante*) of constitutionality of legislation	The ministries have the main responsibility for prior check for constitutionality of legislation	Specialised strong parliamentary committees (Finland: Constitutional Law Committee; Sweden: Committee on the Constitution)
Regulation of parliamentary control of the executive	Not regulated in detail in the constitution, for example, the standing committees are described in the standing orders of parliament	Regulated in detail in the constitution
Legislation procedure	Three readings of a bill in parliament required in general (Denmark and Iceland) or if not adopted in the second reading (Norway)	Fewer readings of bills in Parliament: one reading in Sweden and two in Finland
Chancellor of Justice	Does not exist	Exists

Having pointed out common features of all the Nordic constitutional systems and areas in which we especially see the traditional East/West divide, attention must be paid to features of diversity, which also exist in the Nordic constitutional systems in general and across the East/West divide. It must be emphasised that we can only make general remarks and overviews in the concluding chapter. For more details on individual nuances between the Nordic constitutional systems, see the individual chapters on specific topic. Nevertheless, some areas of diversity are presented in the following table.

Table 8.3: Diversity in the Nordic constitutional systems in general and across the East/West divide

Age of constitution	Old constitutions: Norway, Denmark and Iceland	Newer constitutions Finland and Sweden
Single-document constitution:	Single-document: Norway, Denmark, Finland and Iceland	Multi-documentary: Sweden

(*continued*)

Table 8.3: (*Continued*)

Constitutional amendment procedure	Light procedure: Sweden and Iceland A slightly more arduous procedure: Norway and Finland	Heavy procedure: Denmark
Last revision of the constitution	Recently: Norway (2016), Sweden (2011), Finland (2000) and Iceland (1999)	A long time ago: Denmark (1953)
Form of government	Constitutional monarchy: Denmark, Norway and Sweden (the competences of the monarch are now formal, most explicitly reflected in the Swedish Constitution)	Parliamentarian republic: Finland and Iceland (the competence of nationally elected president mainly formal, with exceptions)
Tradition for majority/ minority government (in contemporary times)	Minority governments: Denmark, Norway and Sweden	Majority governments: Finland and Iceland
State church	State church: Denmark, Norway, Iceland and Finland	No state church: Sweden, separation of church and state in 1974
Negative or positive parliamentarism	Negative parliamentarism: Denmark, Norway, Iceland and Sweden	Positive parliamentarism: Finland since the early 1990s
Special court of impeachment for prosecution of ministers	Exists in Denmark, Norway, Finland and Iceland	Does not exist in Sweden
Level of court activity as regards reviewing the constitutionality of legislation	Active courts: Norway and Iceland (especially since 1995)	Less active courts: Finland (strong tradition for *ex ante* review in the Constitutional Law Committee), Denmark (but development as regards conditions of standing) and Sweden
Modernisation of human rights provisions in the constitution	Recently: Norway, Finland, Sweden and Iceland	A long time ago: Denmark (the last constitutional revision took place in 1953)

An important element in the table is the form of government. As discussed in Chapter 3, Denmark, Norway and Sweden are constitutional hereditary monarchies in which the king or queen is the head of state, while Finland and Iceland are republics with elected presidents who function as heads of state. It is obvious that this division is not the common East/West split that we come across so frequently when dealing with the Nordic countries. This makes Finland and Iceland unique compared to the other Nordic constitutional systems, since the presidents have been actors in the political arena, albeit to a different extent. As illustrated by Bull in Chapter 3, the powers of the presidents of Finland and Iceland have developed from being mainly formal, initially replacing the monarch, into becoming a more powerful figure within the constitutional systems. While the role and powers of the Finnish president were redefined in the 1999 Constitution, the role of the president of Iceland, which has not been amended since 1944, has become more vague. This became more apparent following the presidential veto applied three times since the beginning of the 2000s. As discussed by Bull, this can be seen as a step away from the president's traditional role, but must also be understood in the context of a time of political and financial crises.

The functional comparison seems to reflect our main thesis well. At a macro-level, we are able to identify some common functional features which, viewed from the outside world, provide the Nordic constitutional systems with a special identity. However, it is also clear from our analysis that if we dig a little deeper, a distinction between an Eastern and a Western institutional setting appears. An even closer look reveals many differences at the micro-level in the Nordic constitutional systems.

As shown in several chapters in this volume, EU/EEA cooperation and international human rights (especially the ECHR) have had an impact on the traditional constitutional systems in the Nordic countries. In some areas, this has drawn them closer together across the traditional East/West divide, while in other areas, the East/West divide seems to have survived the winds of change from outside and new divides have also appeared. We will now take a closer look at these movements and will try to provide an overview to the greatest extent possible.

B. The Nordic Countries and Europe: Towards Unity or More Divisions?

Finally, we reach the pressing and timely question of how the EU/EEA and international human rights conventions (especially the ECHR) impact the Nordic constitutional systems. Do we see new divides appearing as a consequence of the European cooperation? Or does it bring the Nordic countries closer together? These are questions that are very difficult to answer, but nevertheless we shall present some reflections on the topic based on our analyses in this book.

In Chapter 7, we analysed Nordic reactions to EU and EEA cooperation as reflected in the constitutional embedding of cooperation, case law from courts regarding primacy/direct effect in the national legal systems, preliminary references to the CJEU, exceptions from EU treaties, outcome of referendums, the use of EU Citizens' Initiatives and use of the EWS and the Barroso initiative. These analyses showed that even though the Nordic countries are now split between three EU Member States (Denmark, Sweden and Finland) and two EEA Member States (Norway and Iceland), we still seem to find traces of a division between East (Sweden and Finland) and West (Denmark, Norway and Iceland). An East/West divide was identified as regards the following:

— Constitutional embedding: the Finnish and Swedish Constitutions clearly refer to EU membership, unlike the Danish, Norwegian and Icelandic Constitutions, which do not refer to EU/EEA membership.
— Primacy and direct effect of EU/EEA law: the most significant judgments reflecting resistance were found in Denmark, Iceland and to some extent Norway. However, as regards prior review of legislation, the Finnish Constitutional Law Committee has expressed resistance towards the primacy of EU law in its opinions in relation to human rights and constitutional rights. This seems to show traces of the traditional East/West differences in terms of review of legislation and the separation of powers between the judicial and legislative power.
— EU Citizens' Initiatives: Swedish and Finnish citizens are the most active Nordic users as regards respectively posing and supporting initiatives.
— Separation of powers: as regards judicial review of the constitutionality of legislation, the traditional East/West divide means that EU/EEA cooperation has probably had a greater impact in the East than in the West. In the West, a strong tradition in this field already existed, while Finland in particular had no such tradition before entering the EU and Sweden only had a weaker and more recent tradition. After joining the EU, the Finnish and Swedish courts have been strengthened. Furthermore, the Finnish courts have adopted a quite active and dynamic legal reasoning style inspired by the CJEU. This is apparently also the case in Sweden.
— However, it should be mentioned that we can also observe a development towards a more active Norwegian Supreme Court based on, among other things, the fact that the Supreme Court has applied a rather active review profile in the fields of EEA law and human rights law, and this seems to have an impact on the review of constitutionality of legislation as well. In Sweden, we also see the Parliament strengthening its position through being the most active Nordic parliament as regards reasoned opinions under the EU EWS and the Barroso initiative. As such, the traditional separation of powers has probably had a greater impact in the East than in the West. As shown above, in the West and especially in Denmark, we even see a landmark Supreme Court judgment insisting on the upholding of the traditional separation of powers setting between the courts and the legislator.

As shown above, the East/West divide only exists in some fields. Several reasons were presented in order to explain how an East/West divide can still exist in the EU/EEA context. First, it seems that national, legal, historical and cultural traditions of the Member States of the EU/EEA still play an important role. Second, the formal division between membership of the EU and the EEA might in reality be less significant than might be thought. Third, though a traditional East/West divide might have existed in the Nordic countries, it has never been a rigid division. Fourth, the Nordic countries are subject not only to the impact of the EU/EEA but also of the ECHR, which they all have incorporated into their national legislation. As a result, while the EU/EEA division could on the one hand be expected to divide the Nordic countries to some extent, the ECHR could on the other hand be expected to strengthen the similarities between the Nordic countries as regards rights protection, since all the Nordic countries have incorporated the ECHR into their domestic legal systems. This naturally leads us to consider how the ECHR has impacted the Nordic constitutional systems. To complicate matters even further, we also see an interplay between the ECHR and the EU Charter of Fundamental Rights, which became legally binding following the Lisbon Treaty.

Before we turn to the ECHR, one more observation must be made. While our analyses showed the existence of an East/West divide in some fields, at the same time they showed how the Nordic countries, to a large extent, express unity as regards typical Nordic values such as democracy, openness, strong welfare states with many social rights financed by the public taxation system, gender equality and protection of the environment (Chapter 7). As such, one may say that EU cooperation might create a stronger Nordic awareness of Nordic values internally and a strong loyalty and unity as regards Nordic values externally towards the rest of the EU. As mentioned earlier, such values are not detached from the Nordic constitutional systems, though they are sometimes primarily regulated by ordinary legislation. In this way, the picture is somewhat complex since: (1) the EU formally creates divisions between Nordic EU Member States and EEA Member States; (2) the EU strengthens awareness and promotion of Nordic values in the EU, thus strengthening Nordic unity; and (3) the traditional Nordic East/West divide still seems to play a role in a number of fields. This might at least partly be interpreted as a natural part of the complex processes and interactions taking place in multi-level constitutional legal systems, in this case with an added regional Nordic factor impacting upon the process.

The strong unity of the Nordic legal systems is not only reflected in the common values mentioned above; as emphasised by Suksi, it is also clearly reflected in the Nordic free movement zone, in which citizens from Nordic countries have for decades been able to enter other Nordic countries without a passport and can become citizens in other Nordic countries on more preferential terms than citizens from outside the Nordic countries. Since citizenship is a core element in constitutional law, this is a quite significant expression of internal unity, which also has an external dimension, since it excludes citizens of other nationalities. Through, among other things, the Nordic Council and the Nordic Council of Ministers, the

Nordic countries are not only a region based on shared geography, culture, history and language, but also to some extent a legal region within Europe.

As mentioned earlier, the impact of international human rights conventions, including the ECHR, and the EU Charter of Fundamental Rights on the Nordic constitutional systems must also be included in order to draw a more complete picture of the emergence of possible new divisions and similarities in the Nordic constitutional systems. As pointed out by Ojanen, Nordic countries have traditionally distinguished themselves by being strong democracies based on the rule of law and de facto upholding human rights to a high standard, even though rights are often regulated by ordinary legislation and judicial protection of rights by the courts has played a much less important role than is the case in most other European countries. The latter shows that judicial protection is only one factor among many that promote a high level of human rights protection in a country. Among other factors, Ojanen mentions a high level of democracy, the rule of law, economic wealth and, in the Nordic context, the fact that the Nordic countries are still relatively homogeneous. That said, according to Ojanen, one of the impacts of international human rights conventions is that judicial review of human rights and the role of the courts in the Nordic countries have in general been strengthened. The international human rights conventions create a more active role for the Nordic courts, the ECHR has been incorporated into the national legal systems, and the recent constitutional revisions in Norway, Finland, Sweden and Iceland are all inspired by the ECHR.

International human rights also seem to have created some new divisions in the Nordic constitutional systems, which results in changes to the traditional East/West divisions. First, Ojanen emphasises that we see a distinction between Finland and Norway on the one hand and Denmark, Sweden and Iceland on the other hand when it comes to the incorporation of international human rights conventions into the domestic legal systems. While all the Nordic countries incorporated the ECHR in the 1990s (though Denmark, Sweden, Norway and Iceland had already ratified the Convention in the 1950s), Finland in particular and increasingly Norway have incorporated other international human rights conventions into their domestic legal systems. Denmark and Sweden have chosen not to do so and Iceland has only incorporated the Convention on the Rights of the Child in 2013. This could be said to create a new division between the Nordic constitutional systems. Second, the ECHR has had a stronger impact on the Constitutions in Finland, Sweden, Norway and Iceland than on the Danish Constitution, which has not been altered since 1953. As such, the ECHR has inspired and impacted some Nordic constitutional systems—at least at a formal level—more than others. This could be said to have created a division between Denmark on the one hand, and Finland, Sweden, Norway and Iceland on the other hand. Third, it might be added that this impact is also reflected in more dynamic court interpretations than the traditional rather positivistic interpretation style in the Nordic countries. Smith and Ojanen emphasise this as regards Norway, Finland and Sweden.

Fourth, the introduction of the EU Charter of Fundamental Rights, which became legally binding when the Lisbon Treaty entered into force in 2009, has the potential to have an interesting impact on the Nordic constitutional systems. As shown by Ojanen, the Charter has especially since the 2010s had an increasing impact on human rights protection in the Nordic EU Member States of Finland, Sweden and Denmark. This could potentially contribute to the new EU/EEA division in the Nordic constitutional systems.

However, it is also possible to argue that international human rights have the potential to create more human rights unity in the Nordic countries. Even though the Nordic countries traditionally share many values and rights in their constitutional systems, with emphasis on democracy, the rule of law and good governance, there has also been differences and especially since the 1990s, we have seen Iceland, Sweden, Finland and Norway revise their constitutional human rights protection to follow more 'modern standards', which often correspond not only to the ECHR but in some cases also other international human rights conventions. As mentioned before, this creates a distinction between the more old-fashioned human rights catalogue in the Danish Constitution and the human rights catalogues of the other Nordic Constitutions, which have in some cases now also chosen to mention the importance of human rights as general constitutional principles in the first articles of their constitutions. Interestingly, it might be suggested that though we might see a formal distinction growing in the constitutional texts (partly created by the international human rights conventions), the ECHR and other international human rights conventions might paradoxically at the same time play an important role in building and upholding unity in reality as regards human rights protection in the Nordic countries. Ojanen mentions that multi-layered human rights protection appears in the Nordic countries, which combines national constitutional law, international human rights and EU human rights. This complex interplay takes place at the ECtHR, the CJEU and the national courts, and according to Ojanen it is 'no longer possible to strongly distinguish between constitutional, European and international systems of human rights protection'. One might argue that these complex interplays could draw the Nordic human rights protection in the same direction across an East/West divide, an EU/EEA divide and formalistic divides in the constitutional texts.

In all the Nordic countries, the ECHR plays an increasingly important role compared to the constitutional texts. Ojanen emphasises that in all the Nordic countries, 'the ECHR, as seen in the light of the case law of the ECtHR, is invoked by parties and adjudicated by the courts more frequently than the corresponding constitutional provisions on human rights'. This means that the ECHR can to some extent 'downplay' the actual importance of the constitutional human rights provisions—especially in the Danish context with a human rights catalogue dating back to 1953. At the same time, the systems of human rights protection in the Nordic countries are drawn closer together across constitutional differences.

Another observation regarding strengthened unity in the Nordic countries relates to the fact that a stronger united Nordic identity can be built through Nordic participation and cooperation in the EU legislative processes. Furthermore, as mentioned by Ojanen, Denmark, Finland and Sweden have played an active role in 'endorsing and promoting' human rights protection in the EU, especially in fields such as the creation of an EU Ombudsman, transparency, access to information, good governance and the accession of the EU to the ECHR. In this way, the Nordic countries have built a common identity and have exported it to the rest of Europe. Even though only Denmark, Finland and Sweden are EU Member States, the identified identity must be said to apply to the Nordic countries as such. As noted by Thorarensen, Iceland and Norway, the non-members of the EU, being part of the EEA, are under an obligation to follow developments in the EU closely and thus are greatly affected by the EU, although they are in a weaker position in terms of participating in the EU legislative processes.[2]

Where does all of this lead us? The picture is complex, but it has been possible to identify a number of trends. The Nordic countries seem to have a quite strong and united cultural and legal understanding of constitutional values, at least at a more general macro-level. These values are to some extent reflected in the constitutional texts, but also extensively in legislation. Based on recent constitutional revisions, the Finnish, Norwegian and Swedish Constitutions express these values more explicitly than the Danish Constitution, which has not been revised since 1953, and the Icelandic Constitution, which has remained largely unchanged since 1944. At the micro-level, we find differences and we also find traces of an East/West divide between Sweden and Finland on the one hand and Denmark, Norway and Iceland on the other hand. The Nordic countries have been under the influence of the EU/EEA and international human rights conventions (including the ECHR), which has been incorporated into their domestic legal systems. This influence has left traces in the Nordic constitutional systems both at a formal level and in reality. We also see new divides appearing between the Nordic countries. Obviously, a new divide is created between the EU Member States (Denmark, Sweden and Finland) on the one hand and the EEA Member States on the other hand. However, interestingly we have shown that even within the Nordic EU Member States, we still find traces of an East/West division, which transgresses the EU/EEA divide. This also shows that national and regional legal and cultural traditions still play an important role in the EU Member States. It might also show that the EU/EEA distinction, though formally important, perhaps means less in reality. Finally, we have shown that the impact of EU/EEA integration and international human rights (including the ECHR) has the potential to create new divisions among the Nordic constitutional systems, but also to unite them and strengthen the regional identity. Both of these tendencies can already be identified.

[2] Their parliamentary oversight tools with respect to EU affairs are different in many aspects and not particularly efficient.

V. Conclusion

In summary, we return to Suksi's thesis of the existence of a special Nordic preference and tradition for local government based on, among other things, the historical context that two Nordic states turned into five Nordic countries. How does this fit into the contemporary picture of the Nordic countries in the EU/EEA and as part of international human rights conventions? Two ideas could tentatively be presented. The Nordic countries like to export values to the EU and other international fora. However, the Nordic countries are at the same time known for sometimes being sceptical as regards both the EU/EEA and the ECHR. Such scepticism is expressed by politicians, voters and judges. In particular, the dynamic interpretation style of the CJEU and the ECtHR has been criticised in the Nordic countries, since it contradicts the Nordic constitutional democratic tradition of strong legislators, self-restraining courts and emphasis on majority rule.

Can the historical tradition for strong local government provide a challenge in relation to committing to international cooperation, at least if it becomes too intense, too binding, too distant from local and national decision-making processes and too far-removed from national values? Another thesis could be that precisely because the Nordic countries have been able to handle and embrace all the moves in terms of borders and kingdoms over time, turn from two states into five countries, and respect local government and home rule in specific areas, the Nordic region would be especially well-trained in handling multilevel constitutionalism. The fact that the Nordic countries are strong, compared to many other countries, in terms of fulfilling their EU/EEA requirements and international human rights standards could perhaps support such a thesis (although this could also be explained by other factors). As such, there are no easy answers. The Nordic countries share a core of strong regional history, culture and constitutional values. They are a region within Europe and the world, they are also active actors in the European and international context in relation to their size, and they are inspired by the trends they are confronted with in such fora. These trends sometimes create new distinctions in the Nordic constitutional systems, but sometimes they unite them further.

Where are we heading to in the future? Based on our analysis, several points can be made regarding future developments. First, the aforementioned divides might be more formal than actually existing in reality. Norway and Iceland are members of the EFTA and are part of the EEA, and so they are de facto deeply affected by EU integration, even though they are not members of the EU. At the same time, the EU is currently facing a crisis at several levels (economic, financial, refugees, Brexit, constitutional reforms in Eastern Europe which contradict EU values etc), which might in the future draw the EU cooperation closer to the original model of economic cooperation. Furthermore, some of the Nordic EU Member States have opt-outs in fields that are especially close to national sovereignty such as criminal law, defence policy, citizenship and the euro.

European integration is more than the EU. All the Nordic countries are parties to the ECHR. Hence, one could claim that European integration could contribute to shaping the Nordic legal systems in the same way in the future and would not draw them apart—though seen from a long-term perspective, they might slowly move closer to a Nordic constitutional model with a stronger European element. That said, the comparative sub-studies also show that the more dynamic and activist court behaviour and the more value-oriented way of thinking at the European international courts at this point seem to have affected some of the Nordic legal systems more than others, with Finland at one end of the scale and Denmark at the other. Whether this will even out in the future remains to be seen, but a development definitely seems to be taking place in all the Nordic countries, affecting the deeper legal culture. Interestingly, Norway and Iceland already had more activist courts and, as such, one might argue that in the long run, the differences will even out between these countries and the Nordic EU Member States, which are moving towards Norway and Iceland after being inspired by a European legal culture.

A final point is that the closer European integration could perhaps trigger further Nordic solidarity within Europe—a solidarity which emphasises a common constitutional inheritance based on shared values. As mentioned before, the Nordic countries normally defend such values in negotiations on, for instance, the EU and international cooperation in general. A more conscious 'new Nordic solidarity' could be triggered in the future, bringing the Nordic countries even closer together.

INDEX

Note: Alphabetical arrangement is word-by-word, where a group of letters followed by a space is filed before the same group of letters followed by a letter, eg 'tax law' will appear before 'taxation'. In determining alphabetical arrangement, initial articles and prepositions are ignored.